Joyce and Aquinas

JOYCE and AQUINAS

WILLIAM T. NOON, S.J.

New Haven and London

YALE UNIVERSITY PRESS

Library of Congress catalog card number: 57-6341

Originally published, as Volume 133 of the
Yale Studies in English, on a grant provided
by Canisius College and on the foundation
established in memory of Philip Hamilton
McMillan of the class of 1894, Yale College.

For my parents

Preface

In THIS STUDY I have attempted to locate and describe the so-called Thomism of James Joyce. I believe that this strand in his writing is least likely to be found at those points where he and his commentators most explicitly invoke it, and that so far as it can be isolated it is a highly qualified derivative of St. Thomas Aquinas' thought. So far as I could I have attempted to derive the literary and critical principles of my discussion from Joyce's theoretical formulations, and when I could not do that I have tried to formulate the theory which his writing seems to me to embody or exemplify. In either case I have been interested in making a critical evaluation of that theory in the light of the determinable aesthetic and poetic principles of Aquinas. I could be easily reconciled if "aesthetics" were to be banished from all discussions of literature, but that is scarcely possible if one takes up this question upon Joyce's own grounds. As my arguments are intended to show, and in any case as one ought to suspect at the outset, Joyce's "Thomism" is for the most part a matter of thematic correspondences and general categories or affinities of outlook. So far as it goes, and it goes far enough, I believe it is significant. If I have at all succeeded in what I set out to do, I hope that this account of it may be of some significance and interest for other readers of Joyce.

In the course of working out this study a kind of double development suggested itself: The chronological order of development in Joyce's work from *Stephen Hero* through *Finnegans Wake* seemed in a general sort of way to correspond with the main points about his Thomism which I believed could be progressively established. *Stephen Hero* and the *Portrait* most conveniently illustrated the explicitly articulated aesthetic theory of his self-styled "applied Aquinas"; the doctrine of Epiphanies seemed most suitably discussed in terms of *Dubliners;* the Comedy and the Trinity themes were suggested by *Ulysses;* and, finally, *Finnegans Wake* lent itself easily to a discussion of the related themes of the poet's role as "creator" and his "creative" resourcefulness in the use of language. I have not restricted myself to a discussion of any aspect of Joyce's Thomism in terms of a single work or period in his life. But in general my argument seemed to chart itself on this double axis: chronological and thematic.

In lieu of a formal bibliography complete references are indicated in the notes when a work is first mentioned, and often these are repeated when the same references are widely separated in the course of a single chapter. The Thomist texts have been cited according to the twenty-five volume Parma edition (1852–73) of St. Thomas Aquinas'

Opera Omnia. Unless otherwise indicated, translations into English in the chapter text are my own. Though I have tried to be as literal as possible, I have aimed chiefly at expressing the sense, so far as I could, in modern idiomatic English. I am not entirely satisfied with the translations, but I am less dissatisfied with them than I am with most others.

To Gene Magner, formerly Curator of the Philip J. Wickser Joyce Collection in the Lockwood Memorial Library at the University of Buffalo, my special thanks are due for his having so very graciously and helpfully made all these unrivaled Joyce materials available for my use. I am indebted to the Librarian of the University of Buffalo and to the executors of the James Joyce Estate for permission to quote from Joyce's unpublished notes and manuscripts. O. A. Silverman has allowed me to quote from the Epiphanies. To the librarians of the Rare Book Room in the Sterling Memorial Library at Yale University my thanks are due also for giving me unlimited access to the John J. Slocum and Herbert Cahoon Joyce Collection. A very personal debt of gratitude is owing to John P. Lahey, a fellow Jesuit, who read patiently and with close attention the first version of this manuscript, and who suggested numberless corrections and needed improvements. Another fellow Jesuit, Joseph T. Clark, a faculty colleague, likewise readily and tactfully rendered me the same service in reading the galley proofs. Laurence A. Michel, also a colleague, has assisted me in re-checking the Aquinas and the Joyce quotations and has helped me much in my reading of proofs. I have profited not a little from many cordial conversations with Richard M. Kain, whose studies in *Fabulous Voyager* and in *Joyce: the Man, the Work, the Reputation* clearly invite attention to the Thomist strand in Joyce's writings.

Finally my gratitude is due most of all and most sincerely to William K. Wimsatt, Jr., Professor of English at Yale University. In its original form this book was a dissertation written under his direction and submitted to the Faculty of the Graduate School of Yale University in partial fulfillment of the requirements for the degree of doctor of philosophy. Mr. Wimsatt's attention to my work far exceeded the call of duty, and I am but making the honest avowal when I acknowledge how derivative my treatment of this subject is from his essays in literary theory and practice.

Financially, the publication of this book would not have been possible without the generous subvention from the fund for the Yale Studies in English, which was most kindly supplemented by the Canisius College administration.

W.T.N., s.j.

Buffalo, New York
October 11, 1956

Bibliographical Note

EDITIONS OF JOYCE'S WORKS USED IN THIS STUDY

Dubliners, intro. by Padraic Colum. Modern Library. New York, Random House, 1926

Exiles, intro. by Padraic Colum. New York, Viking Press, 1951

Finnegans Wake. New York, Viking Press, 1947
(Citations have been corrected according to list of misprints.)

A Portrait of the Artist as a Young Man, intro. by Herbert Gorman. Modern Library. New York, Random House, 1928

Stephen Hero, ed. Theodore Spencer. New York, New Directions, 1944

Ulysses. Modern Library. New York, Random House, 1946

For permission to quote from the above books, I am indebted to the Viking Press, which possesses publication rights to *Dubliners, Exiles, Finnegans Wake, A Portrait of the Artist as a Young Man;* to Random House for quotations from *Ulysses;* and to New Directions for quotations from *Stephen Hero.* In addition, I am indebted to Rinehart and Company for the quotations from Herbert Gorman's *James Joyce,* and to the Talbot Press (Dublin) for the quotations from *A Page of Irish History.*

CUE TITLES TO WORKS OF AQUINAS CITED IN THIS STUDY

Contra Gentes: De Veritate Catholicae Fidei Contra Gentiles

De Potentia (De Pot.): Quaestio Disputata de Potentia Dei

De Veritate (De Ver): Quaestio Disputata de Veritate Dei

Ethics (Ethic.): Commentaria in X Libros Ethicorum (ad Nicomachum) Aristotelis Stagiritae

In Divinis Nominibus (In Div. Nom.): Commentaria in Librum Beati Dionysii de Divinis Nominibus (Opusculum Theologica VII)

Metaphysics (Metaphys.): Commentaria in XII Libros Metaphysicorum Aristotelis Stagiritae

Perihermenias (Perih.): Commentaria in II Libros Perihermenias (seu de Interpretatione) Aristotelis Stagiritae

Posterior Analytics (Post. Analyt.): Expositio in II Libros Posteriorum Analyticorum Aristotelis Stagiritae

Psalms (In Ps.): In Psalmos Davidis Expositio

Quodlibetales (Quodl.): Quaestiones Quodlibetales

Sentences (Sent.): Commentum in Quatuor Libros Sententiarum Magistri Petri Lombardi

Summa (S.T.): Summa Theologiae Sancti Thomae Aquinatis

I: *Prima Pars (S.T.)*, or *Primus Liber (Sent.)*
II: *Secunda Pars (S.T.)*, or *Secundus Liber (Sent.)*, etc.
I-II *(S.T.)*: *Prima Secundae Partis Summae Theologiae*
II-II *(S.T.)*: *Secunda Secundae Partis Summae Theologiae*

a.   articulus
ad   responsum ad objectionem
c.   capitulum
conclus.   toward the end of the argument
corp.   corpus (*or* body of argument)
dist.   distinctio
lect.   lectio
obj.   objectio
q.   quaestio, *or* quaestiuncula

Contents

Nell' altra piccioletta luce ride
quell' avvocato dei tempi christiani.

Paradiso, X, 118–9.

I

Steeled in the School of Old Aquinas

So distantly I turn to view
The shamblings of that motley crew,
Those souls that hate the strength that mine has
Steeled in the school of old Aquinas. . . .
    Joyce's broadside, *The Holy Office* (Pola, 1904)

THE most direct approach to the "Thomism" of James Joyce is by way of a brief consideration of Joyce's formal education. From the age of six to twenty Joyce was a student in Jesuit schools in Ireland, first as a small boy at Clongowes Wood College in County Kildare, from September 1888, until the close of the spring term, 1891; next as a pupil eleven to sixteen years old at Belvedere College, Dublin; and, finally, as a university student at University College on St. Stephen's Green in the heart of Dublin. All the formal education which Joyce ever received was given to him by teachers in these Jesuit schools. Writing in 1927, some five years after the first publication of *Ulysses,* Italo Svevo, Joyce's good friend of the Trieste days (1905–06), remarks: "Joyce still feels admiration and gratitude for the care of his educators; whilst his sinister Dedalus cannot find time to say so." [1] In October of 1921 Joyce was in correspondence with the Jesuit Charles Doyle of Belvedere College, and the exchange of letters appears cordial and unstrained.[2] Even the "sinister Dedalus" is not far at times from feeling an "admiration and gratitude" of a sort for his Jesuit preceptors; in his conversation with the Dean in the *Portrait,* Stephen's thoughts are represented at one point as follows: "he thought how this man and his companions had earned the name of worldlings at the hands not of the unworldly only but of the worldly also for having pleaded, during

1. "James Joyce," A lecture delivered in Milan in 1927, tr. Stanislaus Joyce (Milan, Officine Grafiche *Esperia,* 1950), *ca.* p. 28 (pages not numbered). Hereafter referred to as "James Joyce," Milan lecture. In making use of the sobriquet "his sinister Dedalus," Svevo apparently has in mind Buck Mulligan's reproach to Stephen, "There is something sinister in you . . ." from *Ulysses,* p. 7.

2. Cf. Letters in "The James Joyce Collection," *In Memoriam Philip J. Wickser,* Lockwood Memorial Library, University of Buffalo. (This collection is the so-called Joyce Paris Library.) The subject of the exchange of letters (only Father Doyle's reply is to be found at Buffalo) concerns the possible occupancy in the eighteenth century of Belvedere House by the wife of the first earl of Belvedere.

all their history, at the bar of God's justice for the souls of the lax and the lukewarm and the prudent." [3]

Try as one may, one hardly ever succeeds in shaking off completely the prolonged influence of a highly systematic early education. Rather than call attention to this or that isolated reference to Aquinas, the Thomist-minded student of Joyce may be more inclined to rest his case for an alleged correspondence on the number and nature of the Aquinan ideas *through* which Joyce tended to look at other things.

In presenting the *Ratio Studiorum* in an English translation, Edward Fitzpatrick has characterized this famous Jesuit educational document as "a practical handbook in educational method and school and class management," though Fitzpatrick is at pains to make clear that the *Ratio* is not a complete description of the Jesuit educational system, and that it does not even attempt to provide such a description.[4] The *Ratio Studiorum* is, however, a document of great authority for all Jesuit schools and educators, and has been normative in its various editions and revisions for Jesuit educational enterprises ever since it was first formally issued to the Society of Jesus in 1599. Among its various practical rules and directives, the *Ratio* assigns a privileged position to the teachings of St. Thomas Aquinas, though it avoids making any blind commitment either to Aquinas' philosophy or to Aquinas' theology in the instances of *quaestiones disputatae.*[5]

Joyce's Jesuit educators, in their long course of philosophical and theological studies, would certainly have come to see many things under the influence of a number of Aquinan ideas, and so far as Joyce fell under the influence of his educators he too must have come to see other things in the same light. The respects in which someone may explicitly acknowledge or claim an indebtedness to someone else's "system" or dominant ideas are often the least satisfactory on which to base a comparison. Long exposure to another person's way of looking at reality, or to another person's way of talking out, or writing out, his ideas, often proves to be subtly influential on one's own attitude far more in areas where one least thinks to acknowledge the likeness or the derivation. A thoroughgoing examination of the correspondences in thought or attitude which exist between Joyce and Aquinas will inevitably lead the Thomist-minded critic to consider texts and arguments in Aquinas which it would be fantastic to imagine that Joyce ever noted, much less studied with care. Nothing would be easier to "prove" than Joyce's self-acknowledged indebtedness and pride in his Aquinan cast of thought.

3. *A Portrait of the Artist as a Young Man,* p. 222.
4. Edward A. Fitzpatrick, *St. Ignatius and the* Ratio Studiorum (New York, McGraw-Hill, 1933), pp. 23-4.
5. Cf. The second of the "Rules for the Professor of Scholastic Theology" and the sixth of the "Rules for the Professor of Philosophy" in Fitzpatrick, *St. Ignatius,* pp. 160, 168-9.

Yet a serious study of the Thomism in Joyce invites attention to notions and attitudes which could have become operative in Joyce only to the extent that they were part of the air he breathed, which he accepted, it may be, without knowing that he accepted them, because they were there, like the mountains around Dublin—because he was "steeled" in the school of "old Aquinas' " philosophy, and not just exposed to the teachings of Aquinas, along with a dozen other philosophers, on this or that particular theological or aesthetic point.

The more one comes to learn about Joyce's actual exposure to the thought of Aquinas, the less one is inclined to believe that it was, from a scholarly point of view, systematic or thorough. In approaching Joyce's Thomism, we may rule out Clongowes and Belvedere. These are just preparatory schools, and in Joyce's days the preparatory school study of religion was much less formally organized than it is now. In Joyce's boyhood Clongowes and Belvedere offered hardly more than a most elementary course in apologetics.

Nor was the religion course at University College much more highly organized. From the history of University College, Dublin, compiled by the Fathers of the Society of Jesus and published in 1930 under the title *A Page of Irish History*,[6] one gathers that the study of religion, even at the college level, was not at all systematic in those days, nor was it very much insisted upon. The time appointed for the lectures in religious doctrine at University College was in the afternoon "after the end of the ordinary classes," and attendance at these lectures does not seem to have been strictly enforced.[7] It is unlikely that Joyce would have been brought into any close contact with the text of Aquinas as a result of attending these lectures—if, indeed, he did attend them with any regularity.

No regular course in Scholastic philosophy was offered at all in the old University College during the period of Joyce's attendance. The Royal University, under which University College operated, 1883–1909, was essentially an examining body, and students could be prepared privately for its examinations or could study in recognized colleges. University College in Joyce's student days was merely one of those recognized colleges and simply prepared students for the examinations of the Royal University. From the records of the College there is no proof that Joyce ever took any formal courses in philosophy at all, though there is always the remote possibility that he may have occasionally audited lectures in this branch. There is little if any reason to believe

6. *A Page of Irish History. Story of University College, Dublin, 1883–1909, Compiled by Fathers of the Society of Jesus.* Dublin, Talbot Press, 1930. Subsequently this book will be referred to as *A Page*. The unnamed co-editors of this interesting though somewhat rambling history were Henry Browne and Lambert McKenna, both Fathers of the Society of Jesus.

7. *A Page*, p. 416.

that these occasional lectures would have involved any systematic study of Aquinas' text.

Among the College Societies, as *A Page of Irish History* reveals, there was an "Academy of St. Thomas Aquinas," which was founded in the autumn of 1901, when Joyce was midway through his college course. Joyce appears to have taken no part in the foundation of this society, and his name is not mentioned among the "distinguished" members in the list compiled in 1930.[8] College contemporaries of Joyce, who live in Dublin today, have no recollections of Joyce's having ever attended a meeting of this Aquinas Academy, and since "its appeal was to the more serious-minded students," [9] one can understand why Joyce's living college contemporaries should think it unlikely that Joyce, no longer wishing to be thought "serious-minded" (as he had been at Clongowes and Belvedere), ever attended a meeting of this Aquinas Academy during his college days.

Two questions arise at this point for anyone who is endeavoring to trace the history of Joyce's exposure to Thomist thought: (1) Why did the Jesuit program of studies at University College, Dublin, during Joyce's student days apparently disregard for the most part the prescriptions of the *Ratio Studiorum*, which insist upon a grounding in Scholastic, and specifically in Thomist, thought? (2) In the light of the general lack at University College of any formally organized courses in Scholasticism, how does one account for Joyce's rationalization of his own thought as Scholastic and Aquinan, how does one explain his own polemical assertion that he was *steeled*, as he says, "in the school of old Aquinas"? The aesthetic theory of the *Portrait* (and of *Stephen Hero*) is set forth as an instance of "applied Aquinas"; [1] the most explicit development of the crucial paternity theme in *Ulysses* is worked out under the invoked authority of the "bulldog of Aquin"; [2] and Stephen Dedalus is represented throughout this discourse in the library as an admirer of Aquinas' "wise and curious way" and as claiming a firsthand familiarity with Aquinas' text and arguments: "Saint Thomas, Stephen, smiling, said, whose gorbellied works I enjoy reading in the original." [3] The most damning charge that the philistine Shaun can think of to bring against his poet-brother Shem in the *Wake* is that Shem, with his "jesuit bark and bitter bite," is "weird . . . and middayevil down to his vegetable soul." [4] The world of the *Wake* is described in summary at the conclusion as "thomistically drunk." [5]

8. Ibid., p. 350.
9. Ibid., p. 349.
1. *Portrait*, p. 245; cf. also *Stephen Hero*, p. 212.
2. *Ulysses*, p. 205.
3. Ibid., p. 203.
4. *Finnegans Wake*, pp. 182, 423.
5. Ibid., p. 510.

In order to answer these two questions of why Aquinas was apparently neglected in the University College curriculum, and why in spite of this apparent neglect Joyce could boast of a "steeling" in old Aquinas' school, one needs to consider briefly a bit of the history of University College, Dublin, and to examine to some extent its peculiar educational status during the period of Joyce's attendance. The famous Catholic University of Ireland, founded by Cardinal Newman in 1854, after passing through many trials and coming near to extinction was transferred to Jesuit hands on October 26, 1883.[6] This transfer came about as one of the eventual (though certainly unforeseen) consequences of the Royal University Act for education in Ireland which was passed in the midst of much controversy by the British House of Commons on August 15, 1879.[7] Throughout the quarter century of its existence, University College operated, as has been said, under the provisions of this act. The Royal University prescribed, rather rigidly we should think today, the courses and the examinations which might count toward university degrees, and these courses and examinations were so conceived and so constructed as to be applicable to all member colleges and seminaries, Catholic and non-Catholic alike.[8] Scholastic thought as such was hardly considered of any importance, and Aquinas, far from possessing a privileged position, had no position at all in the program of studies which the Royal University, the official examining body, prescribed and recognized for degrees. Under such an arrangement it was impossible for the Jesuit professors at University College at an official level to follow the authoritative prescriptions of their own *Ratio Studiorum,* which, in any case since the revision of 1832, no longer possessed the force of law in Jesuit educational enterprises, though it was a set of norms which Jesuit schools were still expected to keep in mind.[9]

At no level, official or unofficial, were the Jesuits at St. Stephen's Green free to offer the traditional Jesuit program of college studies constructed around the principles of Scholastic thought. At University College, Jesuit and non-Jesuit professors alike tried to make the best of the situation, but at an early period (1884) they were rather sharply brought to task, not by the Royal University but by the authorities of the Catholic College of Clonliffe, for their alleged failure to offer the type of courses which "ought to be expected in a Catholic seat of learning." [1] As a result of the lively public controversy which this issue aroused, University College was permitted to offer an alternative course

6. *A Page,* p. 63.
7. Ibid., pp. 38–40.
8. Ibid., p. 180.
9. Fitzpatrick, *St. Ignatius,* p. 36.
1. *A Page,* p. 217.

somewhat more strictly Scholastic in content and tone.[2] One gathers the impression that the official courses in the philosophy department (which was then called the Department of Mental and Moral Philosophy and Political Economy) were still largely conditioned by the secular examination requirements of the Royal University during the period of Joyce's attendance. The college records, in any case, give no sign that Joyce took any of these philosophy courses during his student days.

In spite of the officially imposed philosophic neutrality of the College —one may be inclined, in the case of these Irishmen, to suspect largely because of the imposition—a very vigorous extracurricular tradition of Scholastic thought flourished at the College right from the start, and as the founding of the "Academy of St. Thomas Aquinas" during Joyce's student days testifies, this tradition seems to have attained its maximum vitality during the time when Joyce was a student, the period of College history which *A Page of Irish History* characterizes as "the period of triumphant success." [3] Though Joyce did not participate in the activities of the Aquinas Academy, he must have been drawn frequently into discussions with some at least of his classmates on philosophical points, and presumably he would have been as ready as the next man to claim the authority of Aquinas for his own position or point of view. J. F. Byrne, the prototype of the Cranly of the *Portrait* (and of *Stephen Hero*) notes in his published autobiographical memoirs, *The Silent Years,* that ever since his student days fifty years before at University College he has held St. Thomas Aquinas in affectionate regard: "I often day-dreamed of how delightful it would be to walk out with him over the Dublin and Wicklow mountains and maybe talk as we went, or maybe not utter a word." [4]

Byrne's idyllic memories of his schoolboy affection for Aquinas may, one suspects, have been somewhat softened by the passing of the years. As one reads *A Page of Irish History,* the impression grows that at University College the students' affection for Aquinas ordinarily took a much more argumentative, or polemical, form. This appears to have been the case from the beginnings of the Scholastic tradition at the College. Gorman notes in a parenthesis that Father Gerard Manley Hopkins was a member of the faculty "long before" Joyce's time.[5] Hopkins, it is true, came to Dublin in 1884, fourteen years before Joyce's time, but so far as traditions go fourteen years is not a very long time, and so far as Joyce was "influenced" by the Scholastic atmos-

2. Ibid., p. 218.
3. Ibid., p. 327.
4. J. F. Byrne, *The Silent Years: An Autobiography with Memoirs of James Joyce and Our Ireland* (New York, Farrar, Strauss, and Young, 1953), p. 165.
5. Herbert Gorman, *James Joyce* (New York, Rinehart, 1948), p. 54.

phere of the College, he cannot have been totally unaware of the rather stormy history of Scholasticism which the preceding fourteen years had written. *A Page of Irish History* hints suggestively at Hopkins' relation to that tradition in the following words: "As a convert to the Catholic religion he was filled with enthusiasm, but as a theologian his undoubted brilliance was dimmed by a somewhat obstinate love of Scotist doctrine, in which he traced the influence of Platonist philosophy. His idiosyncrasy had got him into difficulties with his Jesuit preceptors who followed Aquinas and Aristotle." [6]

In the same year in which Hopkins came from England to Ireland, another Jesuit, Père Jacques Mallac, came over to Ireland from France. Like Hopkins, Mallac was a convert to Catholicism; until middle life he had been "a confirmed free-thinker, while practising at the French bar." [7] As a result of the controversy which had arisen in Catholic circles over the allegedly eclectic and modern bias of the University College curriculum, Père Mallac had been expressly brought over from France to emphasize the Scholastic side of philosophic thought. He appears to have been something of a "campus character," as the following archaically worded description suggests:

> He, like Father Hopkins, had a metaphysical complex, but unlike him, was a fierce follower of Aristotle. . . . His very appearance was arresting, there was a haggard look in his strong, well-cut swarthy features, and sometimes the glance from his black eyes was so terrifying that he was yclept by the students 'Mephistopheles'. . . . He did not believe that the pabulum supplied the students was sufficiently 'Scholastic'; it lacked the true Peripatetic tone. He undertook to give them the real thing as an antidote, exercising over some of them quite innocently the magnetism of his sincere but strange character. But they were divided into two camps of broader and narrower Aristotelians. . . . The presence of the enthusiast in the College was a disturbing element . . . so that . . . he was, after five years, recalled. [8]

In Joyce's own student days the two principal professors of metaphysics at the College were Father Joseph Darlington and Professor William Magennis. Darlington, prototype of the "convert English Dean" of Studies, with whom Stephen Dedalus is represented in the fire-lighting scene of the *Portrait* as carrying on a discussion of Aristotle's and Aquinas' notions of beauty, was another convert, an alumnus (M.A.) of Brasenose College, Oxford, who had resigned his living as a

6. *A Page*, p. 105.
7. Ibid., p. 108.
8. Ibid., pp. 108–9.

minister in the Church of England in order to enter the Society of Jesus.[9]
Magennis ever since his appointment to the Philosophical Board of the
College in 1893 had been unflinchingly determined at all costs to change
the status of this department as a "Refuge of the Weak," [1] and he is
credited as being "the leading spirit" in the new "Thomistic revival"
which eventuated in the formation of the Aquinas Academy.[2] It was
now his turn, as formerly it had been Père Mallac's, to be "surrounded
by a militant group of his own philosophical students." [3]

Magennis and Darlington had both been lecturers and professors of
English literature [4] before they became full professors in the Department of Mental and Moral Philosophy, and this may well account for
Joyce's own interest in Aquinas' philosophy along aesthetic and literary
lines. Joyce's interest and talent in literature did not escape the attention
of his professors, and in a new and small "familial" sort of college where
the relations between professors and students were very close and personal, there is reason to believe that some well intentioned effort may
have been made to channel Joyce's interest and talent for letters, so far
as possible, along Scholastic and Thomist lines. In any event there was a
good deal of "Thomism" in the air, and it is not surprising that in
Stephen Hero Joyce should fictionally represent the "nimble pleaders,"
as he calls them,[5] pointing out to Stephen Dedalus that "the entire
theory, in accordance with which his entire artistic life was shaped,
arose most conveniently for his purpose out of the mass of Catholic
theology." [6]

One of Joyce's own professors of English at University College was
Thomas Arnold, the last surviving son of Dr. Arnold of Rugby, and
therefore the brother of Matthew Arnold (whose "lawn mowing," or
attempt to tidy up and eliminate all the differences between religion,
poetry, and philosophy, is one of the motifs of *Ulysses*) [7] and the father

9. Ibid., p. 100; Byrne, *The Silent Years*, p. 38. Stephen's "fire-lighting" discussion
with "the convert English Dean" is given in the *Portrait*, pp. 215–22. The subject of
their discussion is the well known dictum of Aquinas: "Pulchra sunt quae visa placent."
Byrne, who characterizes Stephen's conversation with the Dean as "arthritic," and
again as "terpsichorean conversational antics" (*The Silent Years*, p. 36), narrates
that Joyce makes use here of an incident that had taken place in reality between himself (Byrne) and Father Darlington, and that Joyce has seriously distorted the real
incident in telling it in the *Portrait*. Speaking of a visit to Joyce in Paris in 1927,
Byrne relates: "I reminded Joyce that he should have remembered what the fishwives
in Mary's Abbey used to say to a fiddling and fingering customer. 'If ye want the
cod, ma'am, take it, but if you don't want the cod, don't maul it!' Joyce agreed . . ."
(Ibid., p. 35). Are not "fact" and "fiction" here two quite different kettles of fish?
    1. *A Page*, p. 218.
    2. Ibid., p. 349.
    3. Ibid.
    4. Ibid., pp. 215, 218.
    5. *Stephen Hero*, p. 204.
    6. Ibid., p. 205.
    7. *Ulysses*, e.g., pp. 9, 507.

of the militant antisuffragette and popular novelist, Mrs. Humphrey Ward. Arnold was still another convert member of the faculty, an old friend of Newman. Stern and courtly in appearance, he was at heart a shy, childlike person. An amusing incident is told of Arnold's reporting, with some perturbation of soul, to the Dean of Studies at the opening of an autumn term that the first four students whose names he had asked for at the beginning of his course on the Elizabethan period had answered in order, "Bacon," "Raleigh," "Spencer," and "Johnson." [8] The names, as the Dean was at pains gently to assure him, had all been given correctly. "Tommy" Arnold would presumably have had little influence, if any, on the development of Joyce's Thomism, but it may be significant that Arnold, truly his father's son, is remembered by the Jesuit community as having been all his life harassed by the "gadfly" of "the Platonist-Christian Idea." [9] In some at least of his English literature classes, Joyce might have had occasion to qualify his Thomism, much as St. Thomas himself qualified his Aristotelianism, in the light of the traditionally medieval Platonist Christian Idea.

From the foregoing sketchy account of Joyce's exposure to Thomism, it appears that Joyce made little formal study of St. Thomas' works during his student days. As all the surviving contemporaries of that time testify, Joyce was an omnivorous reader, and the chances are that his curiosity and his independent desire to check and to interpret sources for himself led him to do some work privately on the text of Aquinas in an informal way. His readings were so wide at this period, as they were throughout his life, that it is very difficult to trace any one of his sources with much authority or in great detail. The students in the old University College had no regular library of their own to speak of; for the most part they did their reading in the National Library, which was conveniently situated on Kildare Street in close proximity to St. Stephen's Green. So much did they use the facilities of this well stocked library (which possessed the *Opera Omnia* of Aquinas), and so eager was the National Librarian, Charles Lyster, to make his institution helpful to students, that the National Library came to be called jokingly "The Library of University College." [1]

In the *Portrait,* Joyce describes the mind of Stephen Dedalus as "wearied of its search for the essence of beauty amid the spectral words of Aristotle or Aquinas," [2] but in the next paragraph "the lore" which Stephen brooded upon "so that it had rapt him from the companionship of youth" is described as "only a garner of slender sentences from Aristotle's Poetics and Psychology and a *Synopsis Philosophiae Scho*

8. *A Page,* p. 90.
9. Ibid., p. 92.
1. Ibid., p. 235.
2. *Portrait,* p. 205.

lasticae ad mentem divi Thomae." [3] Without pretending to read the portrayal of Stephen Dedalus as the "definitive official biography" of James A. Joyce, anyone investigating Joyce's Thomism would like to know more about the *Synopsis Philosophiae Scholasticae ad mentem divi Thomae.* Is it a real book? If so, could Joyce have read it, and what does it say? No book by this title can be discovered today in the catalogue of the National Library. The small Jesuit library at University College was transferred to the Jesuit residence at Leeson Street, Dublin, when the Jesuits left St. Stephen's Green in 1908, as University College was then being absorbed into the newly formed National University of Ireland scheme. No record of the *Synopsis Philosophiae Scholasticae* is to be found at Leeson Street, or at the College of St. Stanislaus, Tullamore, to which many of the philosophical works of the old University College library were presented in 1931. The title appears on no official list of textbooks for the College for the twenty-five years of its existence.

The probabilities of discovery of any actual book by this title seem extremely slight. But unless one insists upon reading the *Portrait* as straight autobiographical fact rather than as a work of fiction, the failure of the book to turn up will come as no great surprise. The nearest approaches to this title which appear in the catalogue of the National Library are two books by Tilmann Pesch: *Institutiones Philosophiae Naturalis secundum principia Thomae Aquinatis* (2d ed. 1897), and *Institutiones Logicales secundum principia S. Thomae Aquinatis* (1888–90).[4] The contents of these do not tempt us to believe that Joyce could have derived his distinctive version of Thomist aesthetics from studying them.

On the subject of secondary sources of Thomism at the turn of the century—textbooks, synopses, essays, and manuals—much could be said; it is a complicated and thorny question. Since Joyce appears to have avoided any very close study of these secondary sources, it may be sufficient at this point merely to point out that the mid-twentieth-century reading of Aquinas differs in not a few important respects from the reading which was given even in Scholastic circles fifty years ago. Cartesianism in one or another of its derivative idealistic forms had long been in the ascendancy, and one tended, in spite of oneself perhaps, to read Aquinas, much as one read everyone else, through Descartes' spectacles. The Louvain revival of Thomism was in the offing but had not yet come to pass; Étienne Gilson and Jacques Maritain, like so many

3. Ibid.

4. Two other textbooks which appeared while Joyce was working out the aesthetics of the *Portrait* are the Jesuit Joseph Rickaby's *Scholasticism* (London, Constable, 1908) and his *General Metaphysics,* which had appeared in 1898 in a third edition and was subsequently often reissued (London, Longmans, Green, 1918). Thomas Harper's *The Metaphysics of the School* (New York, Peter Smith, 1940) was first published in 1879.

other capable twentieth-century Aquinan scholars, had their work cut out for them, but the work still remained to be done.

In fairness to Joyce's own interpretations of the Aquinan texts, it may be worth noting here at the outset that though Joyce sometimes "went wrong" he was not alone in missing the point. One may have the feeling that certain recent Scholastic faultfindings with Joyce's (or Stephen Dedalus') aesthetic for being a distortion of Aquinas' are a trifle heavy-handed and on the humorless side. In the introduction to a three-volume study authoritatively entitled *The Metaphysics of the School,* the author, a Jesuit, Thomas Harper, could lapse quite innocently in 1879, when the book was first published, into a Cartesian idiom which most modern Thomists, one imagines, would find very foreign to Thomism and would strive earnestly to avoid: "If our thoughts are clear and distinct, our expressions, as a general rule, will be clear and distinct likewise." [5] In quite a different vein, Maritain writes in 1953: "Descartes, with his clear ideas, divorced intelligence from mystery." [6]

Enough may have already been said to suggest that Stephen Dedalus' exposition of Aquinas' aesthetics in the *Portrait*—"Who knows? . . . Perhaps Aquinas would understand me better than you" [7]—is largely a dramatic device. It may do no harm, and possibly may serve some useful purpose, in our subsequent chapters to examine this exposition critically in the light of Aquinas' metaphysical principles. The Dedalan aesthetic is often read and discussed as a statement in the modern idiom of Aquinas' own views. One ought to be on one's guard not to read a hypermetaphysical relevance into Stephen's discourse, a relevance which Joyce, when he wrote it, never intended it to possess. As Joyce represents the fictional situation in the *Portrait,* a number of rather harum-scarum schoolboys gravitate about Stephen Dedalus, the acknowledged "intellectual" of the group, who, in true Peripatetic fashion (with the buzzings of the Platonist "gadfly" breaking in here and there), favors them with a lively, personal version of Aquinas' notions on art and beauty—as they walk, smoking their cigarettes, through no Garden of Colonus nor along the winding lanes of Lacedaemon, but through the "weedy garden" [8] beside the canal which went by Lower Mount Street.[9] To go through Stephen's discourse with a fine-tooth comb to discover all possible discrepancies with Aquinas' few expressed views on "aesthetics" would be to read the *Portrait* badly out of focus. Father Butt is represented in rather broad caricature in *Stephen Hero,* but when he remarks

5. Harper, *Metaphysics of the School,* Intro., p. xlvii.
6. Jacques Maritain, *Creative Intuition in Art and Poetry,* A. W. Mellon Lectures in National Gallery of Art, Washington; Bollingen Series 35.1 (New York, Pantheon Books, 1953), p. 162.
7. *Portrait,* p. 246.
8. Ibid., pp. 234, 239.
9. Ibid., pp. 242, 246.

of Stephen's "Thomistic" essay, read before the Literary Society in this early version of the *Portrait*, that "it was a new sensation for him to hear Thomas Aquinas quoted as an authority on esthetic philosophy," [1] there is much to be said for Father Butt's reserve.

Unless one is disposed to deny all serious significance to the comic, one need not be afraid that Stephen's discourse has no serious relevance. Stephen himself, for the most part (though not always), is represented as making use of his "applied Aquinas" rather solemnly. The theory itself is interesting and significant, and it goes without saying that it shows no little perception into questions which are perennially relevant for aesthetic and literary criticism and discourse. But if one compares the rhetorical presentation of the Aquinan notions of the *Portrait* with the earnest essay manner in which these same notions are presented in the earlier *Stephen Hero* version of the same situation, one is struck by the far greater distance which Joyce puts between himself and Stephen's aesthetic program through the far less solemn dialogue, the far more wittily qualified manner in which he casts the exposition of that program in the later work. Theodore Spencer noted this difference in 1944 when he wrote the introduction to the first edition of the *Stephen Hero* draft: "The theory [in the *Portrait*] is presented objectively and with a comic background." [2]

Joyce did not, of course, stop reading when he left University College after taking his Bachelor of Arts degree in October 1902, nor when he left Ireland a few months later.[3] His "informal" education, which for some time had paralleled or oustripped his "formal" education, seems to have been greatly accelerated about this time. Alone and without many resources in Paris, he turned quite naturally to books. Judging from his self-imposed program of studies about this time, and for some time thereafter, he appears to have regretted not making more of the opportunities for formal study which had been at his disposal at University College. He began to teach himself Greek, which he had avoided taking in college (though he had a special flair for languages), and he embarked, without formal direction, upon a fairly intensive program of private study of Aristotle and Aquinas. Valery Larbaud, who was to become a very close friend of Joyce at a time much later on, and who was chiefly responsible for seeing to it that Joyce became well known in French literary and intellectual circles, says of this early Paris period in Joyce's career: "C'est ainsi que, pendant qu'il était à Paris, il passait plusieurs heures chaque soir à la Bibliothèque Sainte-Geneviève, lisant Aristote et saint Thomas d'Aquin." [4] The library of Sainte-Geneviève is

1. *Stephen Hero*, p. 104.
2. Introductory Essay to *Stephen Hero*, p. 14.
3. Gorman, *James Joyce*, p. 76.
4. "James Joyce," *La nouvelle revue française*, nouv. sér., 9e année, *16*, no. 103 (Avril 1922), 387.

far richer than the National Library of Ireland in the texts of the great medieval Schoolmen, and in particular in the texts of Aquinas, for the pride of the old University of Paris in its well-beloved and much be-leaguered thirteenth-century professor has survived in the French Scho-lastic tradition even to our own day.

Throughout this period of his Paris residence, and apparently later on, again at Paris, and at Pola and Trieste, Joyce made jottings on his readings—summaries, interpretations, reflections, questions, some of these quite lengthy—on odd-sized scraps of paper. Gorman gives the general title "Memorabilia" to these notes. More commonly they are referred to as "The Paris Notebook." [5] They were apparently all, or nearly all, available to Gorman at the time he wrote his revised and continued biography of Joyce, which was copyrighted in 1939. The few entries which Gorman quotes in his text [6] are so suggestive to the stu-dent of Joyce's Thomism that one must regret very much that for the present, at least, this "Paris Notebook" of Joyce can nowhere be found. Slocum and Cahoon in their Joyce *Bibliography* state: "The location of the other entries is unknown, but it is believed that they may have been (and may still be) in the possession of a private owner." [7] There is always the possibility that discovery of the missing notes may modify any conclusions about the Thomism of Joyce which a student of the subject can arrive at today.

At some time in this early Paris period, if not earlier, Joyce would presumably have read a rather important study of Aquinas' aesthetic theories, "Les théories esthétiques propres à saint Thomas," by Maurice De Wulf, which appeared in 1894–95 in the early numbers of a newly founded journal of Scholasticism at Louvain, the *Revue néo-scolas-tique*.[8] Without going so far as to make De Wulf's study a crucial event in the development of Joyce's Thomism, the student of Joyce may yet be struck by certain similarities in De Wulf's exposition, especially the similarities to the Joycean notions of "epiphany" and *claritas* as these appear respectively in *Stephen Hero* and in the *Portrait*. In our subse-quent consideration of "Epiphanies," we shall have occasion to note these similarities of thought and expression. One's first guess might be that Joyce looked into this new review while he was still a student in Dublin. But this periodical, like the *Synopsis Philosophiae Scholasticae*, is not listed in the catalogue of the National Library. A complete set of the *Revue néo-scolastique* is at present listed in the catalogue of the

5. Cf. John J. Slocum and Herbert Cahoon, *A Bibliography of James Joyce (1882–1941)* (New Haven, Yale Univ. Press, 1953), p. 149, E, 11, a, vi.

6. Gorman, *James Joyce*, pp. 95–9; for the additional entries made at Pola, pp. 133–41.

7. Slocum and Cahoon, *Joyce Bibliography*, p. 149, E, 11, a, vi.

8. Maurice De Wulf, "Les théories esthétiques propres à saint Thomas," *Revue néo-scolastique, 1–2* (1894–95), 188–205, 341–57.

Jesuit college at Tullamore, but since this set was purchased by the present librarian from a Belgian bookseller it obviously cannot have come to Tullamore along with any of the other books from the old University College Library. Though there is always the possibility that Joyce came across the review in some other library or bookshop, or in a priest's house in Ireland, the chances are that if Joyce read De Wulf's article—as it seems likely he did—he probably read it in Paris where it would have been easily available and highly recommended at this time to anyone who was inquiring, as Joyce was, into the principles of Aquinas' aesthetic.

There is little more to be said about Joyce's exposure to Aquinas' thought. None of Aquinas' works is included in the collection of Joyce's books, the so-called "Joyce Paris Library" (itemized in the La Hune Catalogue),[9] which is now in the Lockwood Memorial Library at the University of Buffalo. But for that matter, neither are the works of Vico nor those of Freud, Berkeley, Flaubert, Swift, Shakespeare (save for the Sonnets), Blake, nor of the French Symbolists, nor of a hundred other thinkers and writers whose ideas or style of expression at one time or another admittedly challenged Joyce's attention and invited his imitation.

By the time Joyce completed his first published novel at Trieste in 1914, he had, it would appear, a much wider and more mature familiarity with Aquinas' ideas and text than Stephen Dedalus, as he is represented in the *Portrait*, could possibly have had. Literature, not scholarly discrimination in Aquinas' (or Aristotle's) metaphysics, had manifestly been Joyce's chief concern even in the midst of his philosophical inquiries. But as a result of these inquiries, his Aristotelian and Aquinan "lore" was certainly more than the "garner of slender sentences," and the *Synopsis,* which Stephen Dedalus is content to refer to as his authority.[1] To some extent Joyce was in a position, had he chosen to do so, to criticize and evaluate the Thomism of Stephen Dedalus for himself.

An account of the "influence" of Aquinas on Joyce would be rather rigid and misleading if it found that influence at work only in some kind of formal study of Aquinas' works on Joyce's part. Insofar as Joyce's background and early religious traditions were Catholic, he necessarily had numerous indirect contacts with Aquinas' philosophical and theological ideas through catechisms, sermons, conversations on politics and economics, interpretations of novels or poems, and so forth. Most of the educated people with whom Joyce came into contact as he was growing

9. *James Joyce, sa vie, son oeuvre, son rayonnement* (Paris, La Hune, 1949), nn. 348–53. A descriptive bibliography, *The Personal Library of James Joyce,* has been prepared by Thomas E. Connolly of the Department of English at the University of Buffalo '(University of Buffalo Studies, Vol. *22,* April 1955: Monographs in English, No. 6).

1. *Portrait,* p. 205.

up would at one time or another in the course of their education have received a Scholastic orientation. Aquinas did not set out to found a new school in philosophy or theology but strove to work out, so far as he could, a reasoned justification for his Catholic faith. Catholics since his time have leaned heavily on his arguments and have been for the most part more inclined than not to accept the general structure of his defense.

Mary Colum in *Life and the Dream* relates that she later on repeated to Joyce a conversational statement of Maritain's in 1930 to the effect that the "intellectual structure of Baudelaire's mind was Catholic." Joyce was very satirical, says Mrs. Colum, "and made considerable fun of anyone's having a Catholic structure for his mind." But Mrs. Colum, who knew Joyce very well, immediately adds: "Actually, I have never known anyone with a mind so fundamentally Catholic in structure as Joyce's own, or one on whom the Church, its ceremonies, symbols, and theological declarations had made such an impress. . . . The Scholastic was the only philosophy he had ever considered seriously." [2] It was not only upon Catholics, like Mary Colum, that Joyce made such an impression. C. G. Jung's remarks in this context are not without interest:

> Even in his "overturning" (not to be confused with "conversion"), Joyce has remained a pious Catholic. . . . His "counterworld" has the medieval, quite provincial, and quintessentially Catholic atmosphere of an Erin that tries desperately to enjoy its political independence. The author worked at *Ulysses* in many foreign lands and from all of them he looked back in faith and kinship upon Mother Church and Ireland. He made use of his foreign stopping places as mere anchors to steady his ship in the maelstrom of his Irish reminiscence and resentments. [3]

Not everyone would agree, it may be, with Jung's psychoanalytical report; what I quote from it at this point is but a small part of Jung's total appraisal. But even the partial appraisal has value for this study to the extent that it suggests, like Mary Colum's remarks, that Joyce's Thomism and the living Catholicism of his schooling are not always detachable entities, that there are large areas where the two realities either overlap or coincide.

On first glance it may look as if Joyce too completely identified Thomism with a Catholicism merely of the Middle Ages: there is much talk about Stephen Dedalus' mind, in the *Portrait,* being garbed "in the vesture of a doubting monk," of his "monkish pride," [4] of his "monkish

2. Mary Colum, *Life and the Dream* (Garden City, Doubleday, 1947), p. 381.
3. "*Ulysses:* A Monologue." Reprint of the Analytical Psychology Club of New York (Spring 1949), tr. W. Stanley Dell, p. 10. Original article in German appeared in *Europäische Revue* (Berlin), 8 (Sept. 1932), 547–68.
4. *Portrait,* p. 205.

learning, in terms of which he was striving to forge out an esthetic philosophy, [which] was held no higher by the age he lived in than the subtle and curious jargons of heraldry and falconry." [5] Shaun (Justius) tells Shem (Mercius) early in the *Wake,* "you see I have read your theology for you," [6] and for Shaun, who sees nothing to laugh at in Shem's "risible universe," [7] that theology can only be characterized as "weird" and "middayevil." [8] But this equation between medievalism and Thomism is only superficial in Joyce; frequently it is a sign that he is being ironical. Joyce certainly knew the difference between a monk and a friar; Aquinas was no monk, and whatever else his "spectral words" might have been they were not "monkish" words. When Buck Mulligan claims that Stephen has "the cursed jesuit strain" in him,[9] unlike Shaun, he does not make the mistake of equating Jesuitism with Thomism and both with the Middle Ages!

The Jesuit Order was not founded in the Middle Ages but during the High Renaissance, in 1540. The Thomism which Joyce would have encountered as he grew up would not have been oriented to the past but to the present and to the future. The official "Constitutions of the Society of Jesus," when they speak "Concerning the Books Which Are to Be Read," note at one point that although lectures should be given to students on the Master of the *Sentences* (Peter Lombard), there is no reason why some other "summa" or book of Scholastic theology may not be substituted "if it seems better adapted to our times." Likewise, "in the other sciences too, and in humane letters, if some books composed in the Society are accepted as being more useful than others which are commonly in use, let this be done." [1] When Gorman writes that the Jesuits whom Joyce had as teachers were "diggers in accustomed ditches," "limited in horizon" and "subtly biased, of course," [2] one does not need to be oneself a Jesuit to find this a fairly comical overstatement of his case. To some extent the Jesuit partiality to Aquinas is owing to the fact that in Aquinas, more perhaps than in any other Schoolman, the *philosophia scholastica* shows itself to be most truly a *philosophia perennis,* open to history, capable of assimilating, or at least illuminating, the new and rewarding insights of modern thought.

Joyce's Thomism, whatever we may ultimately decide about it, is never found in isolation in his writings. It is not the crucial Joycean "critical problem"—whatever that may be—and it is not always the same thing when it does make its presence felt in Joyce's different works.

5. Ibid., p. 209.
6. *Finnegans Wake,* p. 189.
7. Ibid., p. 419.
8. Ibid., p. 423.
9. *Ulysses,* p. 10.
1. Cf. Fitzpatrick, *St. Ignatius,* pp. 106–7.
2. Gorman, *James Joyce,* pp. 54–5

Its presence is likely to be most strongly felt, by anyone sensitive to the categories and attitudes of Aquinas, in the general texture or tone of Joyce's writings rather than at those places where the authority of Aquinas is most explicitly invoked. The author of this study considers that Bloom, rather than Stephen, is indisputably the central character of *Ulysses*. But for a study of Joyce's relation to Aquinas, the student finds that Stephen and related artist figures in Joyce's work are more immediately significant than Bloom.

Much in the same way, the conclusions of a study of this sort may easily suggest to the careful student of Aquinas' metaphysics that there has been a misunderstanding, if not a wilful distortion, of the Aquinan points of view. In *Stephen Hero* when Father Butt remarks, in his criticism of the essay on Aquinas and literature which Stephen had read to the College Literary Society, that "to interpret [Aquinas'] statements practically" one needs "a fuller knowledge than Mr Daedalus could have of his entire theology," [3] Father Butt (the rather innocent butt of Joyce's satire) is only stating the obvious. Even if one possesses a considerably fuller knowledge of Aquinas' entire theology than "Mr Daedalus" could have had, one may give a misleading impression of Aquinas' total theological perspectives should one set out to consider Aquinas' text, for the most part, only in those respects and at those points where this text possesses relevance to Joyce and to the Joycean canon. Such a reading is an accommodation to the late nineteenth- and twentieth-century subject matter rather than a distortion of Aquinas. The principal focus of this study is not on Aquinas but on Joyce.

3. *Stephen Hero,* p. 104.

2

Dedalus and the Beauty Maze

*The philosophic college should spare a
detective for me.*

Stephen Hero [1]

THE initial effort to locate and label the Thomist aesthetic to be
found in the Joycean material is difficult because it is not altogether clear what a Thomist aesthetic consists of, or indeed that
a Thomist aesthetic exists at all. It should go without saying that the
Princeps Philosophorum never wrote a treatise *De Aesthetica*. It was
approximately five hundred years after the death of Aquinas that A.
Baumgarten, a disciple of Leibnitz, invented the modern term "aesthetica," and assigned to aesthetics a place apart in the cycle of philosophy.

The concept of "fine" or "aesthetic arts" came into use in England in
the eighteenth century. Even as late as 1773 Samuel Johnson makes no
reference in his *Dictionary of the English Language* to "fine art" as a
technical term. Sir Joshua Reynolds in his discourses before the Royal
Academy of Arts appears not to think of "aesthetics" or "fine arts" as
terms which could be generally understood.[2] St. Thomas himself would
have been baffled by the terms, and one can only guess how he might
have defined them in his philosophic system. It would be begging the
question to imagine at the outset that he would have agreed with Baumgarten that the study of the fine arts pertained pre-eminently to the psychology of sensation, and it is not at all likely that he would have been
as happy about the term "aesthetics" as the idealist Croce professes himself to be when he makes use of Baumgarten's title.[3]

The name "fine arts" might well have struck Aquinas as baffling much
in the same way as the term "aesthetics." It was another disciple of
Leibnitz, the Abbé du Bos, who is often credited with having introduced
the expression *les beaux-arts,* in 1719. Charles Perrault's book *Le
cabinet des beaux-arts* appeared earlier, in 1690, and the term beaux
arts seems to have been current in France during the seventeenth cen-

1. *Stephen Hero,* p. 186.

2. Maurice De Wulf, *Art et beauté,* (2d ed. Louvain, Institut Supérieur de Philosophie, 1943), p. 165. Cf. Thomas Munro, *The Arts and Their Interrelations* (New
York, Liberal Arts Press, 1949), pp. 26–7, 113, 157.

3. Benedetto Croce, *The Philosophy of Giambattista Vico,* tr. R. G. Collingwood
(London, Howard Latimer, 1913), p. 47.

tury.[4] In any case students of aesthetics by and large have assumed that "the beautiful," *le beau,* is the particular province of the "fine arts," and in most modern discussions of art this concept plays a leading if not indeed the central role. This is true of the Stephen Dedalus discussions of aesthetics in the *Portrait* (and in the earlier *Stephen Hero* fragment), and the preoccupation with "beauty" looms large in Joyce's private notebooks, in the letters of his earliest Paris sojourn of 1902, and during his subsequent sojourns of 1903 and 1904 in Paris, Pola, and Trieste.[5] This allegedly Thomist alliance between "art" and "beauty" is, however, nowhere stated or taken for granted in the writings of St. Thomas.

St. Thomas and his contemporaries did not make the modern distinction between a "useful" and a "fine" art. In a general sort of way, they acknowledged a distinction between "servile" and "liberal" arts, but the grounds on which they so distinguished had nothing to do with beauty, only with the factor of manual labor: Was or was not physical labor or mechanical ingenuity involved in the production of the artifact?[6] Even as late as the Renaissance, Leonardo da Vinci seemed engaged in a losing battle when he fought for the recognition of sculpture as a "liberal" art. For the thirteenth century itself, artist meant simply artisan, and the artisan no more than the philosopher, the doctor, the husbandman, or the dialectician was much concerned whether his activity achieved beauty or failed to achieve it.

To attempt, as the young Joyce did, to construct a philosophy of art, and in particular a literary aesthetic, on the basis of the Thomistic texts on beauty involves one in a formidable undertaking. "His Esthetic was in the main 'applied Aquinas,'" Joyce said of the literary-minded Stephen,[7] and it is of special importance for students of letters to keep in mind that the traditional Thomist texts on art and beauty (as Stephen employed them) have relevance for literature only insofar as they are "applied." Suggestive as some of the texts may be in themselves, it is advisable for the literary student to remember that Aquinas did not know the text of Aristotle's *Poetics* (nor the text of Plotinus' *Enneads*),[8] and that he was far more interested in philosophical and theo-

4. Leonard Callahan, O.P., *A Theory of Esthetic According to the Principles of St. Thomas Aquinas* (Washington, Catholic Univ. Press, 1927), p. 81. Cf. Munro, *The Arts and Their Interrelations,* p. 29; and Paul Hazard, *The European Mind,* tr. J. Lewis May (New Haven, Yale Univ. Press, 1953), p. 409.

5. Gorman, *James Joyce,* pp. 96–9, 133–5.

6. Jacques Maritain, *Art and Scholasticism,* tr. J. F. Scanlan (New York, Scribner's, 1930), p. 21. It would appear that "art" for the medieval Schoolmen corresponded approximately with the indeterminate Greek "technè," any specific mode of skilled activity with its own rules of operation, the knowledge of which is acquired largely through experience.

7. *Stephen Hero,* p. 77.

8. De Wulf, *Art et beauté,* p. 229. Cf. Arthur Little, S.J., *The Nature of Art, or the Shield of Pallas* (New York, Longmans, Green, 1946), an important and perceptive study by a Dubliner (and a Jesuit) of the "aesthetic" ground in Aquinas which Joyce

logical science than in literature as an art. Of Aristotle's and Aquinas' ideas, the youthful Stephen predicted, perhaps a trifle arrogantly, "I need them only for my own use and guidance until I have done something for myself by their light." [9]

In virtue of his early love of literature Joyce gave to the Thomist texts on art and beauty a searching attention as his early works and private papers testify. Interpreting these texts in his own way, he sought the key to a philosophical justification for the kind of literature which he loved and resolved some day to write. Here if anywhere was the bridge between his Scholastic education and his projected literary life. Joyce approached these texts, in other words, much as they are usually approached, with a mind already more than half made up on what he wanted to find. Scholastic interpreters of St. Thomas at this period in Joyce's life, for example, Cardinal Mercier and Maurice De Wulf, were proceeding in no very different fashion, though their conclusions were sometimes at variance with Joyce's, for the "formal object" of their inquiries was philosophy rather than art; to literature itself they gave hardly more than a passing nod.

A single sentence from an article on art and the beautiful by the distinguished Thomist scholar Cardinal Mercier, one of the leading spirits in the subsequent Neo-Thomist Scholastic revival at Louvain, may be offered as typical of many Scholastic assumptions of the period. This article which appeared in 1895 in one of the earliest issues of the then new and exciting *Revue néo-scolastique* is one that Joyce most likely read. The sentence, in any case, epitomizes neatly several important Scholastic attitudes toward art which find their way into Joyce's own speculations: "L'Art est le moyen de réaliser et d'exprimer le beau, ou, plus explicitement, l'art a pour but d'incarner dans une belle forme sensible la beauté idéale, et d'en procurer à autrui avec la contemplation la pure jouissance." [1] Within a very brief compass, Mercier manages to touch three times on his absorbing aesthetic theme: *le beau, la belle forme, la beauté.* From the start, art is identified with fine art, and without troubling to argue the point, Mercier assumes that fine art is "the expression of the beautiful." The beautiful (artistic) form which human sensibility apprehends is presented as an "incarnation" of an otherwise humanly inaccessible "ideal beauty." The experience of beauty

---

also had gone over in the *Portrait.* Arguing outside the perspectives of the *Portrait,* Little states (p. 48) : "The one mistake that M. Maritain may have made is to assume that Saint Thomas, while admittedly not attempting a complete system of aesthetics, has actually blundered into one. . . . The great doctor's fame can easily bear the mild imputation that, having correctly established some initial propositions in aesthetics, he waived the central problem." On the following page Little adds: ". . . he [Saint Thomas] never suspected that there was such a thing as significant art."

9. *Portrait,* p. 218.

1. D. Mercier, "Du beau dans la nature et dans l'art," *Revue néo-scolastique,* 2 (1895), 339.

is "procured," so it is stated, for another through the other's contemplative act, and would seem to be identical with joy.

Here it would not be difficult to point out analogous assumptions in the aesthetic of the youthful Stephen Dedalus, from Mercier's basic initial assumption that art is the expression of the beautiful [2] to his final one that the aesthetic experience is perfected in joy, what Stephen would later call "the enchantment of the heart" [3]—though Stephen would have understood by "ideal beauty" something less divinely Platonic than Mercier seems to mean. From the point of view, however, of defining a Thomist aesthetic, the first question to be answered is not, Did Joyce (or did Stephen) hold Mercier's basic assumptions? but rather, Would Thomas himself have done so?

The concept of the beautiful is given generous and serious attention in the metaphysics of Aquinas. If we recall some of the authors whom Aquinas studied—Aristotle, Cicero, St. Augustine, and especially Denis the Areopagite [4]—and if we reflect upon Aquinas' early discipleship under Albert the Great, we are not surprised at his interest. To the traditional (ancient and medieval) treatment, which located beauty almost exclusively *in things* or in transcendental ideas underlying *things* (or beauty in its ontological, objective aspect), St. Thomas, not at first, but by the time he wrote his great *Summa Theologiae,* added a decisively new coordinate of his own, beauty as it exists in the human mind (beauty in its psychological, subjective role). Edgar De Bruyne has called this Thomist shift toward the psychological the aesthetic "discovery" of the final *Summa.* [5]

St. Thomas introduced a really new dimension into "aesthetic" discussion by his insistence that the experience of beauty must be as much considered in its psychological as in its ontological aspects, whatever these latter may be: *tranquillitas ordinis, color nitidus, debita proportio in rebus* ("unity in variety," or "order joined with magnitude," as Aristotle had said). Some of the *formulae receptae,* indeed, such as Plato's *splendor veri* or St. Augustine's (and Cicero's) *suavitas coloris,* had long called for the psychological analysis which St. Thomas was the first systematically to afford them. As De Bruyne has demonstrated, Aquinas actually found this neglected principle of beauty as an act of knowledge in the writings of Alexander of Hales. [6]

This concept of the beautiful, however, is never restricted by Aquinas to our "artistic" productions. Sometimes the particular beauty under

2. *Portrait,* p. 242.

3. Ibid., p. 250.

4. De Wulf, "Les théories esthétiques propres à saint Thomas," *Revue néo-scolastique, 1* (1894), 191.

5. Edgar De Bruyne, *Études d'esthétique médiévale, 3, Le xiiie siècle* (Brugge, Rijksuniversiteit Te Gent, 1946), 281.

6. Ibid.

consideration may be that of a divine person in the Most Holy Trinity,[7] or it may be the beauty of the human body;[8] or the discussion may center on the difference between the beauty of the body and that of the soul.[9] A reader would search for a long time in St. Thomas before finding it stated or implied that beauty is in some privileged sense the artist's province. Mercier's unargued assumption that art is "le moyen de réaliser et d'exprimer le beau" may stand at best as a deduction (to-be-reasoned-to) from Thomist principles rather than as a simple enunciation of a Thomist axiom of art.

Like Joyce's putative artist Stephen Dedalus, Aquinas is to a notable extent interested in the psychological experience of beauty, "that which gives delight to the mind." Unlike Stephen, he nowhere seems lost in the Dedalan labyrinth of cognition, "a maze out of which we cannot escape."[1] Moderate realist that he is in his epistemology, he does not, as Joyce's Stephen was later on inclined to do, minimize the force of the extrasubjective factors in the mental experience. The *integritas, consonantia,* and *claritas* (of which Stephen speaks in Aquinas' name) are conceived by Aquinas as qualities of things which the mind comes to know, not as "stages" in the mind's own act of knowing. Furthermore Aquinas does not bear down on these qualities in the same way as Stephen does, though in his effort to keep the objective-subjective scale in a delicate balance he gives in the final *Summa* an increasingly serious attention to the experience of beauty as an act of apprehension: "pulchrum autem dicitur id cujus ipsa apprehensio placet,"[2] or "pulchra enim dicuntur ea quae visa placent."[3] This situation of the experience of beauty as much in the psychological order as in the ontological is in an important sense a clean break with the teaching of Aquinas' master, Albert. Albert was much more inclined to ally beauty with goodness as a reality which satisfies the longings and desires of man's will, of his heart. Aquinas speaks of beauty as satisfying the desire of the mind *to know*.

The Thomist alliance between beauty and truth, beauty and intellect, may be helpful in describing reality so far as it is known by the mind— the *splendor veri* which Plato speaks about, the "ineluctable modality of the visible," "the ineluctable modality of the audible" which Stephen Dedalus broods about in *Ulysses* as he wanders along the Dublin strand: "Signatures of all things I am here to read. . . . Snotgreen, bluesilver, rust: coloured signs. Limits of the diaphane. But he adds: in bodies."[4]

7. *S.T.,* I, q. 39, a. 8.
8. *In Ps.,* 44, 2.
9. *S.T.,* II–II, q. 145, a. 2.
1. *Portrait,* p. 244.
2. *S.T.,* I–II, q. 27, a. 1, ad 3m.
3. *S.T.,* I, q. 5, a. 4, ad 1m.
4. *Ulysses,* p. 38. The Platonism here is at one remove: The "he" here is Aristotle.

There is no reason, however, to imagine that Aquinas more than Stephen ascribed beauty only to works of "fine art." "Seaspawn and seawrack, the nearing tide, that rusty boot" of Stephen's revery might all be included under Aquinas' rubric of the beautiful.

This uneasy alliance between the beauty and the truth of art faces a strain in Joyce which is not felt in Aquinas. The metaphysical situation has changed. Joyce's title for the third episode of *Ulysses,* "The *Proteus* Chapter," suggests what has happened: Dedalus-Menelaus seeks to discover the truth (and beauty) of things under their shifting protean appearances. What is truth? What is reality? What is the capacity of the mind to know? Aquinas considered these questions, but he was not greatly troubled by them. He would not have linked together, as Stephen does, the theme of the beautiful with the truth-and-reality theme which weighs upon the modern sensibility and mind. In spite of Aquinas' new stress upon the psychological aspect of beauty, there was little likelihood in the thirteenth century that this would transform the traditional, ontological question *de pulchro* into a question in the theory of knowledge. Once the epistemological question becomes prominent, the equation between beauty and truth proves less satisfactory. Especially in discussions of poetry, there is danger of being led away from poetry, and into some theory of poetic experience, genetic or affective, so long as the parties to the discussion assume (as Aquinas did not) that beauty is the underlying theme or end (or even "end beyond the end") of the poet's discourse.

How far another philosophical effort, to adjust the bearing of goodness on beauty, will advance anyone in the understanding of a poem or other work of art is also a debatable question. "Is the portrait of Mona Lisa good if I desire to see it?" Stephen asks. It is easy enough at times to understand Lynch's impatient interruptions of Stephen's long discourse on beauty in the *Portrait:* "That has the true scholastic stink." [5] Aquinas, one suspects, might have shared Lynch's impatience, for in his own references to the imaginative representations (the *fictiones poeticae,* as he calls them) of the creative artists, Aquinas says nothing about their "beauty," and never enters into the question of how far these representations possess ontological goodness or truth. Thomas Gilby has suggestively pointed out that it was the artists at the University of Paris, not the students of divinity, medicine, or law, who mourned most for St. Thomas when he died. [6]

The Stephen Dedalus of *Ulysses,* wrestling with the question, What is the soul? What am I? is tormented by the bloated carcass of the dead dog and by the movements of the live dog which he sees in his lonely

5. *Portrait,* p. 251.
6. Thomas Gilby, O.P., *Barbara Celarent* (New York, Longmans, Green, 1949), p. 85.

walk along the shore.[7] What can his soul, dedicated to the priesthood of
the imagination, have in common, he wonders, with a dog's soul? "My
soul walks with me, form of forms," he reflects. In his heart Stephen
hates the formless, hates water because it seems to him to be a formless
substance. Later, also, in the library, he disagrees "superpolitely" as
any good "schoolman" would with Russell's oracular utterance: "Art
has to reveal to us ideas, formless spiritual essences." [8] What is the relation between the essence, the form which the mind knows, and the
sensible garment of things? That is the question which "the artist as
a young man" faces. This question in fact had occurred to Stephen even
when he was a little boy: "But you could not have a green rose,"
he thought one day to himself in class. "But perhaps somewhere
in the world you could." [9] Stephen's question reminds us of the question Socrates asks himself in the *Parmenides:* How many forms are
there?

Literary aesthetics of "the beautiful" tend, as the Dedalan instance
shows, to drive straight away from art and literature and into the
epistemological trap. It is no accident that having remarked on the
respective roles of intellect and imagination, Stephen's next pronouncement should be: "The first step in the direction of truth is to understand
the frame and scope of the intellect itself, to comprehend the act itself of
intellection." [1] To Stephen's charge that Lynch's preoccupation with
female beauty "leads to eugenics rather than to esthetic," [2] Lynch might
have answered (though he is not that astute) that Stephen's preoccupation with poetic beauty leads to the genetics of poetry rather than to the
poem, to the "poetic process" rather than to poetry itself.

In spite of Aquinas' categorical assumption, "nihil est quod non
participet pulchro et bono," [3] the Scholastics generally are not in agreement as to whether or not Aquinas held that beauty is a "transcendental" concept. Did Aquinas hold that beauty is to be predicated analogously, like being, of everything? Does the explicit predication of
being involve an implicit affirmation of beauty? Though recent commentators like Jacques Maritain and Eric Gill argue that Aquinas includes beauty along with truth and goodness among his "transcendentals," [4] the best Scholastics of Joyce's day, like Mercier and De Wulf,

7. *Ulysses,* pp. 45, 46.
8. Ibid., p. 183.
9. *Portrait,* p. 8.
1. Ibid., p. 244.
2. Ibid.
3. *In Div. Nom.,* c. 4, lect. 5 (conclus.).
4. See, for example, Maritain's extended note (No. 56) in *Art and Scholasticism*
(pp. 166-70), an attempt at reconciliation of two apparently disparate sets of texts
from St. Thomas.
    Eric Gill, *Beauty Looks after Herself* (New York, Sheed and Ward, 1934), writes
(p. 53): "The delight of the mind is essentially a rational delight, and it consists primarily in the recognition of being. To the rational soul all being is delightful."

denied that Aquinas' concept "beauty" has any such extension.[5] Mercier says quite positively that "there are three and *only three* transcendental properties" of being: unity, truth, goodness. De Wulf too is disinclined to recognize the metaphysical status of beauty among Aquinas' transcendentals.

Another Scholastic of Joyce's early days, the English Jesuit John Rickaby, speaks in his *General Metaphysics* (1898) of there being some, like De Quincey and Ruskin, "who do not shrink from the proposition that every object ought to be beautiful." [6] One gathers that Rickaby himself would shrink from such a proposition. By and large the philosophy textbooks of Joyce's student days allotted a rather perfunctory treatment to beauty by way of a Scholion in the general consideration of the other transcendentals. Harper's three-volume *cursus philosophiae, The Metaphysics of the School* (first published 1879), omits all mention of "beauty" in his three comprehensive glossaries and excludes the concept from his consideration of the transcendentals.[7]

However hard Joyce himself may have tried in the Pola days to work with beauty as a "transcendental concept," *Ulysses* shows that he has given up this effort. The novel represents this as part of Stephen's growing up: "Houses of decay, mine, his and all. You told the Clongowes gentry you had an uncle a judge and an uncle a general in the army. Come out of them, Stephen. Beauty is not there." [8]

St. Thomas had considered the force of such a disclaimer in the well known question of the *Summa* which contains the classic text on the three things "required for beauty": "For in respect to beauty three things are essential: first of all, integrity or completeness, since beings deprived of wholeness are on this score ugly; and [secondly] a certain required design, or patterned structure; and finally a certain splendor, inasmuch as things are called beautiful which have a certain 'blaze of being' about them [literally, 'which possess a pleasing color,' *colorem nitidum*]." [9] This whole question in the *Summa,* however, treats not of

5. De Wulf, *Art et beauté,* p. 217, n.; also Callahan, *A Theory of Esthetic,* p. 75. See too Cardinal Mercier's *A Manual of Scholastic Philosophy* (8th ed. London, Kegan Paul, 1921), *1*, Pt. II, 472.

6. Rickaby, *General Metaphysics,* p. 150, n. 45.

7. Cf. Harper, *The Metaphysics of the School, 1*, Bk. III, 155 ff.

8. *Ulysses,* p. 40.

9. "Nam ad pulchritudinem tria requiruntur. Primo quidem integritas, sive perfectio; (quae enim diminuta sunt, hoc ipso turpia sunt), et debita proportio, sive consonantia; et iterum claritas; unde quae habent colorem nitidum, pulchra esse dicuntur." *S.T., I,* q. 39, a. 8. For the translation "blaze of being" for *color nitidus,* the author is indebted to a suggestion of John Duffy, *A Philosophy of Poetry, Based on Thomistic Principles* (Washington, Catholic Univ. Press, 1945), p. 145: "The wider is the analogy under which he [the poet] sees individual splendor, the deeper is his penetration into the mystery of being—the blaze of Being, as Chesterton admirably says." The phrase is found in G. K. Chesterton's *Saint Thomas Aquinas* (New York, Sheed and Ward, 1933), p. 239.

No serious Thomist student would defend today an interpretation of *color nitidus* or *quae visa placent* which restricted St. Thomas' remarks on "color" or "sight" to

literary or indeed any other kind of artistic representation, but of the
suitability of "appropriating," or assigning, to one Person in the Uncreate Trinity, in this case the *Verbum,* a work or title which is actually
applicable to the Divine Nature as such and so common to all three
Persons. St. Thomas in other words is talking here about a beauty
"which the eye has not seen, nor the ear heard," and though he works
by analogy from created beauty, one does well to remember if one is
speaking of art that the analogue is precisely that which the eye does
see and the ear hear, that the artistic experience begins in the senses.
The Verbum is the perfect but unique *imago Dei invisibilis.* Human
representations may be flawless enough as representations even when
the reality represented is far from perfect. Whatever else art may be, it is
a human undertaking and achievement, and the best art in this post-
lapsarian world has never been afraid to represent the ugly. No literary
theory of representation has ever satisfactorily accounted for this fearless-
ness of the artists' symbolic vision before the stuff of the nonpoetic
world. Immediately after his enumeration of the three qualities intrinsic
to beauty, St. Thomas goes on to speak in a way which shows that he
was well aware that art might be fair with "the blaze of being" around
it, and at the same time that the reality represented might itself be foul.
His own words are clear enough: "An image is said to be beautiful if it
perfectly represents the object, however ugly the object itself may be." [1]

In an excellent study of Joyce's "impatience for cognition" and of the
commitment in his works to a world of moral values, Hermann Broch
has said: ". . . it has always been the standpoint of the artist to work
well rather than beautifully, and those who worked towards beauty
alone, have always ended in trash. This corruption of all that is 'artistic'
may also be symptomatic of the decay of culture, or possibly it is the
return to ethical severity which is the sign of a new form of culture.
It is a turning away from the pathos of the beautiful and turning towards
the simple bathos of experience; from the pathos of tragedy to the suf-

---

purely visual cognition. De Wulf's already quoted study in the *Revue néo-scolastique*
demonstrates how radically Aquinas modified the medieval "theory of light" in his
remarks on beauty: "La théorie de la clarté ou de la lumière reçoit dans l'esthétique
Thomiste un sens profondément différent de celui que lui donne l'antiquité" (p. 205).
Aquinas never equates the light with the Good, as Plotinus, for example, had done
(*Ennead* V, 8, 10).

The word "sight," for Aquinas, referred to all knowledge obtained through the intellect. He says, in so many words (*S.T.,* I, q. 67, a. 1): ". . . patet in nomine visionis,
quod primo impositum est ad significandum actum sensus visus; sed propter dignitatem
et certitudinem huius sensus extensum est hoc nomen, secundum usum loquentium, ad
omnem cognitionem aliorum sensuum; . . . Et similiter dicendum est de nomine lucis.
Nam primo quidem est institutum ad significandum id quod facit manifestationem in
sensu visus; postmodum autem extensum est ad significandum omne illud quod facit
manifestationem secundum quamcumque cognitionem."

1. *S.T.,* I, q. 39, a. 8, ad 2^m: "aliqua imago dicitur esse pulchra si perfecte reprae-
sentat rem, quamvis turpem."

fering comedy of the human creature and cognition of his existence." [2] On the supposition that beauty is a "transcendental," it would make no sense "to turn away from the pathos of the beautiful towards the simple bathos of experience," for in all experience, in all being, in all reality, beauty would be given, would be only waiting to be seen. If one wishes to speak of art as an "incarnation"—as Mercier does, and as Stephen Dedalus does in *Stephen Hero* (when he talks about "re-embodying the subtle soul of the image" freed from "its mesh of defining circumstances") [3]—it would seem on Thomist grounds both theologically as well as artistically more accurate to conceive of it not as "an ideal beauty" clothed in sensible form but rather as a nature, weak and human, which exists with a wonderful new mode of existence because it has been assumed by art.

The Shelleyan talk of Stephen and his youthful companions about "formless spiritual essences" [4] and about desiring "to press in [his] arms the loveliness which has not yet come into the world" [5] is best understood as their reaction, strong but confused, against the thesis that beauty is a transcendental concept. If the artist still enthralled by beauty repudiates the thesis that poetic beauty is a predicate of every existing thing, his tendency might well be to go to the opposite extreme and give his allegiance to some "ideal beauty" which material forms can but very imperfectly approximate—in which case the artist is always tortured by the notion that art, even at its best, can never be more than "a copy of a copy" in the Platonic sense. Scholastic theorists of the beautiful in Joyce's student days showed a tendency to conceive of art in such Platonic terms though the aesthetic they propounded was couched in Aristotelian-Thomistic language: Mercier, for example, taught that the artist's objective was to express, to reproduce as energetically as possible with the aid of material, concrete, changeable forms, the abstract, unchanging, typical perfection of the purely spiritual, ideal form of forms.[6]

2. "James Joyce and the Present Age," tr. E. and M. Jolas in *A James Joyce Yearbook, 1949,* ed. Maria Jolas (Paris, Transition Press, 1949), pp. 104-5. On the basis of the reading of the presentation copy of this address, I have made certain modifications in the Jolas translation. Hermann Broch corrected certain typographical errors before presenting a copy of this address to Joyce. The most notable correction is the change on page 31 of the German text of the second *Pathos* to *Bathos:* "Es ist die Abker vom Pathos des Schönen und eine Wendung zum schlichten Bathos der Erfahrdung." This presentation copy is in the Joyce Paris Library at the University of Buffalo.

3. *Stephen Hero*, p. 78.

4. *Ulysses*, p. 183.

5. *Portrait*, p. 297.

6. Mercier, "Du beau dans la nature et dans l'art," *Revue néo-scolastique, 2,* (1895), pp. 276, 340: "Viser à exprimer cet idéal, le plus énergiquement, le plus vivement possible, à l'aide de formes materielles, c'est l'objectif de l'art." Cf. *Stephen Hero,* p. 78.

It may well be that a literary aesthetic along strict Thomistic lines drives one straight into a genre theory of literary forms and "representations," but before one commits St. Thomas to this view, it is well to keep in mind that he nowhere asserts such a position and that the little he has to say explicitly on the subject of poetry is quite explicable without such a commitment. For the student of literature the postulate of "ideal beauty" raises more questions than Aquinas' commentators including Joyce have ever faced or answered. What is the specific, ideal form of an artifact like a poem or a novel? Where is the ideal comedy, and how does one find this out? How can one tell if *Antony and Cleopatra* is a better tragedy than *Romeo and Juliet?* than *Lear?* Which of these three tragedies most closely approaches "la perfection typique sans l'égaler jamais" which Mercier teaches is the "objectif de l'art"? [7] These difficulties are very real in any aesthetic in which art has been made the caretaker of beauty, and it may be more just to the intellect of the Angel of the Schools to imagine that he would never have wandered into such a labyrinth, and that he would have chosen to let *both* art and beauty look after themselves.

The youthful Joyce, however, imagined that it was "applied Aquinas" to have art look after beauty, and he believed, too, that he was following in Aquinas' footsteps when he wandered into a labyrinth more intricate than the one which Cretan Daedalus had constructed. "Why are not excrements, children, and lice works of art?" he asks in the Paris Notebook,[8] and both in this notebook and in the *Portrait,* in the dialogue between his own Dedalus and Lynch, he asks : "If a man hacking in fury at a block of wood . . . make there an image of a cow, is that image a work of art?" [9] The principle according to which Joyce answered these questions in the notebook (which Stephen leaves unanswered in the *Portrait*) has a Thomistic ring: "art is the human disposition of intelligible or sensible matter for an esthetic end." [1]

The ring of the phrase is Thomistic, but the sense is Joyce's own, or rather the sense is one which Joyce makes his own on the basis of what he had come to believe was a Thomist principle of art : to express or to incarnate the beautiful for an aesthetic end. "The human disposition of sensible or intelligible matter" is a fairly accurate and conventionally accepted paraphrase of St. Thomas' definition of art : "dicendum quod ars nihil aliud est quam ratio recta aliquorum operum faciendorum." [2] "For an esthetic end," however, is a phrase which owes much more to the eighteenth century than it does to the thirteenth. The addition trans-

7. Ibid., p. 340.
8. Gorman, *James Joyce,* p. 98.
9. Ibid., p. 99; also *Portrait,* p. 251.
1. Gorman, *James Joyce,* p. 98; also *Stephen Hero,* p. 77.
2. *S.T.,* I–II, q. 57, a. 3; see also a. 4, obj. 1 : Ars enim est ratio recta aliquorum operum"; and a. 5, ad 1ᵐ : "cum ars sit ratio recta factibilium."

forms St. Thomas' thought to such an extent that he would scarcely recognize it for his own. In that part of the *Summa* where this definition occurs Aquinas discusses the question of art in some detail, but his attention is largely given to demonstrating that art is an intellectual *virtue* and to distinguishing this intellectual virtue of art from the moral virtue of prudence.

In the course of making his distinction between art and prudence (both are virtues concerned with practical matters, but whereas art has to do with an *object* that man *makes,* prudence has to do with an *action* that man *performs*), Aquinas states a principle which has been greatly magnified and distorted by friend and foe alike of the Thomist synthesis. St. Thomas says: "The goodness of a work of art is to be judged not in terms of the artist, but rather in terms of the art-work itself." [3] If one insists upon taking "artist" in the modern restricted sense, St. Thomas' words would mean no more than saying, for example, that not all the builders of Chartres were necessarily just men, or that you could judge the excellence of the Ninth Symphony without knowing whether Beethoven was in the state of grace when he wrote it. It is in fact farfetched to argue to anything about art in the modern sense from such a statement, and it is a positive distortion to use such statements (for there are others like it) to assert the moral autonomy of the artist. Aquinas was prepared to call the farmer an artist as readily as he was to call the man of letters one. He does in fact often call farming an art, but practically never uses the word of poetry.

The Thomist texts on art, although Thomas is principally concerned with art as an intellectual virtue, never commit one so rigorously to art as artistic *process* as the "applied Aquinas" of the youthful Joyce would suggest. There are hints at least in Aquinas which would lead us to believe that had he undertaken the criticism or interpretation of what moderns understand by a work of art, he of all men would have been an "ontological" critic. In his commentary on the *Sentences*, for example, he writes: "In the coming into being of works of art, the artistic process ought to be looked at in a twofold way, that is, in so far as the artistic process [or impulse of art] proceeds from the [individual] artist as something which he has discovered within himself [in his heart]; and, secondly, in so far as the artistic process of [making] works of art is a discovery of [the rules of] art itself, [and not of the inner individual impulse]." [4] The Trinitarian context of this statement is the question: "Whether the Father and the Son love us by means of the Holy Spirit,"

---

3. *S.T.,* I–II, q. 57, a. 5, ad 1m: "dicendum, quod bonum artis consideratur non in ipso artifice, sed magis in ipso artificiato."

4. ". . . in egressu artificiatorum ab arte est considerare duplicem processum; scilicet ipsius artis ab artifice, quam de corde suo adinvenit; et secundo processum artificiatorum ab ipsa arte inventa." *I Sent.,* dist. 32, q. 1, a. 3, ad 2m.

and St. Thomas' analogy helps him to resolve a theological difficulty only to the extent that art is accepted in the second sense, that is, as the effect of a process (what art discovers) and not as the process itself.

Whether or not Joyce had read this particular question in St. Thomas' commentary on the *Sentences* before he set about writing the *Stephen Hero* version of his first novel must remain an unanswered question; the chances are a hundred to one that he had not. Had he done so he would in the *Stephen Hero* days have read more attentively what Thomas had to say on the artistic process as process than on the "discovery" of that process, which is the art. It is in that genetic orbit at any rate that the aesthetic notions of *Stephen Hero* in general tend to revolve. There are significant exceptions which suggest that the Thomist texts on art might in the long run have drawn Stephen to a critical position closer to the art-work itself: "The critic is he who is able, by means of the signs which the artist affords, to approach the temper which has made the work and to see what is well done therein and what it signifies." [5] So writes Stephen in his college essay in commenting on the internecine warfare between the classical and romantic schools of his own Dublin school days. That Joyce offers this comment as a Thomist derivative seems certain, for almost in the next breath Stephen adds:

> Chief among these profanities [in approaching a work of art] Stephen set the antique principle that the end of art is to instruct, to elevate, and to amuse. "I am unable to find even a trace of this Puritanic conception of the esthetic purpose in the definition which Aquinas has given of beauty" he wrote "or in anything which he has written concerning the beautiful. The qualifications he expects for beauty are in fact of so abstract and common a character that it is quite impossible for even the most violent partizan to use the Aquinatian theory with the object of attacking any work of art that we possess from the hand of any artist whatsoever." [6]

The "Aquinatian" theory of the beautiful, as Joyce could easily perceive, has nothing in common with Puritanic conceptions of the artistic purpose, but one must question Stephen's inference that the "Aquinatian" theory of the beautiful favored or fostered Stephen's own (or

5. *Stephen Hero*, p. 79. Cf. Joyce's own schoolboy essay on James Clarence Mangan (1902) : "This is not to look for a message but to approach the temper which has made the work, an old woman praying, or a young man fastening his shoe, and to see what is there well done and how much it signifies." Joyce goes on : ". . . the inmost region will never yield to one who is enmeshed with profanities." (Quoted from Ulysses Bookshop reprint, p. 3, of "James Clarence Mangan," London, 1930. This essay appeared originally in University College literary magazine *St. Stephen's*, May, 1902.) Cf. Gorman, *James Joyce*, p. 79.

6. Ibid.

anybody else's) conception of the artist's total autonomy. Discussing the virtue of modesty, St. Thomas offers a very shrewd and sober defense of a woman's right to deck herself in fine clothes and ornaments and, if need be, to use rouge and powder her hair. Then in a spirit almost as tolerant as that of Alexander Pope in his portrait of Belinda at her dressing table in *The Rape of the Lock*, Aquinas justifies this widespread feminine practice with the assertion that in so ornamenting herself the woman is behaving as an *artist*. Having had recourse to this analogy of art, St. Thomas goes on to quote St. John Chrysostom, and in so doing makes an important qualification of which Stephen at this time cannot have been aware: "If, however, as it not seldom happens, there are individuals who use the works of some art or other for an evil end—even though the arts are not in themselves unlawful—such arts are to be stamped out by the civil power, just as the documents of Plato prescribe." [7]

In arguing for the licitness of feminine ornamentation, Aquinas comes as close as he does anywhere to relating the two notions, *pulchrum* and *ars*. It ought not to be necessary to argue that the relationship which he here envisages falls far short of the view which Joyce himself held as "Aquinatian" in 1903, that "art is the human disposition of intelligible or sensible matter for *an esthetic end*." [8] The fact of the matter is that Aquinas sees no difficulty in calling the cosmetician an artist. "Artist" was for him a term of such general import that it included both the cosmetician and the preacher: St. Thomas wrote a book, *De Arte Predicandi*. As Edgar De Bruyne has observed: "Saint Thomas ne prend pas l'art dans un sens limitatif. Tout ce qui vient d'être dit, vaut aussi bien pour l'agriculture et la médecine que pour l'architecture ou l'art du sculpteur." [9]

De Bruyne's observation is interesting almost as much for what it does not say as for what it says: there is at least the implication that Aquinas has little to say in his comments on *art* which has any immediate or very evident relevance to literature, to poetry. For though Aquinas allows that "the liberal arts are more excellent than the mechan-

7. "Si tamen operibus alicujus artis ut pluries aliqui male utantur, quamvis de se non sint illicitae, sunt tamen per officium Principis a civitate extirpandae secundum documenta Platonis." *S.T.*, II–II, q. 169, a. 2, ad 4ᵐ.

In the library, Stephen asks John Eglinton, "Which of the two [Aristotle or Plato] would have banished me from his commonwealth?" *Ulysses*, p. 184.

St. Thomas offers, as an example of an artifact which cannot be used without furnishing others with an occasion for sin, an idol—"idola vel aliqua ad cultum idololatriae pertinentia"—but this example would seem to drive straight toward pure intentionalism. Suppose someone dug up a statue in Greece and admired it and then learned afterward that it was an idol? Would the statue at that point cease to be valuable as art, would it be "false" to art?

8. Gorman, *James Joyce*, p. 98; also *Stephen Hero*, p. 77. (Italics mine.)

9. De Bruyne, *Études d'esthétique médiévale*, 3, 334–5.

ical ones," [1] he classifies the construction of a syllogism among the
liberal arts, and classifies architecture and sculpture with the mechanical (or servile) arts, and he does not mention poetry in this classification at all. Moreover, of all the modern "fine arts," architecture and
sculpture are the two that almost always serve Aquinas for examples.
For the most part he talks about such "arts" as farming, medicine, and
preaching. It is perhaps sufficiently "Aquinatian" to say with Maritain
that "art is simply the mind at work," [2] but this will raise some difficulties in our accepting the unargued premises of Stephen's essay that
art is the expression of the beautiful, and that the artist stands "in the
position of mediator between the world of his experience, and the world
of his dreams." [3]

Between the Thomist texts on art and the Thomist texts on beauty,
there is such a difference in contextual situation that it is very difficult
to see how anyone, in any properly Thomist sense, may effect a close
concordance between them. From the fact that Joyce at one period in
his life adapted the texts so freely, and that he did so "with a naïf air of
discovering novelties," [4] it does not follow either that he misunderstood
Aquinas or that he was repudiating in any way the accepted Thomist
aesthetic synthesis of his times. The fact of the matter would seem to be
rather that he saw that the Aquinan texts needed considerable ampli-
fication before they could serve him as a base for the philosophy of art,
for the philosophy of literature, in particular, which he wished to construct. In seeking to exploit the supposed close affinity between the two
series of texts, he involved himself in labyrinthine difficulties, but not
more so than anyone else who attempted to defend this affinity might
have done. His difficulties are reflected in the theoretical *fin-de-siècle*
speculations which Stephen Dedalus advances in *Stephen Hero,* in the
Portrait, and in *Ulysses.*

The fin-de-siècle "art for art's sake," both in its posture and in its
poetry, created the atmosphere in which Joyce pursued his Paris studies
of Aquinas. But when poets like Baudelaire and Wilde used this fin-
de-siècle formula, they meant something much more "précieux" than

---

1. *S.T.,* I–II, q. 57, a. 3, obj. 3: "artes liberales sunt excellentiores quam artes me-
chanicae."

2. *Art and Scholasticism,* p. 90.

3. *Stephen Hero,* p. 77. Maritain's supposition in *Art and Scholasticism* (p. 33)
seems somewhat unargued, like Stephen's premises: "Art in general tends to make a
work. But certain arts tend to make a work of *beauty* and thereby differ essentially
from all the rest. . . . The work which involves the labour of the Fine Arts is ordered
to beauty."

It is difficult to see how Maritain's position avoids making "beauty" a species of its
own genus, as if a squirrel differed essentially from other animals by being *particularly* an animal. Cf. *Creative Intuition in Art and Poetry,* p. 162 ff.: ". . . everything
is beautiful in its own way" (p. 163).

4. *Stephen Hero,* p. 77.

Aquinas ever intended. For them *l'art pour l'art* seems to have been an attempt to put into practice their peculiarly exaggerated version of the Kantian "aesthetic distance" or "aesthetic disinterest." If their formula represents an exaggeration of Kant, it represents as well a version of the Scholastic "art for art's sake" which the Schoolmen would have found quite foreign to their thought. When the Schoolmen used the formula, they wished no more than to insist upon the fact that art has a certain intrinsic finality of its own, that no matter how morally good or well-intentioned the artist may be, he must first know the rules of his craft, that an object is well made if it serves the purpose well for which it was made. Maybe the object should not have been made at all, but that is another question for prudence (not art) to decide. (Literature, as we have said before, was not regarded as a very obvious example of "art." Without the benefit of our modern terms, the Schoolmen seem to have sensed that a poem is as much an "act" as an "artifact.") When Joyce decides in his Paris Notebook, however, that "houses, clothes, and furniture" are not works of art,[5] he comes to his decision not on the basis of prudential considerations but on the basis of the fin-de-siècle consideration that the "aesthetic end" (of beauty) must stand apart not merely from moral but from all practical ends.

5. Gorman, *James Joyce*, p. 99.

3

A Pennyworth of Thomist Wisdom

. . . Though shintoed, spitefired, perplagued and
cramkrieged, I am doing my dids bits
and have made of my prudentials good.

Finnegans Wake [1]

I F Joyce as a young man in Paris passed several hours each evening
at the Bibliothèque Sainte-Geneviève reading St. Thomas and Aristotle, as his friend Valery Larbaud reports,[2] we may reasonably
surmise that he was drawn to the library by a desire not so much to
learn Aristotelian-Thomist metaphysics as to find hints which might
help him answer his questions about the nature and the meaning of art.
Even if he should fall short of constructing a perfectly consistent aesthetic philosophy of his own, he would be better qualified to equip
Stephen Dedalus with an aesthetic philosophy which would make
Stephen intelligible in the world of fiction where Joyce intended to
situate him. Between the *Stephen Hero* draft ("What rubbish it is!"
was Joyce's description of it thirty years later) [3] and the *Portrait,* two
differences of perspective are noticeable: a tendency on Joyce's part to
stand back and let Stephen himself carry the responsibility for the
aesthetic views enunciated in the *Portrait,* and a comic spirit of criticism
of these views which results from the substitution of Lynch for Cranly.
There is also a shift in the style from simple narrative presentation to
ingenious symbolic statement. This new mode of symbolization is not
at first overtly functional; whatever Joyce's intentions may have been,
his symbolic subtleties of color and of legend are largely submerged and
lost in the narrative text. So far as we can detect them, they show at
least that Joyce was desirous of qualifying Stephen Dedalus' utterances
by inviting attention to his own more sophisticated literary concerns.
The painstaking elaboration and interweaving into the finished work
of the three principal symbols—the Daedalus myth; the poet as God-
creator, redeemer, and priest; and the betrayal-crucifixion theme—

1. *Finnegans Wake,* p. 539.
2. "James Joyce," *La nouvelle revue française, nouv. sér.,* 9ᵉ année, *16,* no. 103 (Avril
1922), 387.
3. Cf. Slocum and Cahoon, *Joyce Bibliography.* From a letter to Harriet Weaver,
quoted p. 136.

counterpoints the presentation of Stephen's aesthetic arguments and enables Joyce to stand apart from them in a way which is not possible in the earlier manuscript draft.[4] Finally if we look ahead to *Exiles* and *Ulysses,* we notice an increasingly marked withdrawal on Joyce's part from the aesthetic engagement in which the youthful Stephen becomes involved.

It may be going too far to say with Hugh Kenner, "In explicating the plight of Richard Rowan, *Exiles* becomes Joyce's final abolition of the last shreds of Stephen," [5] since Stephen survives at least long enough to play an important, if no longer central, role in *Ulysses.* Kenner is right, however, in pointing up the paralyzing consequences of Richard's aestheticism when it is transferred to the practical order. So far as Richard is in one sense an extension of Stephen, one sees the peril of confusing the beauty of person or character, which in the practical order naturally inclines to desire, with the beauty of artifacts, with which both would-be artists are chiefly concerned.

As Richard's wife, Bertha is not content to remain for Richard simply an *id quod visum placet;* she is too much of a real woman to be content with the role of a Beatrice in Richard's aesthetic vision. Neither Richard's nor Stephen's aesthetic code permits them freely to give themselves to that which their vision contemplates. Both young men seek to construct not only an aesthetic but a total philosophy of life on the base of the Thomist texts on beauty and art. Their Thomism consequently is oddly distorted; whereas Thomas paid little attention to the beauty of artifacts, which he nowhere seriously analyzes as distinct from the beauty of persons or the beauty of natural things, Richard and Stephen pay little attention to anything else. "Love is more of a unitive force than cognition is," as Aquinas notes.[6] Richard fails to understand this, and is much more interested in making over his wife into an object of aesthetic contemplation than he is in giving himself to her as a person. The "wounding doubt" which paralyzes him at the end of the play rises not so much from his suspicion of her infidelity as from his fear that she may have made an independent use of her freedom, with which he likes to imagine that he has endowed her, and in this way interfered with the artistic transformation he has been at such pains to effect. Stephen's mind too is centered on *ego* rather than on *ens,* as Kenner notes; [7] and as Joyce's good Trieste friend Italo Svevo tells us, "It will be part of the maturer Dedalus of *Ulysses* to remember that he had spent the greater part of his life in a sublime dream." [8]

4. Cf. C. G. Anderson, "The Sacrificial Butter," *Accent, 12* (Winter 1952), 3–13.
5. "Joyce's *Exiles,*" *Hudson Review, 5* (Autumn 1952), 393.
6. "Amor est magis unitivus quam cognitio." *S.T.,* I–II, q. 28, a. 1, ad 3ᵐ.
7. "The *Portrait* in Perspective," *James Joyce, Two Decades of Criticism,* ed. Seon Givens (New York, Vanguard, 1948), p. 154.
8. "James Joyce," Milan lecture, *ca.* 33.

Nevertheless, the most sustained Joycean effort at a philosophical formulation of the nature of art occurs in the *Portrait*,[9] and one does well to begin there if one is interested in seeing how Joyce "used" Aquinas "for all he was worth." [1] "Aquinas would understand me better than you," Stephen tells the unphilosophically minded Lynch. Stephen leads into his discussion with a general proposition that sounds "Aquinatian": "Pity is the feeling which arrests the mind in the presence of whatsoever is grave and constant in human sufferings and unites it with the human sufferer. Terror is the feeling which arrests the mind in the presence of whatsoever is grave and constant in human sufferings and unites it with the secret cause." [2]

In Stephen's mind, these definitions of pity and terror serve the function of emphasizing that tragedy must somehow present what is "grave and constant" in human experience and not rest content with presenting that which is uniquely personal and particular—such as the freakishly accidental death of the girl, of whom Stephen speaks, who was pierced by a splinter of glass as she stepped into a hansom. The raw experience of life must somehow be located in the context of universal human experiences before it can begin to function as an artistic symbol which will have meaning for the experience of others.

This view of Stephen's, that art should anesthetize the painful by eliminating the brutal and by giving an expressive form to the "universal purpose" (of suffering), is a characteristic concern of much late nineteenth-century Hegelian theorizing about tragic art, as Bernard Bosanquet's *Introduction to Hegel's Philosophy of Fine Art* is sufficient to show. Rationality itself, asserts Bosanquet, forces its way into the wild diversity of contingent, brutal facts, "and demands to see the emergence of a higher and more *universal purpose* from these elements in spite of their self-contradiction, and to be assured of its being attained." [3] Bosanquet's general outline of Hegel's aesthetic system reads

9. Pp. 239–54. Unless otherwise indicated, page references to Joyce's works in this chapter refer to the *Portrait*.

1. Cf. Joyce's letters in the collection of the New York Public Library (now at Yale University) ; quoted by A. M. Klein, "A Shout in the Street," reprinted from *New Directions, 13,* 1: "I would not pay overmuch attention to these theories [of Vico] beyond using them for all they are worth, but they have gradually forced themselves on me through the circumstances of my life."

2. P. 239. Stephen remarks, "Aristotle has not defined pity and terror. I have." Aquinas has not *defined* pity and terror either, but in the *Summa Theologiae, Prima Secundae,* where he treats of the emotions, *passiones animae,* he furnishes the elements from which it would not be difficult to construct the Dedalian definitions. Cf. q. 23, a. 1, on the difference between the concupiscible and irascible emotions; q. 35, a. 1 and a. 2 on *dolor, tristitia,* as "concupiscible"; and q. 59, a. 1, ad 3^m for Stephen's "pity," (i.e., *misericordia* as a *virtus* as well as a *passio*) ; and q. 42, a. 3, ad 3^m on *timor,* the contrary of *spes,* for Stephen's "terror," an "irascible" emotion as Aquinas conceives of it.

3. Bernard Bosanquet, *The Introduction to Hegel's Philosophy of Fine Art* (London, Kegan Paul, 1886), p. 91. Italics mine here and below.

in surprisingly large part like the late nineteenth-century versions of the aesthetic system of Aquinas. Stephen's concern with "the grave and constant" as a prerequisite for the tragic emotion is quite what one might expect a Thomist to have. "I speak of normal natures," Stephen tells Lynch.

The second conclusion which Stephen draws from his definitions is not so clearly Thomist as Stephen seems to think. Granted the accuracy of his definitions, Stephen argues from his employment of the word "arrest" to his second general proposition that "the esthetic emotion . . . is therefore static."

At this point Stephen seems to be adjusting a Hegelian notion of tragedy as a "special kind of action" to fit his understanding of the Aquinan *contemplatio*. As A. C. Bradley reads Hegel's theory of tragedy, tragedy is that form of art which shows *in collision* the affirmative forces which rule the world. But having committed himself to a view of artistic contemplation as essentially "static," Stephen cannot come right out and defend Hegel's theory of the tragic as something "kinetic," as Bradley later on feels quite free to do: "He [Hegel] seems to be right in laying emphasis on the action and conflict in tragedy rather than on the suffering and misfortune." [4] The Aquinan contemplatio is as much kinetic as it is static, and Stephen might have made a better formulation of pity and terror as the essentially tragic emotions had he realized that when the mind is arrested by the artistic vision of conflict and collision it is very much in action and not static at all. Paul Elmer More has pointed out in this connection that "all art, so far as it is alive, must be kinetic," and the Aquinan student of Joyce will agree with More's criticism that Joyce "would have formulated his [Aquinas'] principles more correctly if, instead of a contrast between kinetic and static, he had distinguished between art that aims to arouse physical lust or loathing, and art that seeks to move desire and joy of hyperphysical realities." [5] It is easy, however, to see what Stephen is leading up to: a theory of art which situates the artistic (and the tragic-as-artistic) as a department of the beautiful. After a digression Stephen goes on to describe this aesthetic *stasis* of ideal pity or ideal terror as a "stasis called forth, prolonged and at last dissolved by what I call the rhythm of beauty." [6]

As soon as Stephen mentions "beauty," the cautious reader of Joyce may begin to wonder if Stephen has the Scholastic or the Kantian aesthetic in mind. In many important respects the two aesthetics are "astonishingly en rapport," as A. W. Levi (of the University of Chi-

4. A. C. Bradley, "Hegel's Theory of Tragedy," *Oxford Lectures on Poetry* (London, Macmillan, 1926), p. 81.
5. Paul Elmer More, "James Joyce," *The American Review*, 5 (May 1935), 149.
6. P. 241.

cago) has demonstrated. In both, there is a marked teleological approach, a stress on the intuitive, nonconceptual aspect of the act of apprehension of beauty, and some serious effort to explain the aesthetic emotion in terms of the "form," or the "normal" or "rational idea" which the beautiful object illustrates. But as Levi points out several times in his study, there is an important difference between the two aesthetics which to some extent qualifies all the significant likenesses: the Scholastic aesthetic is metaphysical, whereas the Kantian aesthetic is epistemological in nature.[7] The epistemological accentuation of Stephen's exposition is not easy to miss.

Almost all neo-Thomist aestheticians have adverted to the (Kantian) doctrine of aesthetic disinterest and detachment in their explication of the quae visa placent, a special form of contemplation which rests content with the vision of the object as it is artistically symbolized, and which is not led on by the vision to a desire for physical possession of the object itself, nor by any wish to alter the physical (that is, non-ideational) universe, be it material or moral, which the artifact—the poem or the picture, for example—may either symbolize or "represent." The "disinterest" of which Kantian and Scholastic aestheticians speak is not a lack of interest in the artifact nor an indifference in regard to possessing it. But possession of the artifact is not the same as possession of the object which the artifact somehow symbolizes or reveals. Aesthetic interest in the artifact makes one less interested in the object to which it refers. The possession which the mind enjoys in contemplating the artifact as a work of art is an "intentional" possession: so long as the mind can hold the artifact before its spiritual vision, the question of physical possession or contact with the object referred to does not arise, and the question of physical possession of the artifact itself, if it rises at all, is quite separate from and subordinate to the mind's intentional possession by knowledge of what the artifact symbolizes. As W. K. Wimsatt has observed in a valuable explication of this page of the *Portrait:* "The painting looks like a landscape, but we rest in the looks and need not be moved to go out doors. The tragedy is about murder, but we rest short of wishing to save the victim or punish the criminal. In short, the aesthetic symbol absorbs the 'interest' of its referents into itself and 'contains' it in an impractical stasis." [8]

In this sense, Stephen's "luminous silent stasis of esthetic pleasure" comes very close to the concept of "detachment" or "distance" of Kantian "disinterest," and students of St. Thomas have not failed to point out the resemblance and the priority of St. Thomas' formulation. "Motus et quies reducuntur in causalitatem pulchri," says St. Thomas,[9] so it

7. Albert William Levi, "Scholasticism and the Kantian Aesthetic," *New Scholasticism, 8* (July 1934), 201.

8. "Poetry and Christian Thinking," *Thought, 26* (Summer 1951), 225.

9. *In Div. Nom.,* c. 4, lect. 6 (conclus.).

would seem permissible to argue on Thomist grounds of beauty that the dramatic emotion is as much an instance of psychological involvement as it is of aesthetic distance. "The mind is *arrested* and raised above desire and loathing," as Stephen notices, but that is not the whole story, and one could argue in terms of the Thomist analysis de pulchro that the essentially artistic solution of a tragic situation is not adequately accounted for by the view that the mind is arrested in contemplation, and that some element of "release from troubled introspection into action" is inseparable from any truly dramatic emotion.[1] The more mature a man is in his vision of evil, the more necessary it is that his pity and fear should be sublimated, like Dante's vision of hell, by some form of intellectual love.

In a book review in the *Dublin Daily Express,* Joyce (in 1903) expresses his dislike for a contemporary Shakespearean study by remarking: "Here is no psychological complexity, no cross-purpose, no interweaving of motives such as might perplex. . . ."[2] "The tragic emotion, in fact, is a face looking two ways, towards terror and towards pity, both of which are phases of it," continues Stephen in the *Portrait,* and from this approach we might have expected him to point to art as a resolution, at least in symbolic terms, of the complexities and contradictions of experience. Apparently not realizing that this *motus-quies* polarity is as defensibly Thomist as the concept of aesthetic stasis, and in the over-all view compatible with it, Stephen reverses himself in his reasoning and characterizes as "kinetic" or "imperfect" art whatever in any way excites desire or loathing.

It is easy enough to see what Stephen wants to exclude: "the pornographical or didactic" excites desire and loathing by imperfect aesthetic means. But if Stephen wishes to be rigorously Thomist, must he repudiate all kinetic elements in art as pure sensation? The most supremely intellective act of which Thomas can conceive is the Beatific Vision, which as he thinks of it is highly kinetic and has an abundant resonance in the affective nature.[3] Stuart Gilbert quotes to good effect an analysis of Stephen's version of the Thomist definition of beauty by the Cambridge scholar J. P. M. Stern, who concludes by strongly contesting "the validity of Joyce's claim to have drawn his theory of the static nature of art directly from St. Thomas Aquinas."[4]

It ought to be added that though Stephen's theory of static art is not consistent with his Aristotelian and Thomist premises, Joyce's portrayal of Stephen's character is consistent enough. In seeking to cleanse

1. Cf. David Daiches, "Theodicy, Poetry, and Tradition," *Spiritual Problems in Contemporary Literature,* ed. S. R. Hopper (New York, Harper, 1952), p. 82.
2. "Shakespeare Explained!" *Dublin Daily Express,* Nov. 12, 1903. A review of *Shakespeare Studied in Eight Plays* by Hon. A. S. Canning.
3. Cf. *Contra Gentes,* Lib. III, c. 63: "Qualiter in illa ultima felicitate omne desiderium hominis completur."
4. "James Joyce," in Givens, *Two Decades,* p. 459.

his mind of all desire and loathing, Stephen is seeking as an artist the
ideal state of spiritual purgation which fits his notion of the artist's life
as a priestly dedication. "We are all animals," Stephen says in a polite
aside to Lynch, "I also am an animal." But in resuming his discourse
he adds immediately, "We are just now in a mental world." [5] To speak
of the senses as "the prison gates of our soul" is clearly not Thomist at
all. It also makes for incompleteness if not distortion of the Thomist
analysis of intellectual pleasure to suggest that such joy rises only at
the point of silent stasis. In his treatment of *gaudium,* or spiritual joy,
as distinct from *delectatio,* or the gladness of sense perception, St.
Thomas devotes a complete article in the *Summa* to showing how movement, or kinetic activity, may be a cause of this intellectual pleasure.[6]
Dante represents the contemplative choirs of angels in Paradise as
wheeling or revolving in a celestial dance. Our own joy in poetry involves
kinesis as a mode, at least unconscious, of the contemplative stasis.

More attention to the few remarks which St. Thomas has made about
poetry might have helped Stephen as well as other Thomist commentators to a more helpful construct of Thomist poetic theory. "Where
has it ever been established that poetry is a department of the beautiful?"
asks Wimsatt, who presently adds, "The Thomist aesthetician will note
that Aquinas himself, echoing an ancient idea, treats poetry as a first
cousin of sophistical rhetoric." [7] The text which Wimsatt has in mind
is from Aquinas' commentary on the logic of Aristotle's *Organon,* to
which rhetoric and poetic are added. One advantage of following
Aquinas' thought here, rather than through the texts de pulchro is that
at last we find Aquinas saying something directly about poetry. Another modern critic, Richard McKeon, in a valuable commentary on this
text, has observed: "Thomas Aquinas treats poetic not as the science
of a product or process of production but as a subdivision of logic." [8]
Such an approach, though it may need to be modified, at least avoids
confusing poetry, which is verbal discourse and as such a verbal act,
with physical artifacts—an issue which has never been very satisfactorily
cleared up by those who have spoken of poetry as art and who have
conceived of art as an intellectual process that makes a beautiful object.

After discussing the five parts of logic which treat of the certitudes
of science, Aquinas considers the three parts which treat of the process
of discovery (*inventio*): dialectics, rhetoric, and poetry. Dialectics, he
says, leads to certitude or opinion. Rhetoric and poetic are distinguished
as follows:

> Sometimes, however, one arrives not at complete certitude, but
> only at a kind of suspicion, because one is not altogether inclined

5. P. 241.
6. *S.T.,* I–II, q. 32, a. 2.
7. "Poetry and Christian Thinking," *Thought, 26* (Summer 1951), 226.
8. "Poetry and Philosophy in the Twelfth Century. The Renaissance of Rhetoric,"
Modern Philology, 43 (May 1946), 230.

to accept one possibility rather than its opposite, though one may be more inclined to accept it rather than not to do so. This is the province where rhetoric operates. Sometimes, however, solely on the basis of one's own appraisal of the situation, one is more inclined to think one way rather than the opposite, because of the imagery—as happens, for instance, when one comes to loathe a certain kind of food because it is represented under the guise of being loathsome. This latter is the sort of thing that the poetic treats of, for it is the poet's function to induce to virtue by having previously represented virtue [in a fitting manner].[9]

Didactic as the conclusion of Aquinas' argument might at first have seemed to Stephen, it may be that Aquinas' argument in the long run saves a larger area of this world's art and literature for poetic enjoyment than Stephen's own defense: "Plato, I believe, said that beauty is the splendour of truth. I don't think that it has a meaning but the true and the beautiful are akin." [1] Between the true and the beautiful some kinship, to be sure, is recognized both by Plato and Aquinas though it seems to be significant that Aquinas in his discussions of beauty never uses the Platonic formula, splendor veri.[2] In Thomist metaphysics, at any rate, the true is predicated always analogously, just as ens, or being, is. Between the truth of philosophy and the truth of poetry there is room for considerable diversity, so that if one wishes to insist on the kinship between the true and the beautiful it is important to remember that "the true" here is a very special kind of truth—poetic truth.

As a moral theologian, Aquinas wished that poetic "representations" would "induce to truth." The example of the food, commonplace and unpoetic as it is in itself, shows that he recognized that a poetic representation could be successful even though the correspondence with reality were false. This recognition of the possible disparity between "poetic" and "ontological" truth is not, however, the point of his using the example. The point rather is that the poet has a special responsibility to use poetic technique in an expert, "artful" way so that virtue, or anything else, may be symbolized "in a fitting manner." Unless the poet

9. "Quandoque vero non fit complete fides vel opinio, sed suspitio quaedam, quia non totaliter declinatur ad unam partem contradictionis, licet magis declinetur in hanc quam in aliam. Et ad hoc ordinatur Rhetorica. Quandoque vero sola existimatio declinat in aliquam partem contradictionis propter aliquam repraesentationem, ad modum quo fit homini abominatio alicujus cibi si repraesentetur ei sub similitudine alicujus abominabilis. Et ad hoc ordinatur Poetica. Nam poetae est inducere ad aliquod virtuosum, per aliquam praecedentem repraesentationem." *I Post. Analyt.*, lect. 1.

1. P. 243.

2. Cf. John Duffy, C.S.S.R., *A Philosophy of Poetry, Based on Thomistic Principles* (Washington, Catholic Univ. Press, 1943), p. 34. Duffy notes that although the phrase splendor veri cannot be found in the works of Aquinas the concept occurs in the *De Pulchro et de Bono*. Aquinas uses *splendor secundum propriam formam* and, as Duffy notes, he means that the splendor is not merely in the form but in the whole being according to its form (*splendor entis*).

has first done his work well as poet, he cannot possibly hope to serve the cause of virtue.

Plato in his *Republic* also wanted the poets to represent virtue in a fitting manner, but the force of Plato's argument against the actual poets (including Homer) is that, left to themselves, they must necessarily represent falsity and evil as though they were true and good, since being poets and not philosophers they had to deal with semblances of things at a third remove from reality. As charming and as pedagogically useful as poetry might be, it was essentially a lie. Unlike Plato, Aquinas is not prepared to disqualify all discourse which falls short of arriving at philosophic truth. Poetic semblances can have a value in his eyes even when they fall short of mirroring reality. He argues from the very real "plus" value of poetry to a special moral responsibility of poets. He sees that in the alchemy of poetry the true and false, the good and evil can be so transmuted that a poetically successful representation might in actuality incline to moral failure; hence his moral caveat about the poets. A prudent teacher of morals is aware of the widespread tendency of readers of poetry to make poetry a surrogate for morals. Whereas Plato conceives an inaccessible beauty as the splendor veri, which the poets, since they are not philosophers, cannot hope to see, and whereas Joyce's Stephen equates poetry with beauty and arrives at the proposition that poetic truth (imaginative truth) is truth resplendent, Aquinas soberly and realistically assumes that the poetic as such need be no more than the shadow of the truth.

Just as in the moral order Aquinas explains the will's choice of evil as being possible only when the evil appears under some aspect of good (a *bonum apparens*), so on a poetic level he conceives of the poetic representation as having satisfied the exigencies of the mind for truth provided that the representation appears at least provisionally under some "guise" of truth: "The rhetorician and the poet lead one to assent to what they propose not merely by speaking about things as they actually are, but just as much by playing upon the sentiments of their audience. In this way rhetoricians and poets quite often move their listeners to be of one mind about some matter through a manipulation of the feelings of their hearers." [3]

From this comparison of the poetic with the rhetorical (quite alien to the Thomism of the *Portrait*) it does not follow that Aquinas meant to speak of the poets in some pejorative sense, or that he regarded them as constitutionally incapable of arriving at the truth. He recognized that poetic truth need not be logical truth, that the logical structure of

3. "Rhetor et poeta ducunt ad assentiendum ei quod intendunt, non solum per ea quae sunt propria rei, sed etiam per dispositiones audientis. Unde rhetores et poetae plerumque movent auditores in unum, provocando eos ad aliquas passiones." *I Perih.*, lect. 7.

a poem need not be that of a syllogism. The syllogism is not the only verbal means of arriving at the truth. Aquinas praises the poets for their use of metaphors and likens them in this respect to the theologians: "Poetic knowledge concerns those matters which because of some short-coming in truth cannot be grasped by reason; hence it is necessary that the reason be seduced, as it were, by certain metaphors; theological knowledge, on the other hand, concerns matters that are beyond the grasp of reason; symbolic representation, therefore, is common both to poetry and theology since the knowledge in neither case is attainable by reason alone." [4] Like Aquinas, we still sometimes speak, do we not, of the *craft* of poetry and call the poets craftsmen—that is, "crafty" men? Though there is a difference between craftsmanship and craftiness, still there is a likeness too: honesty and cunning can go together in the well constructed work of art.

It appears that one must qualify heavily as "applied Aquinas" the Dedalan proposition: "The first step in the direction of *truth* is to under-stand the frame and scope of the intellect itself, to comprehend the act itself of intellection." In Stephen's own analysis of "the stages them-selves of all esthetic apprehension," [5] he hardly makes mention of the *phantasm,* or sense-image, which in Thomist psychology is not only that from which the intellect abstracts but also that with which the

4. "Poetica scientia est de his quae propter defectum veritatis non possunt a ratione capi; unde oportet quod quasi quibusdam similitudinibus ratio seducatur: theologia autem est de his quae sunt supra rationem; et ideo modus symbolicus utrique communis est, cum neutra rationi proportionetur." *I Sent.,* Prolog., q. 1, a. 5, ad 3^m.

In a lecture delivered July 3, 1949, at the Goethe Bicentennial Convocation in Aspen, Colorado, the German scholar Ernst Robert Curtius maintained in his argument based on the above text that Aquinas discredited poetry (see Curtius' first appendix to his book *European Literature and the Latin Middle Ages,* tr. Willard R. Trask, Bollingen Series 36, New York, Pantheon Books, 1953, pp. 593-4). Curtius is clearly right in perceiving that the great Scholastics of the thirteenth century are not interested either in vindicating or in evaluating poetry. St. Thomas imagined, it is true, that "he had more urgent business" (as Curtius says). But the *opposition* of Scholasticism to hu-manism (in particular, to poetry) is hardly proved by the Thomist texts which Curtius cites. "Scholasticism put an end to the confusion of philosophy and poetry," as Curtius admirably demonstrates (ibid., p. 213), but the incidental remarks of St. Thomas on poetry do not reveal hostility. Many modern defenders of poetry and of humanism would not care to base their defense on poetry as an exact science.

The page (93) in *L'introduction à l'étude de saint Thomas d'Aquin* by M. D. Chenu, O.P. (Montreal, Institut d'Études Médiévales, 1950), to which Curtius refers his reader (*European Literature,* p. 93, n. 20^a) would prove no more than that Aquinas distrusts the use of metaphors and of other figures in *scientific* discourse. There is to be sure a literary aridity in the Latin Scholastic expression of the thirteenth century, especially if we compare it with that of the twelfth century. The greatly accelerated growth of poetry in the vernacular languages (as well as the revival of Aristotelian-ism) tended to suppress the need of creative literary expression in Latin, and it would seem in any case to have required much time for a new poetics to emerge out of this "twilight zone."

5. Pp. 244-5. (Italics mine.)

intellect symbolizes. It is true that Stephen says, "The first step in the direction of beauty is to understand the frame and scope of the imagination." [6] The imagination, or *phantasia,* according to the Thomist analysis of the act of cognition, is the image-making power by which the concrete and singular are represented to the intellect through "phantasms." Stephen in his theoretical reasoning makes no further exploration of this initial aspect of the total process from personal, imaginative intuition to general, conceptual expression. It is this aspect that would seem crucial if one set out to discuss in particular the aesthetic act of apprehension. Here more than in any other cognitive act the symbolic instrumentality of the phantasm is important. At one point in his exposition Stephen speaks of "the esthetic image," [7] but his description of this image as "selfbounded and selfcontained" corresponds much more closely to the Cartesian "clear and distinct idea" than it does to the Thomist "image" or "phantasm," which is obscure and ambiguous, and like the symbols of art, capable of many ambivalent significances and further determinations. Stephen in fact seems to identify his "esthetic image" with integritas, which might strike the ordinary Thomist as such a confusion of what these Thomist terms signify that he would be led to suspect at this point that possibly Stephen, even more than Lynch, is caricaturing the whole Thomist attempt to explain cognition.

The reason that the truth of poetry seems to Aquinas to be an *infima doctrina,*[8] which can be neither perfectly abstracted nor perfectly paraphrased, *propter defectum veritatis,*[9] is that in Thomist psychology the infrarational world of poetry is viewed as a symbolic world which has its roots in phantasms, or symbolic images. So far as metaphors are the language of poetry, there is certain to be an opaqueness for the intellect in the boldly bifurcated language that poets use; in the light of its own intrinsic finality for truth the intellect in its quest for unity remains to some extent dissatisfied. Poetry suggests much, its imaginative vision is splendid and coherent; but the mystery of being like "Ariachne's broken woof," remains to be unraveled and pursued; the intellect cannot but be *arrested,* but the quest for truth goes on. If this be so, one ought to question Stephen's assertion that "the most *satisfying* relations of the sensible must therefore correspond to the necessary phases of artistic apprehension" [1]—the more so, since Stephen characterizes his assertion as "another pennyworth of wisdom" of "our old friend saint Thomas." [2]

If one wishes to utilize Aquinas' analysis of beauty as a basis for

6. Ibid.
7. P. 249.
8. "Procedere autem per similitudines varias, et repraesentationes, est proprium poeticae, quae est infima inter omnes doctrinas." *S.T.*, I, q. 1, a. 9, obj. 1.
9. *I Sent.,* Prolog., q. 1, a. 5, ad 3[m].
1. P. 248. Italics mine.
2. P. 245.

poetics, as the post-Aquinas writers on poetics have done, and as Stephen Dedalus sets out to do, one ought not in the name of Aquinas to confuse the subjective psychological response to the beautiful with the constitutive ontological principles which might be called the "objective correlative" of this response. The Scholastics for their part have almost always spoken, as Aquinas does, of integrity, proportion (*consonantia*), and clarity as objective qualities, or existential properties, *in things,* and though they may not always have been very clear as to whether these existential qualities belong to the things represented by the work of art or inhere in the representation, they have not treated these qualities as though they belong to the act of apprehension, as Stephen does. Nor have the Scholastics spoken, as Stephen does, of these three properties as "stages" or "phases" of the mind's act of aesthetic apprehension. To do so is to shift the whole discussion from Thomist grounds, for in St. Thomas' perspectives not only are these three properties regarded as ontological and objective qualities inherent in the thing known rather than in the knowing mind, but they are conceived of as being known in one single simple act which cannot be divided into "phases."

Writing in the *Australasian Journal of Psychology and Philosophy,* a discerning student of Joyce's aesthetic theory, A. D. Hope, attempts to save the Thomism of Stephen's discussion of the well known Thomist triad by pointing out that "Joyce here is speaking of the 'esthetic image,' that is to say, not the butcher boy's basket at which he and Lynch are looking, but the artist's image of it which, when reproduced in the medium of words or paint, will be the work of art." [3] But Stephen several times calls Lynch's attention to "that basket," the very particular basket which the butcher boy is carrying, and it is only when his remarks on the three qualities are almost concluded that he suggests by an oblique reference to Shelley that what he has been saying could be applied to poetry as well as to the butcher boy's basket. He does not work this application out. Had he done so, he would still *not* have been justified, at least on Thomist grounds, in speaking of the three qualities of beauty as though they were "ways of seeing the object rather than characters of the object itself," which Hope maintains is sufficiently in correspondence with Aquinas' theory.

Stephen confuses, it would seem, the Scholastic *analysis* of the act of apprehension with this act itself. Adequately to analyze the simplest act of apprehension requires many concepts in any epistemology, but the ordering of the concepts of analysis is not a substitute for the act which is under analysis. The concept of beauty is far from simple. As Aquinas conceives it, it is truly complex, with an ontological-psychological polarity which defies simple definition. The best one can do is to describe it,

3. A. D. Hope, "The Esthetic Theory of James Joyce," *Australasian Journal of Psychology and Philosophy, 21* (Dec. 1943), 108.

and the description must necessarily be complicated. But neither the complexity of this concept nor the complications which arise in a description of its genesis warrant one on Thomist grounds to speak as though it were generated in three stages by the mind. The integrity, consonance (or harmony), and clarity of which Aquinas speaks are all three known simultaneously by the viewer or reader or listener in one *intuitive* act.[4]

As has already been noted, Stephen seems to be thinking of the phantasm of the Scholastics when he describes integritas as the first phase of apprehension, which draws a bounding line, as he says, about the object to be apprehended. "An esthetic image is presented to us either in space or in time." [5] The phantasm, or imaginative representation, of Scholastic psychology has, it is true, an ontological priority in the genesis of the act of knowledge. Stephen interprets this ontological priority as though it were a question of temporal sequence. But ontological and temporal priority are not the same thing: one must have light before the act of vision can take place, but the light does not come first and then the act of vision. Granted that there is light, one sees both the light and the object which the light illuminates not in stages but simultaneously. In some respects the aspect of light does not fit the case of the phantasm. Stephen goes on to say: "The esthetic image is first luminously apprehended as selfbounded and selfcontained." But the phantasm, or image, of Thomist psychology is not pure luminosity. It is inchoative cognition or symbolization, and like all imaginative symbolization, though it presents the concrete and the particular for the intellect to scrutinize,[6] it does so tentatively and obscurely. The truth of reality is germinally present, but a simultaneous, not subsequent, immanent operation of the intellect is necessary for this truth to be conceived in the mind.

Even the concept, the *verbum mentis,* though it perfects the image which the imagination has elaborated, makes no commitment or enunciation about the abstract nature of this mental image, or about the nature of the reality which the mind grasps (that is, "apprehends," or knows) through the instrumentality of the image. The Thomist concept is not a

4. "Intuitive" is here used in a general sense, and not in the special sense that one can have knowledge without *any* intellectual abstraction. The latter is much disputed by Scholastics when they concern themselves with the "natural" powers of the intellect. All I mean to imply is "that there is no need for *effort* at abstraction, no *labor,* no *discursus* of reasoning." Cf. John L. Callahan, O.P., "The Esthetic Doctrine of the *Summa.*" Supplement to the *Summa Theologiae of St. Thomas Aquinas, 3* (New York, Benziger, 1948), 3342, col. I. Cf. also *S.T.,* I, q. 58, a. 3, ad I^m: "Si autem uno inspecto, simul aliud inspiciatur, sicut in speculo inspicitur simul imago rei et res, non est propter hoc cognitio discursiva."

5. Pp. 248–9.

6. Cf. Frederick D. Wilhelmsen, "The Aesthetic Act and the Act of Being," *Modern Schoolman, 29* (May 1952), 277–91, esp. 282–3. Cf. too *De Ver.,* q. 2, a. 6, ad 3^m: "Homo cognoscit singularia per imaginationem et sensum; et ideo potest applicare universalem cognitionem quae est in intellectu, ad particulare: non enim, proprie loquendo, sensus aut intellectus cognoscunt, sed homo per utrumque."

mirror of reality, as though one knew the object by knowing its representation in the mind. In Scholastic terminology, the concept is not a *medium quod cognitionis* but a *medium quo* or *in quo:* [7] that is, the mind knows not concepts but things.[8] Explicitly to affirm the conformity or nonconformity of the concept with reality, and a fortiori to predicate such abstract qualities as *wholeness* or *oneness* of an apprehended object, the mind needs two concepts and an act of the judgment, an act which Stephen never explicitly mentions and which he seems to confound now with the phantasm, now with the concept. Furthermore, to affirm the identity of a being with itself "as selfbounded and selfcontained," distinct from all "which is not it," [9] is to predicate of it, in Thomist terms, not integritas but *unitas,* a transcendental property of every being, so far as a being is conceived of as *aliquid,* that is, a being distinct and apart.[1]

Integritas has for Aquinas a perfectly definite and different meaning which Stephen appears not to have noticed in his breezy citation of the Thomist text, "Nam ad pulchritudinem tria requiruntur: Primo quidem integritas sive perfectio." To one familiar with the language of Aquinas, it is clear that by integritas (sive perfectio) he has in mind the completeness or perfection which a being possesses when it is all that it ought to be. Aristotle had much the same thing in mind when, for example, he "required" that the drama have a beginning, a middle, and an end: Did it grow out of something, did it grow toward something, did it finally reach the term of its growth? Was it an organism (in the analogous sense proper to literature)? Was it, as we might say, a mature work of art? In one of his earliest book reviews, Joyce defines "the first quality of beauty" as "the quality of being separate and whole" [2] which comes closer to Aquinas' integritas than Stephen with his talk of the "synthesis" and "analysis" of "immediate apprehension."

7. Scholastics are not in agreement as to whether the concept is a *medium quo* or *medium in quo.* All agree that it is not a *medium quod*—that is, that one does not "know" the concept but the thing. Whether one knows the thing without any knowledge of the concept, as one might look at an object through a perfectly transparent glass without adverting to the medium, or whether one knows the object with some advertence to the presence of the medium is the point in dispute. A medium quod here might roughly be likened to a mirror.

8. Cf. Albert J. Steiss, "Outline of a Philosophy of Art," *Thomist, 2* (Jan. 1940), 21: "The concept is not to be thought of as an object of knowledge; an image, as it were, which the mind sets up in lieu of the external object; or as a mirror in which the mind sees the object indirectly. The mind does not know the concept: the action of conceiving *is* knowledge. The concept, or expressed species, is the Form of the object existing by an act of the knower (i.e., intentionally) whereas outside the knower it exists by its own act (i.e., substantially)."

9. P. 249.

1. Cf. Emmanuel Chapman, "The Perennial Theme of Beauty and Art," *Essays in Thomism,* ed. Robert E. Brennan, O.P. (New York, Sheed and Ward, 1942), p. 340.

2. "An Irish Poet," *Dublin Daily Express,* Dec. 11, 1902. A review of *Poems and Ballads of William Rooney.*

Stephen's description of consonantia (or debita proportio) as "rhythm of . . . structure" [3] is Thomistically accurate, though here again Stephen speaks for himself and not for Aquinas when he calls it a "stage" or "phase" of apprehension rather than an existential quality inherent in the object apprehended. Also one is surprised to hear Stephen say: "Having first felt that it is *one* thing you feel now that it is a *thing*." [4] Inasmuch as Stephen himself describes consonantia as that by which the object is apprehended as "harmonious," "made up of its parts, the result of its parts and their sum," it would seem more consistent to apply his distinction in reverse. Then we should say that integritas is that in virtue of which one comes to know the object as one *thing* (aliquid), and consonantia is that which enables one to see the object's *oneness,* since consonantia (or proportio) is the principle of order, *quaelibet habitudo unius ad alterum.*[5] Aquinas at any rate states the matter in exactly the reverse order, and does so in the paragraph which immediately precedes the enumeration of the three qualities, which Stephen quotes: the object, as he says, must be first conceived of as a *thing* (*ens quoddam*) before one can think of it as *one,* "a thing" (*in quantum est una*).[6]

Stephen's account of consonantia presents this quality as a rather static, completed or pre-established harmony in constructed things, whereas the account of Aquinas pays more attention to it as a dynamic principle of order operative throughout all reality.[7] In his commentary on the *Sentences,* Aquinas applies consonantia to the immanent procession of the Son from the Father within the unity of the Divine Trinity, as well as to the immanent, dynamic presence of God in all creatures, and to the union of all creatures among themselves, which has the Divine Trinity as its ideal analogate.[8] The consonantia of a poem, a verbal act, would seem to postulate some such principle of fluid order, or dynamic structure, more "energetic" than the static structure of the basket which Stephen uses for an example. An account of consonantia which fails to take into consideration the asymmetrical function of dissonance or discontinuity in the rhythm of the whole would not be a very valuable tool for literary criticism or interpretation; it would ignore the existence of the real toads in so much of the world's imaginary garden of poetry.[9] Such a tool would be particularly inept for a critical understanding of Joyce's own significant contributions to modern literature.

3. P. 249.
4. Ibid.
5. *S.T.,* I, q. 12, a. 1, ad 4[m].
6. "Nam primo consideratur res ipsa absolute in quantum est ens quoddam. Secunda autem consideratio rei est in quantum est una." *S.T.,* I, q. 39, a. 8 (corp.).
7. Cf. De Bruyne, *Études d'esthétique médiévale, 3,* 303.
8. *I Sent.,* dist. 31, q. 2, a. 1, conclus. of solutio.
9. Cf. Marianne Moore, "Poetry," *Collected Poems of Marianne Moore* (New York, Macmillan, 1953), p. 41.

When Lynch interrupts Stephen after the latter's account of consonantia, he remarks, "Tell me now what is claritas and you win the cigar." [1] Lynch's wager is a better calculated risk than he himself might have realized. Aquinas' theory of claritas or *resplendentia* is the most crucial and subtle element in Stephen's "Aquinatian" theory of art. With the usual reminder that Aquinas presents this third quality of the beautiful as an existential property in the object rather than as a "stage" or "phase" of the mind's own act of knowing, most Thomists would probably agree that in the main Stephen gives at this point the most satisfactory interpretation of Aquinas' thought.

Stephen prefaces his own interpretation of claritas by setting aside another possible interpretation which, as he admits, "baffled me for a long time. It would lead you to believe that he [Aquinas] had in mind symbolism . . . a light from some other world." Inasmuch as Aquinas holds that "every form through which anything has existence is some kind of participation in the divine clarity," [2] it follows that Aquinas' understanding of claritas is more compatible with a "sacramentally" symbolic view of poetry than Stephen suspects. Dante, whose Thomism is admitted by most of his commentators, certainly seems to understand the radiance of created beauty in some such anagogical sense. [3]

The identity which Stephen establishes between claritas and the Scholastic *quidditas,* the "whatness" of a thing, is also questionable if Stephen claims Aquinas as his authority. Unlike the Suarezian Scholastics (and Joyce's Jesuit professors in Dublin at the turn of the century would presumably have been followers of Suarez), Thomists in general insist on the "real" (or actual), as opposed to the "rational" (or notional), distinction between the essence (or the quiddity, whatness) of a thing and its existence. Stephen certainly places his emphasis on the quiddity or essence as actuated, as "existential," as a structurally intelligible whole belonging to that order where "existence is prime among perfections." [4] Even if one allows that as a good Suarezian Thomist Stephen did not need to concern himself about the nice refinement of a "real distinction" between essence and existence, it is still difficult to see on what

1. P. 249.

2. *In Div. Nom.,* c. 4, lect. 5.

3. Cf. Karl Vossler, *Mediaeval Culture. An Introduction to Dante and His Times,* tr. William Cranston Lawton (New York, Harcourt, Brace, 1929), *I*, 107, 127-8.

Curtius asserts (*European Literature,* p. 595) : "The Thomism of Dante is an exploded myth." I must leave it up to the Dante specialists to decide whether Vossler or Curtius is more nearly correct. The famous letter of Dante to Can Grande would incline one to suspect that Dante, like Joyce, was accommodating his Thomism to his poetics rather than "exploding" it.

4. "Prima quidem [perfectio est] secundum quod in suo esse constituitur." *S.T.,* I, q. 6, a. 3.

"Unde patet quod hoc quod dico esse est actualitas omnium actuum, et propter hoc est perfectio omnium perfectionum." *De Pot.,* q. 7, a. 2, ad 9^m.

Scholastic grounds, Thomist or otherwise, he means "claritas is quidditas." Aquinas, to be sure, considers quidditas in the existential order
when he talks about existent things, but even in this existential order
the existent quidditas is conceived of as the nature of a thing, or the
principle of operation which the thing possesses in virtue of its "substantial" form. The *forma substantialis* is not a principle of individua-
tion; it is sometimes called the "specific form," or *forma specifica,* but
the specification is to species, or class. Though Stephen alleges that he is
following Aquinas, he clearly has more than that in mind: "You see
that it is that thing which it is and no other." [5]

So far as Stephen is talking about poetry, and his citation of Shelley
at this point suggests that he is, he must intend to include in his notion
of quiddity some "accidental" or secondary form over and above the
"specific form," some intrinsic modification imposed from within.
Though Stephen cites Shelley's comparison in *A Defence of Poetry*
between the creative mind and "a fading coal," [6] he is throughout his
exposition of the Scholastic quidditas much more of a realist than Shelley ever was. The symbolism which Stephen advocates is tied down to
the objects of this world, like the butcher boy's basket, much more than
Shelley's symbolism could be: a knowledge (root, blossom, fruit, and
seed, as Shelley says) "from those eternal regions where the owl-winged
faculty of calculation dare not ever soar." [7] Shelley's "transcendental"
symbolism would seem, from Stephen's calculated analysis of quidditas,
to be a kind of symbolism which Joyce did not particularly like. It was
too much "out in the yonder," too much inclined to evaporate the things
of this world, to be quite congenial to Joyce. Besides, when Joyce speaks
of poetry he appears to be thinking of a knowledge which does not come
from the "yonder" but is constructed through a careful molding by
words. This interest in a claritas of the here and now shows how close
is Joyce's own affinity with Aquinas even when he portrays Stephen as
a kind of nineteenth-century idealistic symbolist eager to cite Shelley in
support of his Scholastic views.

The claritas which a poem possesses is a most individual and concrete

5. P. 250: "The radiance of which he [Aquinas] speaks is the scholastic *quidditas,*
the *whatness* of a thing." Cf. *Stephen Hero,* p. 213: "*Claritas* is *quidditas.*"

6. This image of the mind in creation being like "a fading coal" is a favorite one
with Joyce. He uses it in his college essay in *St. Stephen's* (May 1902), p. 8, applying it to James Mangan; in the *Portrait* (p. 250) he uses it to illustrate claritas; in
Ulysses (p. 192) he incorporates it into his theory of *Hamlet.* In all three cases the
mind is "the fading coal," but in the Mangan essay the mind is considered as creative
under the breath of the imagination; in the *Portrait* the mind is considered as apprehending beauty, not creating it; and in *Ulysses* the mind is identified with the creative imagination in such wise that its light, though fading, not only illuminates what
we see and what we are but is prophetic and reflective of what we are ourselves fated
to become.

7. "A Defence of Poetry"; see John Shawcross, ed., *Shelley's Literary and Philosophical Criticism* (London, Henry Frowde, 1909), pp. 152, 153.

concentration of meaning brought to some particular point of intellectual focus. In this sense the poem's quidditas might be likened to a prism which gathers in light from various sources—metaphors, images, antitheses, rhythm, syntax, and so forth—but which is cut in such wise by the poet's craft that all the light is brought to a point of radiant intuition, the claritas, for the mind to see. It is this concrete, individual quidditas of an existent thing which has always defied precise philosophical analysis, be the thing a poem or a basket or anything else.

What Stephen seems to mean by claritas may have been expressed better by the *haecceitas* of Duns Scotus than by the quidditas of Aquinas. Étienne Gilson, an authority on both Aquinas and Scotus, has described the haecceitas of Scotus as "l'extrême point d'actualité qui détermine chaque être réel à la singularité," [8] and he goes on to say, "Même si nous connaissions le singulier, nous pourrions le voir, mais non le définir." [9] Or in the words of Heidegger, "Das Individuelle ist ein unzurückführbar Letzes." [1]

Stephen's final summary of claritas as an "enchantment of the heart," though it is easily explicable in an "Aquinatian" context, has also even greater affinities with Scotus' principles. It is interesting to speculate whether the poet Gerard Hopkins, who died while a professor at University College, may have left behind him a little of his love for the *Doctor Subtilis,* strong enough to keep alive a modest tradition of Scotist poetics in Joyce's student days. Be that as it may, the affective, aesthetic affinities of Joyce's Stephen are better described as Scotist than as "Aquinatian." The actual composition or interpretation of poetry, with which Stephen is not much concerned, would seem to be largely the same whether one's bias in poetics was Scotist or Aquinan.

Aquinas would have said that quidditas is a condition for claritas, rather than claritas itself, but in either case the claritas is to be explained as a radiance of the form, and Stephen is correct in describing it as a synthesis of integritas and consonantia.[2] It is the form of an object, according to the Scholastic account of cognition, which the intellect assimilates when it knows the object. The assimilation to be sure is an intentional and not physical appropriation of the object and owes as much to the intrinsic finality of the knowing mind as to the principle of intelligibility, the form, which is in the object known. Ultimately any theory of knowledge must admit that it is up against one of the irreducibles of human experience. The Scholastic account, like others, makes the effort to describe upon reflection what must take place, or at least what must

8. Étienne Gilson, "Jean Duns Scotus," *Études de philosophie médiévale,* No. 42 (Paris, Librairie Philosophique J. Vrin, 1952), p. 464, n. 2.
9. Ibid., 466.
1. Quoted, ibid.
2. P. 250.

be accounted for, without claiming to explain it. Some union between object and mind is to be described: the Scholastics begin by looking for a principle of intelligibility in the object, and this they discover in the form, the intrinsic principle of organization, which determines that the object exists in this way and not in another. Between the form of an object and the clarity there is, therefore, a most intimate connection: the claritas is nothing else but the *irradiatio formae:* "For every essence either is a simple form or has its completion through the form. The form, however, is a certain radiance flowing from the first clarity. Clarity, moreover, is one of the aspects of the beautiful." [3] So Aquinas expresses himself in his *Commentary on the Divine Names*. The Dedalan exposition of claritas would have gained in precision had it taken up Aquinas' notion of claritas as the irradiatio formae. Forma and quidditas are not convertible notions as Aquinas uses them. He conceives of the quidditas or essence of an angel as being the same as its form, but in the case of all other creatures the essence is regarded as compounded of matter as well as of form, and it is obvious that a poem or any other work of art cannot be judged as though it were pure form.

Inasmuch as a poem is not something which is found in nature as is, for example, a tree, there is no particular advantage in talking about its forma substantialis. The form a poem has is a "secondary" form. Its intelligibility is man-made, contrived; there is no reason why a poem as a human utterance may not have, may not be, an aggregate of forms. It must have unity, and here precisely the work of the poet (and his reader) with language begins: to discover some principle of organization, some pattern according to which the insights and suggestions associated with individual words and collocations of words may be utilized so as to offer a new verbal dramatization of experience. It is in this way, is it not, that the claritas of a poem, its "radiance of form," manifests itself to the mind?

When Stephen speaks about the claritas of a being as the only logically and aesthetically permissible synthesis of integritas and consonantia, he would seem to be echoing the Scholastic theory of the form, though he does not mention it. So far as the existential form of a being successfully manifests itself to the mind, the full perfection (integritas) of the being is revealed, and the principle of order (consonantia) in the midst of multiple, even discordant or asymmetrical, elements is discovered. To talk about the "substantial form" of a poem manifesting itself to the mind would not, however, take one very far; at most the disclosure would reveal that one was reading a poem, and even this disclosure would be assuming that the reader knew the "specific essence" of poetry

3. "Omnis enim essentia vel est forma simplex, vel habet complementum per formam. Forma autem est quaedam irradiatio proveniens ex prima claritate. Claritas autem est de ratione pulchritudinis." *In Div. Nom.,* c. 4, lect. 6.

as distinct from all that is not poetry. Theories of *la poésie pure* are not easy to defend, and one may presume that Joyce would have been least of all likely to wish to defend them. For Stephen the case is not so clear; his romantic version of the neo-Thomist aesthetic, couched as it is in literary language and not, as he tells us, in the language of the market place,[4] sounds at times like a plea for the refined essence of poetry, pure and distilled.

On the analogy of the irradiatio formae of Scholastic psychology, it would be legitimate and perhaps helpful for the literary critic or aesthetician to speak of the work of the poet as a preparation through the "formal" organization of his language for the moment of illumination, or clarity. In this sense, the meaning or the idea of a poem is comparable to Aquinas' (and Aristotle's) material cause, and the poem's style is comparable to their formal cause. W. Y. Tindall has noted that the aesthetic theory of the *Portrait* is a definition of significant form.[5] A theory of literature in the light of the Thomist texts de pulchro seems to move toward some such solution of the question of content and style. If our analysis of the form be correct, then it would seem as if one should conceive of the words or the language as the formal, determining principle of embodiment, and that the meaning or the poetic truth should be regarded as "the potential" waiting to be actuated by the form. (It is, of course, possible to view this application of matter and form to literature, as the Chicago critics have done, in just the opposite light.) [6] It goes without saying that any application of the hylomorphic theory at this point must necessarily be analogous, but the analogy may be instructive so long as one remembers that in the Thomist cosmology the matter and the form are never conceived of as independent causes but always as "co-causes," *con-causae,* which interpenetrate at every point.

Stephen sums up this account of claritas ("the only synthesis which is logically and esthetically permissible") by remarking: "The instant wherein that supreme quality of beauty, the clear radiance of the esthetic image, is apprehended luminously by the mind which has been arrested by its wholeness and fascinated by its harmony is the luminous silent stasis of esthetic pleasure . . . the enchantment of the heart." [7] In spite of the stress which the intellectualist Aquinas places on the cognitive aspect in his analysis of beauty, he sees no difficulty in accounting for the overflow of the mind's joy into the emotions, so that they too are *actively* engaged, even though silently, as long as the harmonious vision of the mind endures. In response to a difficulty proposed against

4. P. 250.
5. W. Y. Tindall, *James Joyce, His Way of Interpreting the Modern World* (New York, Scribner's, 1950), p 119.
6. Cf. W. K. Wimsatt, Jr., "The Chicago Critics," *Comparative Literature,* 5 (Winter 1953), 50–74.
7. P. 250.

the argument of the *de Veritate,* Aquinas speaks, for example, much as Stephen does when he describes the intellectual meditation on the meaning of the beautiful as an "enchantment of the heart." Man is an *unum per se,* as the Scholastics say, and it is a common experience of men whose attention is absorbed by the forms of art to experience this "intransitive attention" and affective enchantment which Stephen's phrase expresses so well. In the words of Aquinas: "Insofar as one desires the good, he desires at the same time beauty and peace: . . . for it is with one and the same longing that one wishes for goodness, for beauty, and for peace." [8] The *Summa Theologiae* makes the same correlation between knowledge and joy: "It appertains to the nature of beauty that in the sight of it—or in the knowing of it—yearning should come to rest." [9] This aspect of joy in knowledge, contemplative joy, had a special relevance for Joyce's early theory of poetry, as his youthful essay on the Irish poet James Clarence Mangan shows: "Beauty, the splendour of truth, is a gracious presence when the imagination contemplates intensely the truth of its own being or of the visible world, and the spirit which proceeds out of truth and beauty is the holy spirit of joy." [1] From what Stephen has said, it is clear that his aesthetic emotion of joy is different, or at least distinct, from the emotions represented in the poem, which may be quite sorrowful (as they often are in Mangan's verse). The joy of listening to *Dark Rosaleen* comes not from sharing the joy of the speaker, who "night and noon" is in "pain and woe," nor from sharing the joy of Rosaleen herself, who sighs and weeps without hope. The listener (or reader) overhears and rejoices not at the speaker's or Rosaleen's sorrows but at Mangan's perfect expression of their sorrows through the "truth and beauty" of his vision elaborated in *words.* It is there that the "gracious presence" of the aesthetic emotion of joy in the poem resides.

All that Stephen has said in the *Portrait* on the nature of beauty and the nature of art leads in the end to his division of art into three forms: "Art necessarily divides itself into three forms progressing from one to the next. These forms are: the lyrical form, the form wherein the artist presents his image in immediate relation to himself; the epical form, the form wherein he presents his image in mediate relation to himself and to others; the dramatic form, the form wherein he presents his image in

8. "Ex hoc enim ipso quod aliquid appetit bonum, appetit simul pulchrum et pacem: . . . Unde et eodem appetitu appetitur bonum, pulchrum, et pax. *De Ver.,* q. 22, a. 1, ad 12[m].

9. "Ad rationem pulchri pertinet quod in ejus aspectu seu cognitione quietetur appetitus." *S.T.,* I–II, q. 27, a. 1, ad 3[m].

Cf. Maritain, *Creative Intuition in Art and Poetry,* p. 58: ". . . in the last analysis, in art as in contemplation, intellectuality at its peak goes beyond concepts and discursive reason, and is achieved through a congeniality or connaturality with the object, which love alone can bring about."

1. "James Clarence Mangan," *St. Stephen's,* p. 15.

immediate relation to others."[2] From the corresponding account in *Stephen Hero*[3] it comes out that Stephen is thinking of literature and that he considers the other forms of art which do not "offer this division with the same clearness" as on this account less excellent. Having taken the position that the reality of art is apprehended in a moment of detached and silent stasis, he does not surprise us in describing as profanities "the antique principle that the end of art is to instruct, to elevate, and to amuse." As any student or alumnus of a Jesuit college ought to know, the aims of rhetoric and of poetic do not coincide.[4] Having based his aesthetic of poetry on a theory of contemplative joy, a *revelatio,* as he says, analogous to the Thomist *contemplatio pulchri,* Stephen feels justified on Aquinas' authority in dismissing the aims of rhetoric as Puritanic, as absurd, as a criticism established not on poetry but on homilies.[5]

The "impersonal" theory of poetry which emerges from Stephen's threefold division is a logical development from the premises of aesthetic distance and detachment which Stephen imagined that Aquinas had established. Aquinas has so little to say about poetry that it is difficult at this point to decide how he might have felt about the Flaubertian principle back of Stephen's three-form theory, the artist's progressively refining himself out of existence in his work.

Though Stephen's particular division of literature into lyric, epic, and dramatic is as old as Plato's and Aristotle's "manners of imitation," he describes these three forms in such a way as to suggest that he is strongly influenced here by Hegelian theories of art's progressively transcending itself through the symbolic, classical, and romantic forms.[6] There seems to be some echo too of Schelling's concept of art in the sphere of ideality as progressing through the stages of lyric finiteness and particularity, to epic infiniteness and generality, and finally to dramatic union, where the particular is lost in the general and the real is totally taken up into the ideal.[7] It would seem to be only in virtue of Stephen's Scholastic training in rhetoric and poetic (a sturdy ballast) that he is saved at this

2. Pp. 250–1.

3. *Stephen Hero,* p. 77.

4. The last two years of the Jesuit course of study in "colleges" organized on the European plan are devoted respectively to "poetry" and "rhetoric." (Jesuit houses of study in America also have "a poetry year," and "a rhetoric year," and the students are referred to as "poets" and "rhetoricians" respectively.) Cf. *Portrait,* p. 13: "He felt small and weak. When would he be like the fellows in Poetry and Rhetoric?"

5. *Stephen Hero,* pp. 79–80.

6. Cf. Bosanquet, *The Introduction to Hegel's Philosophy of Fine Art,* pp. 145–57.

7. Cf. Katherine E. Gilbert and Helmut Kuhn, *A History of Aesthetics* (New York, Macmillan, 1939), p. 433. Also see Joyce's early review, "George Meredith," in *Dublin Daily Express,* Dec. 11, 1902, in which he remarks that Meredith "is plainly lacking in that fluid quality, the *lyrical* impulse," and goes on to say that "Meredith's novels . . . have no value as *epical* art, and Mr. Meredith has not the instinct of the *epical* artist." (A review of Walter Jerrold's *George Meredith: An Essay toward Appreciation.* Italics mine.)

point in his discussion from being carried off into the idealistic empy-
rean of German romantic aestheticism.

It would not be too much to say that the problem of rhetoric versus
poetic is the underlying aesthetic problem which the young man of the
Portrait sets himself to solve. In Stephen's terms, rhetoric aims at forming the man of action through a kinesis of the will in the presence of
good and evil; poetic aims at leading a man to contemplation, to a stasis
of the mind before the *visum placens*.[8] The moral claims of theology are
viewed by the youthful Stephen as compatible with the aims of rhetoric
but not with those of poetic. After listening to the retreat-master's rhetorical peroration calling to repentance—the conclusion of the lurid
sermon on hell—Stephen returns to his room despondent. His heaviness
of heart is not caused by an onrush of penitential sorrow but rather by
his disappointment when he fails to feel any penitential emotion at all:
"Could it be that he, Stephen Dedalus, had done those things?"[9] He is
torn between two impulses: the explicit, rhetorical demands of the sermon ("to meet his sins face to face, to recall their times and manners
and circumstances, to weep over them") and his implicit, poetic refusal
to assume kinship with so "leprous" a company ("He could not weep,
he could not summon them to his memory"). The conflict is resolved
not on the level of rhetoric, a conversion of the will into action, but on
the level of poetic: "He saw." He begins to consider the subject aesthetically and it comes into focus. This is the key to his understanding it—
to understanding, so he imagines, his life: "He wept for the innocence
he had lost."[1]

Seen in this light, the "conversion" of the *Portrait* needs to be qualified. It is not theological in the strict sense of the word: a turning to God;
much more, it is a turning to art, a commitment to the life beautiful, to
the life of the artist, seen perhaps for a time in theological perspectives
but accepted here and now because it is a solution congenial to art: "It
would be beautiful to die if God so willed. It was beautiful to live in
grace."[2] This is not to impugn Stephen's sincerity or to deny that God
might have used Stephen's passion for the beauty of art as an occasion
for grace. When the practical demands of living this life beautiful grow
too exigent for the artist to heed, Stephen turns from the vision of his
retreat to the vision of "mortal youth and beauty," and in an instant of
ecstasy is prepared to follow this "envoy from the fair courts of life"
into "all the ways of error and glory."[3] The break with theology and
with rhetoric is complete, but the solution of the *Portrait* is not final.

8. P. 243.
9. Pp. 157–8.
1. P. 160.
2. P. 168.
3. P. 200.

In the Library chapter of *Ulysses,* when Stephen returns to the question of poetics, he uses both rhetoric and theology to beat down his adversaries and to state his own case. A theory of poetry is not a poem, and Stephen's rhetorical-theological presentation, a "mixture of theolologicophilolological," as he calls it,[4] need not touch the validity of his argument; all through the aesthetic discourse of the *Portrait* Stephen uses the kinetic devices of rhetoric to solicit assent to his own theory of static art. Even though its rhetorical strategy is manifest, the defense in *Ulysses* of Shakespeare as a dramatic poet is based not on the principle of the *Portrait* that the dramatic artist "is refined out of existence" [5] but on the principle that the artist puts himself, not that which he has apprehended but that which he is, into his work: "He goes back, weary of the creation he has piled up to hide him from himself." [6] The analogy to the divine artist is adverted to in each case, but whereas Stephen uses the analogy in the *Portrait* to drive home his point about the poet's "transcendence"—"like the God of the creation, . . . indifferent, paring his fingernails"—he appeals to the analogy in *Ulysses* to illustrate the omnipresence of Shakespeare in all the *personae* of the dramas. An approach to drama as an embodiment of human experience has greater possibilities for criticism and interpretation than an approach which would try to isolate it as an "impersonal" artifact. "His own image to a man with that queer thing genius is the standard of all experience, material and moral": [7] such is Stephen's point as he leads into his theory of Shakespeare as immanently present in every Shakespearean poem. The point is one which Aquinas would not have phrased in such highly subjective language, but it is consonant with his idea of man as an image of God. Once in speaking of the angels Aquinas discusses charity as a motive for language: "The more beings capable of action are given a participation in the divine goodness, the more they endeavor to transfer their own perfections to others—as far as this can be done." [8]

One of the indisputable values of literature which emerges from Stephen's discussion of Shakespeare is this transference to other men of that which is most excellent in the human experience of the artist. Unlike the angelic transference of concepts, the manifestation of a human excellence of insight requires always the employment of some sensible sign: "Oportet aliquod signum sensibile adhibere," as Aquinas goes on to say.[9] The symbols which poetry has offered have been universally

4. *Ulysses*, p. 202.
5. *Portrait*, p. 252.
6. *Ulysses*, p. 194.
7. Ibid., p. 193.
8. "Quanto igitur aliqua agentia magis in participatione divinae bonitatis constituuntur, tanto magis perfectiones suas nituntur in alios transfundere, quantum possibile est." *S.T.*, I, q. 106, a. 4.
9. *S.T.*, I, q. 107, a. 1, ad 1m.

accepted by men as among the most valid of such signs, possessing an
interest and import that relate the personal with the universal, the word
with the world. So Stephen understands Shakespeare in all his works to
have made use of symbols to embody his own interior experience: "He
has hidden his own name, a fair name, William, in the plays, a super
here, a clown there, as a painter of old Italy set his face in a dark corner
of his canvas. He has revealed it in the sonnets where there is Will in
overplus." [1]

As Stephen develops his argument, he deliberately makes his case too
strong and concludes, it would seem, with a view of literature, even
drama, as a kind of veiled biography. When Eglinton asks him if he
believes his own theory, he promptly replies, "No." [2] There is no reason,
however, to believe that he would deny his central intuition: the concrete reduction of inner personal experience into a coherent symbol is a
method of penetrating into the universality of human experience, "as far
as this can be done," and of imparting to the personal a potential of
significance for other men. "The note of banishment, banishment from
the heart, banishment from home" which, as Stephen says, "sounds un-
interruptedly" in Shakespeare has had interest for all readers of Shakespeare partly at least because there is no reader who has not had some
experience of what it is like to feel banished, unreconciled: "an original
sin, . . . committed by another in whose sin he too has sinned." The
closest that Stephen and Bloom come to finding themselves and each
other occurs when they gaze without speaking into the mirror, and each
beholds Shakespeare's face, not his own, reflected in the glass.

The Dedalan theory of Shakespearean poetic presented in *Ulysses*
does not contradict the theory of aesthetic stasis developed in the *Portrait*. But it introduces into the discussion of stasis a theological dimension of man's incompleteness and of art's insufficiency which the *Portrait*
lacks. "Age has not withered it," says Stephen of the insight into reality
which Shakespeare still makes available through his poetry. "Beauty
and peace have not done it away." [3] As the discussion moves away from
the preoccupation with beauty and with the peace which comes from the
aesthetic contemplation of beauty, it moves forward in another direction
into the domain of what Hermann Broch, speaking of Joyce, has called
the "supra-social general commitment" of literature to existence.[4] It is
in this domain that Aquinas conceived of the mythmakers and the theologians as involved, each in their own way, with the meaning of existence and the meaning of man. So far as men's intellects are clouded, so

1. *Ulysses*, p. 207.
2. Ibid., p. 211.
3. Ibid., p. 209.
4. Hermann Broch, "James Joyce and the Present Age," *A James Joyce Yearbook*,
1949, p. 97.

long as their wills remain free, it is always possible for them to reject the solicitation of the good and the true and the beautiful. In such a scheme of things there may be a function for the rhetorician to perform side by side with theologian and poet : the contrivers of the verbal symbols of reality should be able to win men to meditate on the symbol without paralyzing their wills into inaction, and without breaking their hearts. The comic parody of journalistic rhetoric in the Aeolus chapter of *Ulysses* is so devastating precisely because it measures the contemporary decline of rhetoric from its once high estate. Stephen's most telling reflection about it is a theological one, echoing St. Augustine, who was himself a poet and rhetorician as well as a Father of the Church : "Those things are good which yet are corrupted which neither if they were supremely good nor unless they were good could be corrupted. Ah, curse you! That's saint Augustine." [5]

5. *Ulysses,* p. 140.

4

How Culious An Epiphany

> *For numpa one puraduxed seer in
> seventh degree of wisdom of Entis-
> Onton he savvy inside true inward-
> ness of reality, the Ding hvad in
> idself id est, all objects (of
> panepiwor) allside showed them-
> selves in trues coloribus re-
> splendent with sextuple gloria of
> light actually retained, untisintus,
> inside them (obs of epiwo).*
>
> *Finnegans Wake* [1]

ARTHUR POWER, one of Joyce's Irish friends, recalls that one day he remarked to Joyce that he wanted to become "international." "For myself," Joyce answered, "I always write about Dublin, because if I can get to the heart of Dublin I can get to the heart of all the cities of the world. In the particular is contained the universal." [2] In exploring the theme of the city Joyce discovered early that two things were necessary, an undistracted sensibility to the self-disclosures which the city offered, and a painstaking expertness in recording these disclosures in meaningful patterns of art. For both these aspects of the city's claim on the poet's resources, Joyce as a young man coined a poetic name, "Epiphany." Sometimes he used the name as if it chiefly pertained to the moments when the city gave itself away, disclosed its mystery for him who was alert in noticing, in some casual, unpremeditated word or gesture. Sometimes he used the term as if it were chiefly a particular kind of verbal strategy by means of which the various carefully premeditated devices in the poem's or story's utterance at some point coalesced, and the structure of the whole disclosed itself in a sudden illumination of meaning. In this latter sense Joyce's epiphany is not unlike what Hopkins meant when, in a letter to Robert Bridges, he described the kind of clarity which he aimed at in poetry as an "explosion

---

1. *Finnegans Wake,* p. 611. Cf. *ibid.,* p. 508.
2. Arthur Power, *From the Old Waterford House* (London, Mellifont Press, undated), p. 64.

out of darkness," [3] just as epiphany in the first Joycean sense of an unpremeditated, personal disclosure of the city's secret is not unlike what the Scotist-minded Hopkins meant by his formally patterned "inscapes" of individual being: "I thought," wrote Hopkins in his journal, "how sadly beauty of inscape was unknown and buried away from simple people and yet how near at hand it was if they had eyes to see it." [4]

In either case the epiphany is related, as Joyce makes clear, to the claritas which Stephen Dedalus describes as "the supreme quality of beauty," [5] to Aquinas' forma as quaedam irradiatio, [6] and to the resplendence of the "true inwardness of reality," the "untisintus" of which Balkelly the archdruid speaks in Finnegans Wake. [7] As defined by Joyce in Stephen Hero, epiphany is a precise concept which applies almost exclusively to the meaningful, artless dramatization of inner, spiritual life through some particular bodily attitude or sign: "By an epiphany he meant a sudden spiritual manifestation, whether in the vulgarity of speech or of gesture or in a memorable phase of the mind itself. He believed that it was for the man of letters to record these epiphanies with extreme care, seeing that they themselves are the most delicate and evanescent of moments. He told Cranly that the clock of the Ballast Office was capable of an epiphany." [8]

Beyond saying that it is for the man of letters to record these epiphanies of experience with extreme care, Joyce in this early work does not develop the idea of epiphany as a literary strategy or term. In Ulysses he presents Stephen walking along the beach and meditating on the books he had once imagined he would write: "Remember your epiphanies on green oval leaves, deeply deep, copies to be sent if you died to all the great libraries of the world, including Alexandria? Someone was to read them there after a few thousand years, a mahamanvantara." [9] The epiphany of a book is by no means an artless, unpremeditated gesture, and Joyce implies that it is Stephen's failure to realize how artfully contrived the literary re-presentation of an epiphany of experience must be that accounts for the wistful fact that Stephen's numerous books, "with letters for titles," had achieved no existence outside his mind. The literary epiphanies which Joyce, unlike Stephen, succeeded in constructing are recorded with measureless care. As his brother Stanislaus has put

3. *The Letters of Gerard Manley Hopkins to Robert Bridges,* ed. Claude Colleer Abbott (London, Oxford Univ. Press, 1935), p. 90.
4. *The Notebooks and Papers of Gerard Manley Hopkins,* ed. Humphrey House (London, Oxford Univ. Press, 1937), p. 161.
5. *Stephen Hero,* p. 211.
6. Cf. *In Div. Nom.,* c. 4, lect. 6.
7. *Finnegans Wake,* p. 611.
8. *Stephen Hero,* p. 211.
9. *Ulysses,* p. 41.

it: "Joyce worked with tireless patience; above all with patience." [1]

The druid in *Finnegans Wake* speaks of epiphany as of a sensible clue given by experience which leads the mind to interior philosophical insight, to the wisdom of "the Ding hvad in idself id est," but here Joyce establishes a connection between this philosophical meaning of epiphany as an insight given by the "trues coloribus resplendent" of an object, and the function of epiphany as a verbal strategy of art. He does so first by linking the druid's utterance which begins "Tunc" with the *"Tunc* page" of the Book of Kells, and secondly by giving to St. Patrick an opportunity to refute in Dantean imagery the Berkeleyan-Kantian idealism of the druid-seer: "the sound sense sympol in a weedwayedwold of the firethere the sun in his halo cast." [2] The mature Joyce of *Finnegans Wake* had no inclination to treat the symbol, verbal or nonverbal, merely as a clue to understanding essences in nonsymbolic terms. All symbols, and especially verbal symbols, are shaped by tradition, and as Joyce moved further away from the Cartesian idealism of his first aesthetic formulations, couched though these were in "Aquinatian" language, he became more and more resourceful in exploiting the various symbolic traditions for the associative values of words. "No esthetic theory is of any value which investigates with the aid of the lantern of tradition" had been Stephen Hero's prelude to the rejection in the early novel of symbolism as a means of understanding or representing the actual world: "What we symbolize in black the Chinaman may symbolize in yellow: each has his own tradition." So the youthful Stephen had been resolved to substitute for "arbitrary" symbolism a kind of Cartesian dialectic of his own, "The apprehensive faculty must be scrutinized in action," and in making the substitution, Stephen had broken so completely with tradition himself as to claim Aquinas for his guide: "You know what Aquinas says. . . ." [3] But Joyce had not felt himself bound by Stephen's resolve: "So why, pray, sign anything as long as every word, letter, penstroke, paperspace is a perfect signature of its own?" [4]

In his first description of epiphany, Joyce represents Stephen as seeking to discover the meaning of the city's self-disclosures, not in the signatures of things nor in the "sextuple gloria of light . . . inside them," but in the light within his own soul, "as the gropings of a spiritual eye which seeks to adjust its vision to an exact focus. The moment the focus is reached the object is epiphanized." The earlier Joycean emphasis is on the light within the mind of the spectator. It is in virtue of

1. Stanislaus Joyce, *Recollections of James Joyce*, tr. (from Italian) Ellsworth Mason (New York, James Joyce Society, 1950), p. 19.

2. *Finnegans Wake*, p. 612.

3. *Stephen Hero*, p. 212. Joyce gives in *Stephen Hero*, pp. 211–13, his most sustained development of epiphany. From Stephen's remarks, here and below, it is clear that he claims St. Thomas Aquinas as his source.

4. *Finnegans Wake*, p. 115.

```
#E56   Thu Jun 10 2004 10:38AM
Item(s) checked out to Arana, Ignacio An

TITLE: Bernstein in Paris [videorecordin
BARCODE: 0000001932145
DUE DATE: 07-01-04
```

this light that the radiant manifestation of inward being is said to be grasped and held for meditation. Without such an inward light, no object—Ballast Office clock or human word or gesture—can be apprehended in the attitude of self-disclosure. "What is a Joycean 'epiphany,' after all," asks one student of Joyce's artistic theory, "but the equivalent of a Crocean 'moment of expression'? You see a clock daily; but at last you 'intuit' it." [5] As time went on, Joyce, without discounting the role of the inward light, paid less attention to it. His later remarks on epiphany, incidental as they appear in context, show that he is thinking more of the "Entis-Onton," the "sextuple gloria of light" which is hidden within the object. It then becomes the poet's business to represent this light in the only way he can, through the symbolic constructs of language. Opaque, unwieldy, ambivalent as words may be, the "sound sense sympol" of poetic discourse can concentrate much of the sunlight and firelight of reality, the radiance of claritas, the blaze of being, in the "wold of words," and what matter if the paths of this wold have become dense and weed-grown, if the light can still be trapped within the wold and the weeds?

In one of the unpublished Zurich notebooks, there is an entry which suggests that as Joyce ceased to take so seriously the theory of the three prerequisites for beauty (Nam ad pulchritudinem tria requiruntur) he had found in practice another triad that would be more decisive for his mature work. The note is cryptic but revealing: "Good diction: tria— metaphor, antithesis, energy." [6] The entry immediately preceding sheds some light on Joyce's reason for this substitution of triads: "Metaphor prefer to comparison. Comparison makes folks wait and tells you only what something is like." Is not the implication clear, that good diction should tell you not what a thing is like but what it is? Good diction is not obsessed with beauty but with being. Unless a poet takes this means of good diction, he cannot present epiphanies. In speaking thus of diction, or of verbal strategy, Joyce also shows that he is beginning to think of diction not so much as process but more as product or endresult. Aristotle had noted in his Poetics: "But the greatest thing by far is to have a command of metaphor." [7] Aristotle too had included diction as one of the elements in the finished structure of a poetic imitation, rather than as part of the poetic process.

At the outset of his commentary on Aristotle's Metaphysics, Aquinas lays down the principle that the philosopher must marvel at being just as the poets do, and be himself a lover of myths and of poetry: "Inas-

5. Geddes MacGregor, "Artistic Theory in James Joyce," Life and Letters, 54 (July 1947), 21–2.

6. Unpublished and unedited Zurich Notebook, University of Buffalo Library. Punctuation is mine.

7. Cf. S. H. Butcher, Aristotle's Theory of Poetry and Fine Art (4th ed. New York, Dover, 1951), p. 87 (Steph. 1459 a).

much as philosophy rises from the sense of wonder, it is clear that the philosopher must be to some extent a lover of the myth (*philomythes*), as all poets are." [8] (In an early review of one of Lady Gregory's translations from the Irish, *Poets and Dreamers,* Joyce begins: "Aristotle finds at the beginning of all speculation the feeling of wonder.") [9] To make it possible for us to rejoice either in the representation or in the discovery of the real the poets must, says Aquinas, use metaphors,[1] since "metaphors or symbolic locutions are, as it were, the poetic vestures of the truth" of things as they are, from which wonder rises: "metaphorae, vel symbolicae locutiones, sunt quasi quaedam velamina veritatis." [2] Even the "fictions" of the poets must be respected, Aquinas holds, since these fictions aim at no other thing than the symbolization of reality: "Fictiones poeticae non sunt ad aliud ordinatae nisi ad significandum." [3] The truths of philosophy are not the only way, then, of apprehending the "Entis-Onton" of reality. Do we not still refer to "fiction" as "poetic truth"?

To quote Aquinas at this point to indicate an Aquinan correspondence with the Joycean theory of epiphany would be misleading if one sought in this way to establish that in the later literary development of the term Joyce was consciously elaborating on the text of Aquinas. Joyce

8. "Ex quo admiratio fuit causa inducens ad philosophiam, patet quod philosophus est aliqualiter philomythes, idest amator fabulae, quod proprium est poetarum." *I Lib. Metaphys.,* lect. 3.

With this willingness to join hands with mythmakers, it is interesting to compare Carlyle's pontifical utterance: "The Fine Arts once divorcing themselves from *truth,* are quite certain to fall mad, if they do not die." Much might be said in defense of this ex cathedra pronouncement but hardly in the sense in which Carlyle appears willing himself to defend it: "Fiction, even to the Fine Arts, is not a quite permissible thing. Sparingly permissible, within iron limits; or if you will reckon strictly, not permissible at all! The Fine Arts too, like the coarse . . . are to understand that they are sent hither not to fib and dance, but to speak and work; and, on the whole, that God Almighty's *Facts,* such as are given us, are the only pabulum which will yield them any nourishment in this world." (Cf. "Jesuitism," No. 8 in *Latter-Day Pamphlets,* New York, Harper, 1850, p. 34.)

Joyce's caricature of himself as "Shem the Penman" in *Finnegans Wake* has not a few overtones comically resonant of Carlyle's diatribe against the "prussicacid and chloroform" of "Jesuitism": cf. page 182 of the *Wake:* "in which the soulcontracted son of the secret cell groped through life at the expense of the taxpayers, dejected into day and night with jesuit bark and bitter bite."

9. "The Soul of Ireland," *Dublin Daily Express,* March 26, 1903.

1. *S.T.,* I, q. 1, a. 9, ad 1m: "Dicendum quod poeta utitur metaphoris propter repraesentationem." Cf. *I Sent.,* Prolog., q. 1, a. 5, ad 3m.

2. *I Sent.,* dist. 34, q. 3, a. 1, obj. 3. (Minor conceded.)

3. *Quodl.,* VII, q. 6, a. 16, ad 2m.

At one point Cervantes represents "a man of good sense" who attacks Don Quixote's beloved books of chivalry before a listening priest who "approved all that he said": "If you reply that the men who compose such books write them as fiction, and so are not obliged to look into fine points or truths, I should reply that the more it resembles the truth the better the fiction." *Don Quixote,* tr. J. M. Cohen (Penguin Classics, Baltimore, 1954), Pt. I, ch. 47, p. 425.

himself asserts through Stephen Dedalus that the early idea of epiphany is derivative from, indeed identical with, the Aquinan *claritas*. The subsequent development of the notion as a verbal strategy or symbolic technique takes place without reference to Aquinas but it has clear correspondences with the Aquinan notions about metaphor and *locutiones symbolicae*. The decorum of the "middayevil" verbal gesturings of the *Wake* is deemed appropriate when Joyce is asked to justify the dance and drama of his "Thomistically drunk" symbolic world.[4]

It seems curious at first that the word epiphany which occurs at the most crucial point of the discourse on aesthetics in *Stephen Hero,* the key which Stephen uses for an understanding and exposition of Aquinas on the beautiful, should have disappeared altogether from the corresponding "Aquinatian" exposition of the *Portrait.* Various reasons have been suggested. Rudd Fleming, for example, writing in the *University of Kansas City Review,* declares that "epiphanized" is *certainly* not the same as "symbolized," and surmises that the reason for the omission of epiphany in the *Portrait* discussion of beauty is that the word "suggests a dynamic movement of vision through, or beyond, the thing itself," and so would be out of harmony with the static theory of contemplation which the *Portrait* defends.[5] Fleming is certainly right in noticing that the adolescent Stephen Hero is not disposed to subscribe to a symbolic theory of art. Stephen's remarks on symbols indicate clearly enough that he thinks of them as a series of quite arbitrary signs: "Greek beauty laughs at Coptic beauty and the American Indian derides them both." But Stephen Hero's reluctance to subscribe to an aesthetic theory of symbolism seems not in itself to explain the disappearance of epiphany from the aesthetic discourse of the *Portrait.* Though Stephen dismisses symbolism in the *Portrait* as mere "literary talk," [6] the technique of Joyce in reworking the early manuscript version is precisely in the direction of symbolic transformation.

Hugh Kenner argues that the *Stephen Hero* text is "drastically pruned" in the *Portrait* of several of its key doctrines, including that of epiphany, because Joyce was already at work on *Ulysses* and wished to "leave Stephen Dedalus unpropped against the ironic realities which were to overwhelm his soul in the epic." [7] "I haven't let this young man off very lightly, have I?" Joyce remarked once in a conversation to his friend Frank Budgen.[8] So Kenner's argument seems plausible. Yet one is left with the difficulty that Stephen is equipped with the key theory of

4. *Finnegans Wake,* pp. 423, 510.
5. "*Quidditas* in the Tragi-Comedy of Joyce," *University of Kansas City Review,* 15 (Summer 1949), 289–90.
6. *Portrait,* p. 250.
7. "The *Portrait* in Perspective," in Givens, *Two Decades,* p. 153.
8. Quoted by Tindall, *James Joyce,* p. 17.

epiphanies in *Ulysses,* where Joyce in his irony would presumably desire least of all to be identified with Stephen.

Tindall, unlike Fleming, equates Joyce's epiphany with symbolism, though he adds that epiphany is not only the meaning of a symbol but the artist's apprehension of that meaning. Tindall offers also a distinction which may put us on the track of discovering why the epiphany doctrine of *Stephen Hero* is omitted from the *Portrait:* "In spite of Stephen's identification, radiance and epiphany are not identical. Whereas radiance is the property of art, epiphany may belong to any experience." [9] Tindall's distinction, possibly valid in itself and possibly more helpful than Stephen's failure to distinguish, certainly does seem to misrepresent Stephen's view of the matter, for the Ballast Office clock, presumably not a work of art, possesses no little radiance for Stephen.

The earlier version of Joyce's Thomist aesthetic theory operates very much in a void. At no time does Stephen Hero attempt to apply his abstract aesthetic theory to actually existent works of art. The *Stephen Hero* epiphany is conceived, as Tindall notices, solely as a quality of experience. Stephen's opposition to symbolism is tenable only so long as Stephen keeps his aesthetic insulated from contact with the symbolic transformations of literature and of art. The aesthetic discourse of the *Portrait* is differently situated: the purpose of the theoretical analysis of the Thomist texts de pulchro is to lead up to and illustrate a theory of literature, or in particular, a theory of poetry. Having written *Dubliners* in the interval between the two versions of the autobiographical novel, Joyce had learned how to tell someone else's story in the oblique references of a premeditated symbolic structure, and how to dramatize his own story within the formal dimensions of an ironic narrative.

Stephen Dedalus, the artist *as a young man,* has not learned this lesson. To have represented him as interpreting the epiphany as an artificial, artful symbolic reconstruction of the unpremeditated, artless self-disclosures of experience would have blurred the basis for Joyce's ironic portrayal of "the Dedalus." To have managed it so that Stephen would have defended the same lyric theory of epiphany which is set forth in *Stephen Hero* would have been inconsistent with Stephen's own impersonal theory (in the *Portrait*) of the progressive development of the poet. Stephen is made to maintain that this progressive development of the poet is away from the lyric impulse, "at first a cry or a cadence or a mood and then a fluid and lambent narrative," and toward dramatic reprojection or objectivity, where "the personality of the artist . . . finally refines itself out of existence." [1] Stephen misses the clue, as Joyce

9. Ibid., p. 120.

1. *Portrait,* p. 252. Cf. Gustave Flaubert's letter to Mlle. de Chantepe, 1857 (tr. E. W. Parks) : *"Madame Bovary* is not fact. Its story is *entirely fictitious;* I have put into it nothing of my beliefs or of my experience. The deception (if there be one)

intends he should, which is not annihilation of the artist's personality, but the symbolic presentation of reality, be it the artist's personality or the personality of others or "the signatures of things." The comparison of the artist with the God of the creation, who "remains within or behind or beyond or above his handiwork, invisible, refined out of existence, indifferent, paring his fingernails," is the climax of Joyce's ironic development of the Dedalan aesthetic.

"So far as this side of esthetic philosophy extends Aquinas will carry me all along the line" [2] had been Stephen's propaedeutic as he led into his three-form theory of art. Stephen's argument, set forth in Aquinas' own terms, never carries him close at all to Aquinas' "line" and brings him at the last to a point which is exactly antithetical to the "Aquinatian" notion of this world of creation as a sacrament, which symbolizes the omnipresence of the divine artist who made it. Speaking of the imaginative vision of the prophets, Aquinas remarks: "The illumination of the divine ray of light in this present life is not had without the veils of imaginative symbols (*sine velaminibus phantasmatum*), since it is connatural to man in this present state of life that he should not understand without an imaginative sign." [3] Then he goes on to say, "The signs which are in the highest degree expressive of intelligible truth are the words of language." [4]

At a time when Joyce is demonstrating an increasingly sensitive expertness in exploiting the techniques of verbal symbolism, he represents the rationalistic-minded Stephen as all but blind to these resources. "His soul shrivelled up sighing with age as he walked on in a lane among heaps of dead language." [5] It is not that Stephen does not love the word, for he is deeply saddened to notice that the shop legends along the lane had been emptied of sense. Even as a little boy in the Class of Elements at Clongowes, he had been touched by the mystery of words: "He wanted to cry quietly but not for himself: for the words, so beautiful and sad, like music." [6] Stephen cannot integrate into his rationalizations about art the poetic sensibility which he experiences in the music of words. It is through the word and not alone through self-introspection

---

comes, on the contrary, from the *impersonality* of the work. That is one of my principles: one simply must not *write himself in*. The artist ought to be in his work like God in Creation, invisible and all-powerful; let him be felt everywhere but not seen." (Quoted from *The Great Critics*, ed. James Harry Smith and Edd Winfield Parks, 3rd ed., New York, W. W. Norton, 1951, p. 887.)

2. Ibid., p. 245.

3. "Illustratio divini radii in vita praesenti non fit sine velaminibus phantasmatum qualiumcumque, quia connaturale est homini secundum statum praesentis vitae ut non intelligat sine phantasmate." *S.T.*, II–II, q. 174, a. 2, ad 4m.

4. *S.T.*, II–II, q. 174, a. 3, corp.: "Signa maxime expressa intelligibilis veritatis sunt verba."

5. *Portrait*, pp. 207–8.

6. Ibid., p. 22.

that the poet gives form to his own experience and negotiates an insight into the experience of others.

Harry Levin has said of Joyce's later works that they "are artificial reconstructions of a transcendental view of experience." [7] For Stephen, as for Mallarmé, not Being but the Beautiful had been the Absolute. As Joyce progressively dissociated himself from Pater's and Mallarmé's aestheticism and from the neo-Thomist and French Symbolist emphases on a world of ideal beauty, he was carried "along a line" where a transcendental view of experience became possible and where the imaginative "epiphanies" of poetry, incapable though they might be of proving anything to the reason, might yet, "seduce the reason," as Aquinas says of poetry, by symbols, by images, and by "fictions" that signify. [8] In a study entitled "Portrait of the Artist as John Keats" a critic in the *Virginia Quarterly Review* points out that it is curious that Stephen should have mentioned Shelley's poetic visions as epiphanies: "That was the very obstacle to Shelley's imaginative seizure of life: the gross earth could reveal nothing to him; his focus was within. . . ." [9] Stephen's talk about the object's being epiphanized at the moment when "the gropings of a spiritual eye . . . adjust its vision to an exact focus" [1] suggests that Stephen's own focus is largely within. Stephen's difficulty in working out a coherent theory of epiphanies in *Stephen Hero* stems largely from his failure to notice that the aesthetic image keeps its contact with the object.

Irene Hendry in her study of the Joycean Epiphany notes that Joyce seems to shift back and forth in his use of the term "from the actuality of life experience to the experience of literature, of the book, the story, the poem." [2] She points out that whereas the quidditas of the *Stephen Hero* version achieves its radiance of epiphany in the perceiving consciousness, the quidditas of the *Portrait* has its claritas, or radiance, attached to itself. [3] It is true there is a shift, yet not so much back and forth as steadily forward, and not alone toward a greater objectivity but also toward a progressively greater degree of verbal symbolization in character and situation. Even as the characters tend to become essences (*H.C.E.* or *A.L.P.*) and the situations tend to become typical

7. Harry Levin, *James Joyce: A Critical Introduction* (Norfolk, New Directions, 1941), p. 29.

8. Cf. *I Sent.*, Prolog., a. 5, ad 3^m: "Poetica scientia est de his quae propter defectum veritatis non possunt a ratione capi; unde oportet quod quasi quibusdam similitudinibus ratio seducatur."

Quodl., VII, q. 6, a. 16, obj. 2: "Poeticae artis est veritatem rerum aliquibus similitudinibus fictis designare." (Major conceded.)

(Usually Aquinas designates poetry as a *science* rather than as an *art*.)

9. Wylie Sypher, "Portrait of the Artist as John Keats," *Virginia Quarterly Review*, 25 (Summer 1949), 422.

1. *Stephen Hero*, p. 211.

2. Irene Hendry, "Joyce's Epiphanies," *Sewanee Review*, 54 (Summer 1946), 453.

3. Ibid., p. 455.

("The Vico road goes round and round to meet where *terms* begin"),[4] there is an ever increasing verbal elaboration of particularity and detail: "The ring man in the rong shop *but the rite words by the rote order!*" [5] The shift is achieved by the language, for as the intellect (as reason) abstracts the quidditas or essential notes of a character or a situation, the intellect (as imagination) projects the quidditas by verbal connotations or relations into the structure of individual metaphors, cadences, or images capable of identifying the abstraction in some existent and particular verbal symbol or sign. The Joycean epiphany expands thus in symbolic dimensions in proportion as it concentrates its radiance in verbal signs which exist not in isolation but in combinations of patterned sense and sound. This later Joycean theory of the literary epiphany is not theoretically unfolded in a context of the Aquinan theory of the beautiful in the same way that Stephen Hero unfolds his theory of epiphany in the nonliterary sense of "sudden spiritual manifestations" of actual life. Between the later literary sense of the epiphany and the Thomist theory of cognition there is nevertheless such a close affinity that it is difficult to believe that anyone who was exploiting the Thomist texts for the purposes of fiction, as Joyce was doing, could have failed to notice the correspondences. Unless this is so, it is difficult to imagine why Joyce makes so much of quidditas in the speeches he contrived for Stephen in explication of the Thomist texts de pulchro, since the notion of quidditas rarely if ever occurs in Aquinas' remarks on beauty but is a central concept in his theory of knowledge and of signs.

The following text (from the *Summa Theologiae*) which treats of the intellect's dependence on the phantasms, or symbols of the imagination, is typical of many texts which Joyce can hardly have failed to notice as he read Aquinas in his preparation of the Dedalan aesthetic: "When anyone tries to understand something, he forms to himself certain images (*phantasmata*) by way of examples, in which he observes as it were what he is searching to understand. And so it is too when we wish someone else to understand a thing, we propose examples to him by means of which he may form symbols (phantasmata) so as to be able to understand." [6] The poet, the literary artist, is the manipulator par excellence of the symbol, or metaphorical sign; he is the craftsman of the phantasmata (which have the same contents as the sign), the contriver of the meditative verbal image that suggests, reveals, "epiphanizes" short of logical abstraction, interpretation, or argument.

In the language of Aquinas, "to speak metaphorically is not to speak

4. *Finnegans Wake,* p. 452. (Italics mine.)
5. Ibid., p. 167. Italics mine.
6. "Quando aliquis conatur aliquid intelligere, format sibi aliqua phantasmata per modum exemplorum, in quibus quasi inspiciat quod intelligere studet. Et inde est etiam quod quando aliquem volumus facere aliquid intelligere, proponimus ei exempla ex quibus sibi phantasmata formare possit ad intelligendum." *S.T.,* I, q. 84, a. 7, corp.

falsely." [7] The Joycean epiphany in literature may be described as a formulation through metaphor or symbol of some luminous aspect of individual human experience, some highly significant facet of most intimate and personal reality, some particularly radiant point to the meaning of existence. At the *Stephen Hero* stage, Joyce (or Stephen?) tends to undercut the role of the word, as if the meaning of literature could be an "unuttered" or wordless thought. "The classical temper," writes Stephen, ". . . chooses rather to bend upon these present things and so to work upon them and fashion them that the quick intelligence may go beyond them to their meaning which is still unuttered." [8] The complex experiments with language which are carried on in the later works of Joyce are part of Joyce's effort to find vital symbols at the verbal level, capable of interpreting the ineffable epiphanies of experience, and of making these "sudden spiritual manifestations" permanently available through words for the apprehension of other minds.

A related "epiphanic" question, second only in interest to the question of the nature of epiphany, is how Joyce came by the term. The religious implications would have been obvious to Joyce: no Irish Catholic child could fail to hear of and to understand the name of the liturgical feast celebrated on January 6. But why does Joyce appropriate this term for his literary theory? Oliver St. John Gogarty (the prototype of the Buck Mulligan of *Ulysses*) recalls Joyce as "the best example of the type extinct since the Middle Ages of a Goliard, a wandering scholar," and as for the term epiphany has this to say: "Probably Father Darlington had taught him, as an aside in his Latin class—for Joyce knew no Greek—that 'Epiphany' meant 'a shining forth.' So he recorded under 'Epiphany' any showing forth of the mind by which he considered one gave oneself away." [9] Joseph Prescott in an informative note on the subject regards Gogarty's remark "as no more than a guess," and adds, "It seems at least [as] likely that Joyce got his information from Skeat's *Etymological Dictionary*, which the autobiographical Stephen 'read by the hour.' " [1] As Joyce first uses the term, it seems certainly to have reference, as Prescott notices, not to literature but to those "moments of spiritual life" of which Joyce speaks in his notebooks,[2] when the soul of the commonest object reveals itself by some trivial attitude or gesture, discloses its secret, "gives itself away."

In the light of Joyce's fondness for verbal correspondences and his

7. *I Sent.*, dist. 16, q. 1, a. 3, ad 3m: "Aliquis loquens per metaphoricas locutiones, non mentitur."

8. *Stephen Hero*, p. 78.

9. Oliver St. John Gogarty, *As I Was Going down Sackville Street* (New York, Reynal and Hitchcock, 1937), pp. 293, 295.

1. Joseph Prescott, "James Joyce's Epiphanies," *Modern Language Notes*, 64 (May 1949), 436. Cf. *Stephen Hero*, p. 26.

2. Cf. Gorman, *James Joyce*, p. 136.

ingenuity in interpolating into a context where one word is expected or customary another word similar in sound or appearance so as to make unexpected new sense, it may be—who knows?—that in first writing epiphany Joyce was playing on the French *épiphénomène* (that which at certain times attaches itself as if inevitably, though momentarily, to some other phenomenon). Inasmuch as the word epiphany first occurs in Joyce in a context which is explicative of the Aquinan "quae visa placent," and is so intimately associated with the Dedalan exegesis of claritas as quidditas, the possibility that Joyce is here substituting the English word epiphany for the French term épiphénomène is not a bad guess. Maurice De Wulf's important study, *"Les théories esthétiques propres à saint Thomas,"* first appeared while Joyce was a student at University College, Dublin, and was recognized at once as an important step in the direction of constructing a contemporary aesthetic along Thomist lines.[3]

De Wulf stresses throughout his study the psychological aspects of the claritas pulchri, and interprets the épiphénomène esthétique much as Stephen interprets "epiphany." For example, at one point De Wulf says: "Saint Thomas étudie le second phénomène qu'on retrouve dans toute impression du beau: la jouissance caracteristique, qu'on appelle parfois *l'épiphénomène* esthétique ('quae visa placent')." [4]

In his analysis of the épiphénomène De Wulf makes much of the intimate relationship which Aquinas establishes between the claritas pulchri and the *causa formalis* in things.[5] Numerous Aquinan paraphrases for claritas are suggestively developed by De Wulf as indications of how far the Aquinan notion of aesthetic radiance moved away from the mere charm in color, the suavitas coloris or color nitidus of Aquinas' medieval predecessors, and toward some theory of intuitive, spiritual apprehension of the intelligible light in the object, the *lumen apparens,* the *lumen manifestans,* the *resplendentia,* or splendor of being. De Wulf then quotes from the *Summa* to show how intimately associated are the attributes of claritas and proportio with this resplendentia formae, or self-disclosure of being: "Pour revêtir les attributs de la beauté, toute chose doit réaliser cette double condition: la debita proportio et la claritas." [6] The *Stephen Hero* account of epiphany coincides in so many respects with De Wulf's description of the épiphénomène esthétique that it is difficult not to detect a correspondence between the two formulations. Stephen summarizes as follows: "This is the moment which I call epiphany. . . . When the relation of the parts is exquisite, when the parts are adjusted to the special point, we recognize that it is *that* thing

3. Cf. *Revue néo-scolastique, 1-2,* pp. 188-205, 341-57.
4. Ibid., *2,* 345. (Italics mine.)
5. Ibid., 351.
6. Ibid., 349. Cf. *S.T.,* II-II, q. 145, a. 2, corp.: "Ad rationem pulchri, sive decori, concurrit et claritas, et debita proportio."

which it is. Its soul, its whatness, leaps to us from the vestment of its appearance. The soul of the commonest object, the structure of which is so adjusted, seems to us radiant. The object achieves its epiphany." [7]

The *"claritas* is *quidditas"* remark in the context of the *Stephen Hero* exposition is quite easily interpreted as a Thomist derivative, whereas the same statement in the *Portrait* is made to carry the sense of a particularity in determination of essence which aligns it much more closely with the Scotist haecceitas. The specific or universal form rather than the individual form is the inner heart of the object as Thomists view the individual thing. Though the inner core of the reality is conceived of by the Thomist as a specific or universal essence, or quidditas, the relevance of the particular in exemplification of the universal is not ignored. The difference here between the Thomist interpretation of claritas in *Stephen Hero* and the Scotist interpretation in the *Portrait* rises mainly from a difference of emphasis and of approach. Whereas the Scotist takes joy in disengaging the particular from the general, in seeing that an object "is that thing which it is and no other," as Stephen says in the *Portrait,* the Thomist delights in recognizing in the fully differentiated singular the universal essence or quiddity—"Its soul, its whatness," which, as *Stephen Hero* says, "leaps to us from the vestment of its appearance." The Thomist would argue too that the Scotist haecceitas, in any case, presupposes the specifying quidditas, and that the haecceitas of itself is ineffable and incommunicable, capable of intuition but in no way capable of conceptualization, whereas the quidditas of the singular is utterable, intelligible in one's own mind, and communicable to the minds of others.

At a time when Joyce was moving closer to a quasi-Thomist interpretation of quidditas as the concern for the universally significant and "essentially" important aspects of reality, he assigned to Stephen in the *Portrait,* possibly to heighten the irony in Stephen's predicament, a solicitude for the uniquely singular and individually ineffable thing. In first introducing the *Stephen Hero* manuscript, Theodore Spencer made some important observations on epiphany, which are still valid so long as one talks about epiphany in its original, nonliterary sense: "A theory like this is not of much use to a dramatist, as Joyce seems to have realized when he first conceived of it. It is a theory which implies a lyrical rather than a dramatic view of life. It emphasizes the radiance, the effulgence, of the thing itself revealed in a special moment, an unmoving moment of time." [8] Such a theory, one might add, reflects a tendency in nineteenth-century aesthetic theory to substitute a "taste for tokens" of the sense and of the passions for the intuitions of thought. [9]

7. *Stephen Hero,* p. 213.
8. Theodore Spencer, *"Stephen Hero:* The Unpublished Manuscript of James Joyce's *Portrait of the Artist as a Young Man," Southern Review,* 7 (Summer 1941), 185–6.
9. Cf. Gilbert and Kuhn, *A History of Esthetics,* p. 313. The authors describe the

As soon as one tries to apply the theory of epiphany as a literary tool for the interpretation of Joyce's own work, the matter becomes complicated. In what sense, literary or nonliterary, should one understand "the radiant epiphany of the whole and structurally intelligible *individual* thing?" [1] Is "this thing" the poem, the story itself, or is it the evanescent experience or insight or, indeed, the trivial object which the poem or the story patterns or illuminates? Granted that the theory of epiphany has a relevance for literature, is there any good reason why if the theory is valid it should have any special relevance for Joyce? A literary application of the Joycean epiphany in its original sense of "sudden spiritual manifestation, whether in the vulgarity of speech or of gesture or in a memorable phase of the mind itself," [2] would seem to differ little from the literary strategy which Wordsworth described as the aim of the *Lyrical Ballads:* "to choose incidents and situations from common life, and to relate or describe them, throughout, as far as possible, in a selection of language really used by men, and, at the same time, to throw over them a certain colouring of imagination, whereby ordinary things should be presented to the mind in an unusual aspect." [3]

Why even should epiphany in its later, more strictly literary meaning of a "sound sense sympol" [4] have any distinctive value as a clue to the meaning of Joyce's own works? Tindall comments, *"Ulysses* and *Finnegans Wake* are great epiphanies, disclosing their whatness and the whatness of reality. But this is only a fancier way of calling them significant forms." [5] If that is all that the theory of epiphany as symbol means, why should this theory be any more or any less relevant for Joyce than it is for any other imaginative writer—Shakespeare, Blake, Chekhov, Katherine Mansfield, to name but a few? Furthermore if modern critics are correct in reading the *Portrait* as an ironic portrayal of Stephen Dedalus, the artist *as a young man,* ought we not to take Stephen's *Portrait* theory of radiance or claritas (all, indeed, that survives in the *Portrait* of the *Stephen Hero* "epiphany") with a grain of salt? Joyce the artist need not always have agreed with Joyce the theorist, and especially when the theorist is the adolescent Stephen we should be on our guard not to identify the theory too closely with Joyce's own practical techniques in art. It may be too in Joyce's case, as in the case of other poets, like Wordsworth, Shelley, and Hopkins, who have offered theories of art or of poetry, that the works, with a certain minimum of good will, can be seen to illustrate the theories

aesthetic of J. C. Hamann (1730–88) as a theory of "sense as epiphany": "Esthetic was reduced by Hamann to a commentary on the mysteries of Theophany and Incarnation."

1. Cf. Wimsatt, "Poetry and Christian Thinking," *Thought, 26* (Summer 1951), 223.
2. *Stephen Hero,* p. 211.
3. [Cf.] *Preface to the Lyrical Ballads,* fifth paragraph.
4. *Finnegans Wake,* p. 612.
5. Tindall, *James Joyce,* p. 121.

more successfully than the theories can be used to interpret the works.

The generally formless character, from a literary point of view, of the original epiphany is manifest in the example which serves to introduce the discussion of epiphanies in the *Stephen Hero* draft:

> The Young Lady — (drawling discreetly) . . . O, yes . . . I was . . . at the . . . cha . . . pel . . .
> The Young Gentleman — (inaudibly) . . . I (again inaudibly) . . . I . . .
> The Young Lady — (softly) . . . O . . . but you're . . . ve . . . ry . . . wick . . . ed. . . .[6]

That is all! However interesting this "sudden, spiritual manifestation" may have been when Joyce actually overheard it or remembered it or conceived it in his imagination, the literary transcription is far from significant, and the reader would not be much the wiser in spiritual insight if he counted on "the man of letters" to do no more than "record" such moments "with extreme care."[7] In order that the "epiphanic" moment of phenomenological experience may enter into poetry, the writer has no other choice than to represent the subjective experience within a symbolic structure of words. Otherwise these "most delicate and evanescent of moments" pass evanescently away, and like the "green oval leaves" Stephen Dedalus' "epiphanic records" are blown about on the winds of memory but do not exist as poems. An informing transformation of the mood through the symbolic projections of language is needed if the "sudden spiritual manifestation" is not to perish like the lost treasures of Alexandria. In poetry the conflict or drama either of mood or of spirit is seen through the language; as Joyce later on says, "The war is in words and the wood is the world."[8]

There is no exact agreement as to the actual dates of the writing of *Stephen Hero*. Spencer's investigations seem most authoritative, and though he allows wide margins (1901–06) he inclines to date the manuscript as representing the work of the years 1904–06.[9] In any case it seems certain that the epiphany incorporated into *Stephen Hero* was composed subsequently to, if not lifted from, a series of similar "plotless sketches, flashes of life, manifestations of mood and place" which Gorman describes as having been written by Joyce in Paris as "the major labour of this green season of his career" between December, 1902, and April 1903.[1] To fifteen of these extant sketches Joyce himself gave the title

6. *Stephen Hero*, p. 211.
7. Ibid.
8. *Finnegans Wake*, p. 98.
9. Intro. to *Stephen Hero*, p. 9.
1. Cf. Gorman, *James Joyce*, p. 92; see also Slocum and Cahoon, *Joyce Bibliography*, p. 153, E, 11, a, x. Cf. also "Notes et rêves," translations of three of Joyce's epiphanies

"Epiphanies." There may have been more. These fifteen epiphanies, as well as seven other brief descriptions similar in style to the epiphanies, are written out neatly in Joyce's own hand on twenty-two separate foolscap sheets and form part of the Joyce Paris Library now in the Lockwood Memorial Library of the University of Buffalo.

The collection shows how admirably sensitive Joyce already was to "the single word that tells the whole story," to "the simple gesture that reveals a complex state of relationships." [2] But the symbolic representation of these emblematic, "epiphanic" moments although hinting at a story does not really tell one, and the complexity in human relationships, suggested as it may be, finds little corresponding echo in a complexity of verbal reconstruction or in a patterned "re-presentation" of insight. They are not without a delicate irony, however, and show already the solicitude for verbal compression and the economy of explicit comment which is characteristic of Joyce's mature work. The following two epiphanies are typical of the strategy of all, and have besides an auto-biographical note which adds a special interest:

1.   (Dublin: in the National Library)
            Skeffington — I was sorry to hear of
the death of your brother . . . sorry we didn't know
in time . . . to have been at the funeral . . .
            Joyce — O, he was very young . . . a boy . . .
            Skeffington — Still . . . it hurts. . . .

2.   (Dublin: on Mountjoy Square)
            Joyce — (*concludes*) . . . That'll be
forty thousand pounds.
            Aunt Lillie — (*titters*) . . . O laws!
. . . I was like that too . . . when I was a girl I was
sure I'd marry a lord . . . or something. . . .
            Joyce — (*thinks*) . . . Is it possible
she's comparing herself with me?

One further example may be worth quoting since it suggests so well the manifold possibilities of further verbal growth in narrative symbolization which may be contained if only in a tiny literary seed:

                                        (Dublin: at Sheehy's
                                          Belvedere Place)
            O'Reilly — (*with developing seriousness*)
. . . Now it's my turn, I suppose . . . (*quite seriously*)
. . . Who is your favourite poet?

---

by André du Bouchet in the review *84* (Paris), No. 12 (Nov. 1949), pp. 477-9. Slocum and Cahoon note on page 114 of their bibliography that the third of these epiphanies has not been identified.

2. Cf. Levin, *James Joyce*, p. 28.

(*a pause*)
Hanna Sheehy — . . . German?
O'Reilly — . . . Yes.

(*a hush*)
Hanna Sheehy — . . . I think . . . Goethe. . . .[3]

Whatever may be the latent possibilities of dramatic narrative completion, is not the story as it stands more of an evocative cue to emotion than a dramatic narration? Joyce would seem to have sensed this: to have realized that his flair for the epiphany technique was better adapted for the lyrical gesture than for the narrative or dramatic reprojection of imaginatively formed reality. In any case every epiphany of literature needs words, not just stage directions, parentheses, and dots and dashes. Joyce's next serious endeavor was not yet *Dubliners* but the poems which were later published together in *Chamber Music* in 1909. Many of these poems appeared separately in various English and Irish periodicals several years before the initial publication of *Chamber Music,* some of them as early as 1904.[4] The composition of the poems must have overlapped, however, with the writing of *Dubliners,* since, as Padraic Colum points out, this book of stories was completed and first accepted for publication about 1905.[5] The composition of the *Chamber Music* poems— lyrics for music, as their title suggests—was done on the Elizabethan models, especially Ben Jonson, whom Joyce revered and whom he studied with unusual care.[6] In this way he must have been compelled to focus his attention in writing upon the objective reality of *verbal* imagery, and to notice the richness and complexity in interpreting experience which can be achieved through the artful alchemy of "metaphor, antithesis, and energy."

It was also just at this time that Joyce was reading extensively in Aristotle and in Aquinas, both at Paris in 1903 and at Pola in 1904, as the quotations cited by Gorman from the Paris and Pola notebooks clearly show.[7] The entries in the notebooks are almost exclusively concerned, at least on the surface, with a philosophical analysis of the notions of art and of beauty. The genetic and affective aspects of the aesthetic experience are manifestly Joyce's principal concern at this period, as they tend almost invariably to become for anyone who makes

3. For permission to quote these Epiphanies (unpublished as this book goes to press), I am grateful to O. A. Silverman, who has prepared the introduction and notes to *James Joyce: The Epiphanies,* to be published by the Lockwood Memorial Library, 1956. The quoted Epiphanies are numbered 4, 9, and 21 in the Silverman text. Except for my reading of *laws* for *laus* in my second quotation, our interpretation of Joyce's early handwriting agrees. (Owing to his progressive loss of vision, Joyce's handwriting becomes increasingly difficult to decipher as he grows older.)

4. Cf. Slocum and Cahoon, *Joyce Bibliography,* p. 93, C, 26, 27, 28.

5. Cf. Intro. to *Dubliners,* p. v.

6. Cf. Gorman, *James Joyce,* pp. 94–5.

7. Cf. Ibid., pp. 96–9, 133–8.

of beauty the dominant rubric in art. There is little if any explicit comment on the formal aspects of the ontological construct, the poem as an imaginative symbol, and little inclination to conceive of the poem as a verbal act which dramatizes the dialectics of a situation, the phases of the experience as they exist in a structure of words. The question of the nature of poetry is hardly more than glanced at and is nowhere seriously considered as related to the question of language as a system of verbal symbols or signs. Two of the entries, though disconnected in themselves, appear to mirror Joyce's dissatisfaction with his own heavily psychological approach: "Beauty is so difficult," "Art has the gift of tongues." [8] In the absence of clear-cut Joycean references it is not possible to assert that Joyce at this period of his reading in Aquinas was directly influenced by Aquinas' own numerous references to language, his comments on metaphors as *symbolicae locutiones*,[9] his treatment of words as *sensibilia signa*,[1] his description of poetic representations as *similitudines fictae*,[2] *velamina veritatis*,[3] *figurae aliarum rerum*.[4]

It is not likely that the cumulative force of such "arguments" would have failed to register on a reader of Aquinas who was interested in poetry and in poetic expression. In the light of Joyce's own religious background, ritual and sacramental, in the light of his familiarity with the symbolic role of the word in liturgical acts, and finally in the light of his Jesuit education in the function of the word in poetic and rhetorical contexts, it seems only reasonable to conclude that Joyce must have been struck by Aquinas' treatment of poetic expression as symbolic utterance, and that he would have found in the Aquinan texts he was reading a congenial philosophic justification and incentive for the new symbolic dimensions of his own writing. If this is so, it becomes easier too to account for the new Joycean shift as to the location of radiance (claritas), from the actual experience of the spectator in life to the verbal act or construct that imaginatively re-presents this experience in the symbols of language, re-enacts it through illuminating images (though not purely luminous) for the contemplation of the imaginative mind.

In the Aquinan perspectives there are at least two different ways in which a word may function as a sign: the first way is in virtue of the referential meaning which the word has in the particular verbal context where it is situated, and the second is in virtue of the interpretative instrumentality which this referential meaning has to negotiate a further insight through the pressure of the total nonverbal situation that the

8. Cf. *Ibid.*, pp. 135, 136.
9. *I Sent.*, dist. 34, q. 3, a. 1, obj. 3.
1. *S.T.*, II–II, q. 174, a. 1, ad 3^m.
2. *Quodl.*, VII, q. 6, a. 16, obj. 2.
3. *I Sent.*, dist. 34, q. 3, a. 1, obj. 3.
4. *Quodl.*, VII, q. 6, a. 14, corp.

verbal discourse calls to mind.[5] Aquinas appears to be thinking of these two different functions of the verbal sign when he writes: "The sign expresses something known to us, through which we are led to a further knowledge of something else." [6] Unless one is prepared to hold that language is the only reality, a view which at times has been ascribed unjustly to Joyce, one will see, as Aquinas does, that objects, events, and other nonverbal facts of many sorts may also be signs, suggestive of further reality, expressive of another order of being: "Signa autem exteriora non solum sunt verba, sed etiam facta." [7] Though Aquinas asserts that nonverbal objects may and do function also as signs, time and again he assigns a primacy of symbolic power to the word: "Signa maxime expressa intelligibilis veritatis sunt verba," [8] or again, "Voces . . . sunt praecipua inter signa." [9]

All imaginative writers, dependent as they are on words, are necessarily interested in symbolic vision and in symbolic technique, and to the extent that they are so interested one may say that they are interested

5. The author is manifestly indebted at this point to Susanne K. Langer for her illuminating comments on the symbolic nature of language. Possibly the distinction here attempted between "the referential meaning" and "the interpretative instrumentality" of the word coincides with her distinction between signs as *signals* and signs as *symbols* (*Feeling and Form. A Theory of Art*, New York, Scribner's, 1953, pp. 22, 26; *Philosophy in a New Key. A Study in the Symbolism of Reason, Rite, and Art*, New York, Mentor, 1951, ch. 3, "The Logic of Signs and Symbols," pp. 42–63). If this is so, Mrs. Langer's description is more concise and more easily manageable in discourse. (Mrs. Langer in *Feeling and Form*, p. 28, n. 1, states that she has adopted her present distinction between "signal" and "symbol" from Charles W. Morris. See, for example, his *Signs, Language and Behavior*, New York, Prentice-Hall, 1946.)

But her insistence that the function of symbols is "the articulation and presentation of *concepts*" (*Feeling and Form*, p. 26)—"symbols are not proxy for their objects, but are *vehicles for the conception of objects*" (*Philosophy in a New Key*, p. 49)—would be a misleading report of the Aquinan view on the twofold nature of the word as symbol and sign. The intentional, or interpretative, instrumentality of the symbol is certainly not regarded by Aquinas as a vehicle for the presentation of concepts but as an efficacious manifestation, however analogous, of ontological reality (ens). As Frederick D. Wilhelmsen says in his excellent article on Aquinas ("The Aesthetic Act and the Act of Being," *Modern Schoolman, 29* May, 1952), "When the poet writes of the 'tears of God,' he may be talking *about* tears, but he means God. The Clowns of Rouault are not characters in a local circus; they are a human prefiguring of Christ on the cross" (p. 290). It is only fair to state that Wilhelmsen makes all his comments in quite different perspectives from mine and possibly he would not agree with either the premises or the conclusions of the present study. Since Mrs. Langer, with considerable acumen, has already pre-empted the "signal-symbol" distinction in talking about signs, a more cumbersome distinction has been substituted here, not for signs but for words: "referential meaning," "interpretative instrumentality."

For a more extended treatment of the doctrine on language and the theory of the sign from a strictly Scholastic point of view, the reader may consult Jacques Maritain, *Ransoming the Time* (New York, Scribner's, 1941), ch. 9: "Sign and Symbol," pp. 217–54.

6. *IV Sent.*, dist. 1, q. 1, a. 1: "Signum importat aliquod notum quo ad nos, quo manuducimur in alterius cognitionem." (Solutio II to quaestiuncula 5.)

7. *S.T.*, II–II, q. 111, a. 1, corp.

8. *S.T.*, II–II, q. 174, a. 3, corp.

9. *S.T.*, II–II, q. 85, a. 1, obj. 3.

too in "epiphanies." For the imaginative writer there will then under-standably appear to be a very close link between the way the word func-tions as a sign and the symbolic value of nonverbal objects or *facts* (evoked by the word). For in its interpretative function of negotiating an insight over and beyond its referential meaning, the word plays within literature a role that is handled outside of literature by some significant event or tangible symbol (a jewel, flower, or emblem, and so forth) or figurative gesture or sign. In acting as a vicar or proxy for the non-verbal symbol, the word never ceases to be a word, subject to the same tensions of referential meaning which must arise in all metaphorical predications of language, but subject too to the manipulation of the writer in a way that nonverbal signs, or *facts,* ordinarily cannot be.

The "referential meaning" of a word is not an inevitable meaning. As Aquinas puts it, "Voces autem quae sunt praecipua inter signa, . . . non significant naturaliter sed ad placitum." [1] Custom, convention, the so-called "laws" and accidents of philological and phonetic develop-ment, and a host of sociological factors determine what referential meanings a given word in any language may have. Each language has verbal resources of its own which no other language can exactly dupli-cate. Milton's and Crashaw's artistic punning on "sun" and "son" in their Nativity Hymns would be quite impossible, for example, with the French *soleil* and *fils.* [2] The French punning on *pleure* and *pleut,* on the other hand, is quite impossible in English. As W. K. Wimsatt observes: "If the rain is something like human tears, that is true in England as well as in France. But certain poems could be written in French and not in English, because we have *weep* and *rain,* they have *pleurer* and *pleuvoir.* (*Il pleure dans mon coeur/Comme il pleut sur la ville.*)" [3] The work of modern critics has tended (presumably without their in-tending it) to revive a tradition of alert verbal exegesis which in many respects is medieval and very similar to the Aquinan canons of meta-phorical meaning and poetic sense.

Of the word in its role as "interpretative symbol" Aquinas notes: "Those things which are signified by a verbal expression can be symbols of still other things." [4] In the medieval attitude there seems to have been a twofold kind of appropriateness looked for in a symbol: the "natural" fitness of an object to signify other realities, and its "conventional"

1. Ibid.

2. The English homonyms "sun" and "son" make it possible to ring many new changes on the common medieval analogy between the sun and God: e.g., "Non per far, ma per non fare, ho perduto Di veder l'alto Sol." (Dante's *Purgatorio,* Canto vii, vs. 25–6.)

3. W. K. Wimsatt, Jr., "Verbal Style: Logical and Counterlogical," *PMLA, 65* (March 1950), 17.

4. *S.T.,* I, q. 1, a. 10, ad 1ᵐ: "Ipsae res significatae per voces aliarum rerum possunt esse signa."

Cf. *Quodl.,* VII, q. 6, a. 14: "Res [significatae per verba] sunt figurae aliarum rerum."

fitness to do so in virtue of tradition or established usage. To say that
the Aquinan criterion of poetic symbolism is not the word but the thing
represented by the word is not the same as to say that this thing represented by the word is cut off or divorced from the word, or that it must
be conceived of as existing outside the poem. The Joycean phoenix,
"O foenix culprit," [5] certainly cannot exist in any such independent
fashion, nor indeed the pelican which feeds its young by plucking at its
own breast to give them blood, though this does not prevent Aquinas
from using the pelican as a symbol of Christ in his eucharistic hymn,
Adoro Te Devote: "Pie pellicane, Jesu Domine . . ." [6] "Phoenix" and
"pelican," once their referential meanings are established (partly through
convention, partly through context)—the bird that rises from its own
ashes every thousand years, the bird that feeds its young with its own
life's blood—can then begin to function as "insight symbols," not in-
dependently of the referential meaning but consequent upon this meaning in tradition or in the nature of things.

It may be worth while at this point to note by way of parenthesis that
the application to poetry of the Aquinan (and medieval) fourfold sense
of Scripture (literal, allegorical, moral, and anagogical) is not strictly
speaking an application visualized by Aquinas. It is to Dante rather than
to Aquinas that the renown belongs for having systematically distinguished, in the *Convivio,* these four "senses" of *poetic* meaning, and in
doing so Dante himself takes pains to distinguish carefully between
theological and poetical "allegories," conceiving of the latter as veiled
by a fable of the poet's invention and the former by an extrapoetical fact
or event of real occurrence. [7] Aquinas for his part is quite explicit in
denying to poetry any "sense" but the literal one. In the seventh of his
Quaestiones Quodlibetales, for example, he devotes an entire article to
the question: In other writings, besides the Scriptures, and in the case of
ars poetica in particular, may not a fourfold sense be found? His conclusion is that it may not: "Unde in nulla scientia, humana industria
inventa, proprie loquendo, potest inveniri nisi litteralis sensus." [8]

In qualifying his conclusion as he does, *proprie loquendo,* Aquinas
leaves the door open to Dante's later distinction of the fourfold sense
of poetry. There is no serious incompatibility on this point between
these two thirteenth-century medieval thinkers, the poet-theologian of
the *Summa* and the *Adoro Te Devote,* and the theologian-poet of the
Divina Commedia and the *Convivio.* Aquinas' reason for denying that
poetry can have any but a "literal sense," since it casts light on the na-

5. *Finnegans Wake,* p. 23.
6. Cf. F. J. E. Raby's discussion of this Eucharistic hymn, "The Date and Authorship of the Poem *Adoro Te Devote,*" *Speculum, 20* (April 1945), 236–8.
7. Cf. *Convivio,* II, i. Cf. too Vossler, *Mediaeval Culture, 1,* 131–2.
8. *Quodl.,* VII, q. 6, a. 16, obj. 2 and corp.

ture of poetic diction as he conceived of it, and as Joyce appears too to have conceived of it, is worth recalling here. Only the Holy Spirit, argues Aquinas, can tell us if an event or an utterance in Scripture has a further significance over and beyond what the words themselves suggest or signify. Once the Holy Spirit tells men that a scriptural event or object has this ulterior sense (the *sensus typicus*), the believer is obliged to accept the Holy Spirit's testimony. In regard to utterances not inspired by the Holy Spirit, and in regard in particular to the *fictiones poeticae*, no meaning emerges except what the words themselves signify, since these *fictiones poeticae* have signification as their only end—non sunt ad aliud ordinatae nisi ad significandum [9]—and achieve their end only to the extent that they do signify without a gloss or imputation of meaning from outside the poem. Strictly speaking, therefore, *proprie loquendo*, poetry has not, of itself, a *sensus moralis* (or *tropologicus*) exhorting men to right action, and no *sensus allegoricus* (or *typicus*) inviting men to view the events of the old order as a shadow of the events of the new, and no *sensus anagogicus* disposing men to see the historical happenings of both the old and the new orders on earth as types of the Church Triumphant in heaven, the New Jerusalem signified by the imperfect human realizations of the Jerusalem on earth. The poet as poet is the negotiator through words of the "literal sense," and of that alone.

In a preceding article of the same (seventh) *Quaestio Quodlibetalis*, Aquinas has defined the "literal sense" in such a way as to include all

9. *Quodl.*, VII, q. 6, a. 16, ad 2[m].
Cf. Charles S. Singleton's discussion of "Dante's Allegory," *Speculum, 25* (Jan. 1950), 78–86. Singleton maintains that the allegory of the *Divine Comedy* is so clearly the "allegory of theologians" that he greatly wonders at the efforts made to see it as the "allegory of poets" (p. 81). "The crux of the matter," as Singleton views it, is whether the "literal sense" is fictive (as with the poets) or factual (as with the theologians). But Aquinas' view of the matter is that the imaginative *fictiones poeticae* are necessarily and always to be read for their "literal sense" (whether historically considered that be fictive or factual) since only God, the author of Scripture, can use events as men use words. Even the "literal sense" of some parts of Scripture need not be read as "factually true"—for example, the parables of the Lost Sheep or of the Prodigal Son.
Cf. too Erich Auerbach's "Typological Symbolism in Mediaeval Literature," *Yale French Studies*, No. 9 (Spring 1952), 3–10: "In an allegory of love or in a religious symbol at least one of the terms does not belong to human history; it is an abstraction or a sign. But in the sacrifice of Isaac considered as a figure of the sacrifice of Christ, it is essential, and has been stressed with great vigor, at least in the Occidental tradition, that neither the prefiguring nor the prefigured event lose their literal and historical reality by their figurative meaning and interrelation" (p. 6).
As Aquinas views the matter, the sensus typicus is a sense exclusively proper to Scripture. Poets like Dante whose minds were rooted in scriptural traditions sought a way to accommodate this scriptural "figurative sense" to poetry. In doing so they tended to shift their attention from the literal meaning to be found in words to the spiritual meanings to be found in the things and events which the words pointed to. Joyce shows an increasingly marked inclination to return to the sensus litteralis (fictive or factual) which is to be found *in verbis*.

the devices of metaphor, irony, imagery, and "wit," which later literary traditions would characterize as "the figurative sense": "Totum id ad sensum litteralem pertinet quod ex ipsa verborum significatione recte accipitur." [1] It may be that Aquinas' way of conceiving of the poetic sense as the *sensus litteralis* escapes more successfully than Dante's "the intentional fallacy" [2] as well as the imputation latent in later literary traditions that the poetic meaning of words is mere adventitious ornament and as such not essential to the real meaning or sense. On the human level, *humana industria inventa*, there is no strict "poetic" diction, no poetic way of using words different from the way words are used outside of poems. Poet and reader alike must take the old words as they come, with all their impurities and all their opaqueness of sense, with their more or less resonant metaphorical overtones, and in their more or less metaphysical flatness or thrust. Renewal, if it comes, comes not by refining the old word of its impurities or by seeking to substitute a one-to-one transparency for the old opaqueness of meaning. Words are not mathematical symbols or points on a graph. A new relationship established between the old words may, however, suggest or symbolize an aspect of being, analogous, antithetical, or unexpected, which without this fresh verbal formulation might for a long time have remained unsuspected or unexplored. So it comes about that the symbolical efficacy of language increases in proportion as one can take advantage of the meaning of words in their basically "literal" sense.

So long then as one is following the Aquinan line of thought, one should characterize the "four senses" of which Harry Levin speaks in the following helpful comment as but various poetic aspects of the fundamental and unique "literal sense": "When Joyce exclaims 'O foenix culprit!' over the (moral) downfall of (literal) Earwicker, thereby locating his story in (allegorical) Dublin and adhering to Vico's schedule of (anagogical) revival, he demonstrates how the four levels of symbolism can be subsumed by a single phrase." [3]

In Aquinan perspectives, Joyce's "O foenix culprit" demonstrates how close is the link between poetic symbolism and an expert management of the literal sense of words. The referential meanings of the basic phrase *"O felix culpa"* are multiple: the fall of Adam; the Incarnation and Redemption of Christ, the Saviour; the hyberbolic *Exultet* of the Holy Saturday liturgy. Interacting with these referential meanings, through the seriocomic compression of "O foenix culprit," are the associations with the immortal phoenix of mythology and of poetry (now seen as a culprit detected in crime), the Phoenix Park in Dublin which is the

---

1. *Quodl.*, VII, q. 6, a. 15, corp.

2. Cf. W. K. Wimsatt and M. Beardsley, "The Intentional Fallacy," *Sewanee Review*, 54 (Summer 1946), 468–88.

3. Levin, *James Joyce*, p. 157.

scene of Earwicker's transgression (and the scene too of the Phoenix Park murders), and the Viconian theory of historical decline and resurrection. It is through this interaction that the nonparaphrasable insight of the exclamation is "negotiated." The symbolic sense of poetry is not an interpretation of the literal sense. It *is* the literal sense *in the fullest sense of the words.*

Between the half-wordless and largely parenthetical transcriptions of Joyce's earliest Epiphanies, and the highly compressed, many-visioned verbal formulations of the *Wake,* a complicated series of linguistic experiments was to take place. From *Dubliners* onward, Joyce's style shows a steady development in the direction of symbolic verbal notation. Levin has compared *Dubliners* to the collection of epiphanies which Stephen, as he walked along the beach in *Ulysses,* had lost hope of ever recording in words. The fact that Joyce succeeded in recording some of them in *Dubliners* is a sign that Joyce had come to see that the "sudden spiritual manifestation" was not in itself enough to constitute a poem or a story. The radiant structure of the object in literature is not self-adjusting. Only insofar as the poet or storyteller can turn the symbolic resources of his language to advantage will the literary experience "epiphanize," "seem to us radiant." [4] If *Dubliners* is the turning point in Joyce's attitude toward the epiphany, it appears reasonable to assume that his independent study of Aquinas during the period when he was writing these stories would have been one of the influences inclining him to a higher degree of symbolization in his art.

A brief look at one or two of the *Dubliners* stories may help to show how this new epiphanic strategy operates. The moment of "sudden spiritual manifestation" for the reader of *Two Gallants* [5] occurs at the very end when Corley with a grave gesture extends his hand toward the light and opens it to the gaze of Lenehan: "A small gold coin shone in the palm." So far as the incident might have been viewed by a spectator in the Dublin streets that evening, who was aware of what Corley had been up to, as Lenehan certainly was, this wordless "vulgarity of gesture" would be deeply and horribly illuminating of the ironic perversion of romantic gallantry in twentieth-century Dublin. But for the reader of a story to be thus enlightened a strategic psychological preparation is necessary, which the writer has no other means to effect except through the calculated arrangement of words so as to achieve the right adjustment of symbolic insight. How does Joyce, the "Spickspook-spokesman of our specturesque silentiousness," [6] manage this? The

4. *Stephen Hero,* p. 213.

5. *Dubliners,* pp. 58–73. My remarks here on *Two Gallants* are largely a paraphrase of an excellent unpublished interpretation of this story by Robert R. Boyle, S.J.

6. *Finnegans Wake,* p. 427.

central image elaborated by the language of the story is that of the harp whose mournful music struck silent the two gallants. This image of the harp with her coverings about her knees is also made to suggest, through an allusive verbal recall, Moore's treatment of the harp as a symbol of poor, paralyzed, charmed Ireland, "Lir's lonely daughter." The naked harp of Joyce's story is mournful with reason, since in Corley the reader sees her ignored, despised, and sold for a gold coin. But besides the symbolism of the harp image, Joyce negotiates a further insight through language by his development of the imagery of the moonlight and of the rain. The faint romantic light of the moon is represented as gradually fading as the story develops, and as completely disappearing behind the rain clouds at the end, to be replaced by the hard glitter of the shining gold coin, become thus the emblem of the "base betrayer." It is in this way that the success of the gallants "epiphanizes" as the betrayal of gallantry: "the object achieves its epiphany"—but within the symbolic dimensions of language and not as a depressing vulgarity of nonliterary fact.

The same sort of symbolic technique accounts for the "radiant epiphany" of meaning which accompanies the snow image at the conclusion of the last and longest of the *Dubliners* stories, "The Dead": "His soul swooned slowly as he heard the snow falling, faintly through the universe and faintly falling, like the descent of their last end, upon all the living and the dead." [7] Gabriel's own sudden spiritual illumination is represented as having taken place in silence several moments before the story closes. It is the moment when the full impact of Gretta's disclosure of her secret strikes him: in the light of this long hidden love of hers for the poor youth of the gasworks—"I think he died for me"—Gabriel sees his wife as a person in a way he had never been capable of seeing her before. The revelation humiliates him but does not make him resentful. Gabriel's moment of epiphany is that "most delicate and evanescent of moments" when his love for Gretta turns from *Eros* to *Agape.* "What is a woman standing on the stairs in the shadow, listening to distant music, a symbol of?" he had asked himself earlier. Now he knows to his sorrow: the sad and gracious memory of the romance and poetry in Gretta's life was in no way related to him.

But that silent moment of insight, so uniquely personal and shattering and generous, cannot be the epiphany of the story for anyone else but Gabriel. How does Joyce manage the epiphany, the radiant moment of insight, *for the reader,* and in what does that insight of the story as a story consist? The central clue to an answer here would seem to lie in the image of the snow. "Yes, the newspapers were right: snow was

7. *Dubliners,* pp. 224–88 *passim.* Here I acknowledge my indebtedness to Cleanth Brooks, not only for insights of which I make use in discussing this story but for my appreciation of Joyce as one of the most significant of modern writers.

general all over Ireland." Prosaically literal as the verbal statement of Gabriel's reflection sounds, the mention of the cold, impersonal, but not implacable snow at this near-final moment of the story's utterance succeeds both in suggesting the ineffable mystery of the lonely human person and at the same time in symbolizing the transcendental unity of the dead with the living, and of all nature with all mankind.

This radiance of poetic meaning at the mention of snow is possible only in virtue of Joyce's strategic elaboration of the image from its first verbal appearance, when Gabriel is described quite casually as "scraping the snow from his goloshes," to the final reference of all, when the snow is represented as stretching out spatially, not just all over Ireland but "falling faintly through the universe," stretching back to the past and over the future, stilling the fainting heart, for snow is impartial alike to desire and regret. Between the first and the final references there is a whole series of seemingly unpremeditated snow images —"the light fringe of snow lay like a cape on the shoulders of his overcoat," "Gretta'd walk home in the snow if she were let," "the snow would be lying on the branches of the trees and forming a bright cap on the top of the Wellington Monument," and so forth. Integrated very subtly with this series of snow images are many other allusive verbal stratagems which half suggest snow: Gabriel tells Gretta *coldly* that she can go to Galway herself if she likes; Aunt Julia sings the old song, "Arrayed for the Bridal"; "My babe lies cold" are the last words of Bartell D'Arcy's song which Gabriel half catches at the stairs; "It was in the winter," Gretta tells Gabriel, that Michael Furey fell ill and died. Between the two series of remarks there is quiet interaction, a kind of reciprocal illumination, or half-illumination of meaning, "a structure so adjusted" that at the final mention of snow the meaning of the story as a whole "epiphanizes," "seems to us radiant" with light.

Gabriel's story is the story of a man who has fallen ill, like Stephen Dedalus, of one of the chief maladies of his age, the substitution of aesthetics for religion. But Gabriel passes the crisis, gets past aestheticism, and is on the road to recovery when the story is over. Stephen Dedalus never recovers, never transcends the aesthetic Ersatz. "The Dead," it may be worth noting, was the last of the *Dubliners* to be written, a kind of afterthought or postscript to the original stories. Joyce abandoned his work on *Stephen Hero* in order to write it. It seems not unimportant to notice that Gabriel Conroy stands for Joyce as much, if not much more, than Stephen Dedalus ever does.

5

A comedy of Letters

Loud, heap miseries upon us yet entwine
our arts with laughters low!
Finnegans Wake [1]

EUGÈNE JOLAS relates that at a dinner which he and Madame Jolas gave on the occasion of Joyce's fiftieth birthday, "Someone . . . gave voice to his dislike for the adage: *in vino veritas,* which he held to be untrue and bromidic. Joyce agreed warmly and added: 'It should really be: *in riso veritas;* for nothing so reveals us as our laughter.'" Jolas adds, "He was always astonished that so few people had commented on the comic spirit in his writings." [2]

As early as 1922 Ezra Pound almost alone had the penetration to see the import of the comic drift which Joyce's writing had begun to take. Speaking in the *Mercure de France* of the relationship between Flaubert and Joyce, Pound remarks, "Entre 1880 et l'année où fut commencé *Ulysses* personne n'a eu le courage de faire le sottisier gigantesque . . ." Nor did Pound fail to notice that "le sottisier gigantesque" of Joyce employed as it were a revolving double axis of comic contrast, not only of the real with the ideal but of the present with the thirteenth-century (Aquinan) past: "Joyce emploie un échafaudage pris à Homère, et les restes d'une culture moyenâgeuse allégorique." [3]

The shift into an explicitly comic tone, though it begins with *Ulysses,* is consistent with what one might have predicted on the basis of the aesthetic theory of "static" and "kinetic" art which Joyce elaborates toward the end of the *Portrait.* [4] One might almost say that the two revolutionary novels of Joyce (*Ulysses* and the *Wake*) are no more than an effort to put into practice the canons of art, static and contemplative, for which Stephen Dedalus is allowed to express a preference in the *Portrait.*

Joyce as a young man perceived that the comic situation becomes

---

1. *Finnegans Wake,* p. 259.
2. Eugène Jolas, "My Friend James Joyce," in Givens, *Two Decades,* p. 8. Cf. *Finnegans Wake,* "In voina viritas," p. 518.
3. Ezra Pound, "James Joyce et Pécuchet," *Mercure de France, 156* (June 1922), pp. 312, 314.
4. *Portrait,* pp. 240 ff.

such in the light of an intellectualized measurement of the actual by the ideal, of the individual by the social norm. Such a view is no more than a corollary of the Thomist theory of contemplatio adumbrated in the *Portrait,* according to which the emotions present in any poetic situation are there to be intellectually grasped and studied rather than personally experienced or felt. The aesthetic emotion (quae visa placent) is conceived of as conferring an imperturbability upon one's vision of the most strongly (even violently) felt emotions represented in the poem. The factor of personal involvement is kept at a minimum, if indeed it is allowed to overlap at all with the deeply felt emotions which may have led up to and occasioned the poem and which the poem is not so much meant to duplicate as to embody for study, to *re-present* in symbolic dimensions for the scrutiny of the contemplative mind.

In the light of such a theory it is not difficult to see why Joyce should have preferred the *stasis* of comedy to the *kinesis* of tragedy. The intellectual detachment seemed to Joyce so much more evidently operative in the symbolic attitude which comedy assumes toward life or reality. In comedy intellectual vision is clearly in control of the situation, though the comic control becomes increasingly precarious the more deeply the comic artist concerns himself with the fundamentally serious issues of life. The very precariousness of the control is a constant challenge to the serious comic artist, and Joyce welcomed the challenge.

Joyce would have been prepared to concede to Bergson that comedy is an appeal to the intelligence, and to the social intelligence at that, but he would not have agreed with Bergson that you must therefore anaesthetize your heart in order to laugh. Joyce's own comedy, with its Molly Blooms and Gerty MacDowells, its Biddy Dorans and Ginger Janes, though it stands at a far remove from Meredith's ideal comedy of high salon sophistication, unfolds in the Aristotelian tradition which Meredith articulated in the face of a romantically agonized century, a tradition which sees no incompatibility between wit of intelligence and "enchantment of the heart." A serious sympathy with the plight of man need not take a solemn turn or utterance. Nor if it takes a comic utterance must one conclude, as David Daiches does of Joyce, that for the comic artist "There is neither decency nor indecency, neither piety nor blasphemy, but simply one vast neutrality." [5] W. H. Auden conceives of the comic far more wisely when he writes, "A sense of wit and humor develops in a society to the degree that its members are simultaneously conscious of being each a unique individual and of being all in common subjection to unalterable laws." [6] The magnitude of Joyce's comic achievement appears the more remarkable when one realizes how he

5. David Daiches, *The Novel and the Modern World* (Chicago, Univ. of Chicago Press, 1939), p. 138.
6. W. H. Auden, "Notes on the Comic," *Thought, 27* (Spring 1952), 57.

had to strive for the assertion of personal values and unalterable laws
in the midst of a literary generation which often seemed eager to surrender to the collectivity and to the void. The Frenchman Jacques Mercanton has spoken far more to the point than many an English critic
of Joyce: "Si *Ulysses* comme on l'a dit mettait fin à notre humanisme,
Finnegans Wake semble exclure toute possibilité d'humanisme." [7] In
the shattering upheavals of personal or social disaster, the comic has
ever been the most efficacious of religious safety valves.

In the perspectives of Kierkegaardian thought, a genuinely religious
sympathy with the plight of man need not take a solemn turn or utterance. Indeed it is positively interdicted from doing so. In a suggestive
note to his treatment of the "existential pathos" in *Concluding Unscientific Postscript,* Kierkegaard goes so far as to say, "In general
there is nothing so faithfully guarded by the comical as the religious . . ." [8] Having drawn attention to the fact that there are three
spheres of existence, the aesthetic, the ethical, and the religious, Kierkegaard finds in irony the means of effecting a transition from the aesthetic to the ethical and in humor the means of transcending the merely
ethical and of entering into the religious sphere: "Irony is a specific
culture of the spirit, and therefore follows next after immediacy; then
comes the ethicist, then the humorist, and finally the religious individual." [9] The ethicist must use irony as his incognito, according to Kierkegaard, because irony maintains an inner relationship between the finiteness and relativities of particular human performance and the infinite
exigencies of absolute ethical laws. In maintaining such a relationship
the ethical ironist cannot help grasping the contradiction, cannot help
placing the comical between himself and the world.

With admirable realism, Kierkegaard adds that this irony is certain
to be misunderstood by all those naively solemn individuals who are
ceaselessly distracted by the relativities of immediate experience, the
interest and judgments which the passing scene offers from morning to
night: "The judgment of men upon the ironist will always be: for him
there is nothing important. And why not? Because for him the ethical
is absolutely important, differing in this from men in general, for whom
so many things are important, aye nearly everything, but nothing absolutely important." [1] The circular movement of history in the *Wake,* it
may be noted, is represented always as a movement back to the Viconian
thunderclap, back to the moment of God's transcendent revelation. For
those who see through the ironic incognito, the *Wake* is surely one of

7. Jacques Mercanton, *Poètes de l'univers* (Paris, Editions Albert Skira, 1947),
p. 61.
8. Søren Kierkegaard, *Concluding Unscientific Postscript,* tr. David F. Swenson, ed.
Walter Lowrie (Princeton, Princeton Univ. Press, 1944), p. 436, n. 1.
9. Ibid., pp. 448, 450.
1. Ibid., p. 451.

the most remarkable books ever written about the aridity of the waste-
land which is not watered by the rain of divine grace. Could Joyce or
any other serious writer afford to be so ironically detached at the sight
of the shambles in the city of man unless at least implicitly he had been
conditioned to believe that another city goes on a-building out of the
wreckage, the city to which Joyce often refers half poignantly in the
"grandfunferall," "Heliotropolis," the city of light? "Kilt by kelt shell
kithagain with kinagain. We elect for thee, Tirtangel. Svadesia salve!
We Durbalanars, theeadjure. A way, the Margan, from our astamite,
through dimdom done till light kindling light has led we hopas but hunt
me the journeyon, iteritinerant, the kal his course, amid the semitary of
Somnionia. Even unto Heliotropolis, the castellated, the enchanting." [2]

The Odyssean parallels in *Ulysses* are ironic in the ethical sense, as
though Joyce were telling his readers on every page that this is no
golden Homeric age. This is a very different age! Joyce gives us a father
like Odysseus, a son like Telemachus, and a mother like Penelope. Alike,
yet how unlike! All the basic relationships are there. But Bloom and
Stephen cannot remain together, cannot speak to one another really no
matter how many words they use, and Molly and Bloom can never unite.
With the many critics like Stuart Gilbert who maintain that *Ulysses*
"ends on a triple paean of affirmation," [3] it seems important to insist
upon the "ironic incognito" which Joyce assumes throughout the novel,
and to ask for what reason Joyce is supposed to have dropped this incognito in the last few pages and by what stretch of the imagination he
is supposed at the end in some special way to be identifying his own
point of view with that of unhappy, dissatisfied, sex-sated Molly. Who
would be prepared to say that Chaucer identifies his point of view with
that of Dame Alice, the Wife of Bath? [4]

In spite of the irony of his portrayal, Joyce has given to each of his
principal characters, even to poor Molly, an interior life of a sort, a kind
of hidden awareness such as Kierkegaard has called a "martyrdom in
itself." [5] There's even "a touch of the artist," Joyce tells us, "about old
Bloom," [6] almost as if Joyce, not Kierkegaard, had been the one to say:
"But is it not then possible that every other human being you meet is
such a knight of hidden inwardness? Yes, why not? To whom could
this assumption do any harm?" [7]

2. *Finnegans Wake,* p. 594: "Heliotropolis,"—now Tim Healy's Dublin; now Heliop-
olis, the Egyptian sun-city of the phoenix.

3. Stuart Gilbert, *James Joyce's Ulysses* (New York, Knopf, 1952), p. 389.

4. The standard Marxist criticism of the conclusion of *Ulysses* likewise fails to see
through the "ironic incognito": "The ending of *Ulysses* signifies the triumph of the
vital bourgeoisie over the decadence represented by Stephen and Bloom. . . . At the
zenith of his victory [over language], Joyce surrenders his vantage points to the vulgar
female Marian." D. S. Mirsky, "Joyce and Irish Literature," *New Masses* (April 3,
1934), pp. 33-4.

5. Kierkegaard, *Postscript,* p. 453.

6. *Ulysses,* p. 232.

7. Kierkegaard, *Postscript,* p. 453.

Irony, as Kierkegaard reminds us, operates on the side of self-assurance.[8] Or as Arthur Koestler puts it, "Irony consists in defeating an opponent on his own ground, that is, by accepting his premises, his values, his prejudices, his methods of reasoning, for the purpose of unmasking their implicit absurdity." [9] Humor, so far as it is distinguished from irony, lacks this self-assurance or at least does not make much of it. "The great secret of morals is love," Shelley (not to mention St. Paul) notes,[1] and the comic apprehension is not so much engaged in defeating an opponent or in unmasking him as in reconciling itself to the pain of contradiction between the actual and the God-exacted. "The pleasantry of humor consists in revocation," says Kierkegaard, "(a start being made with profundity, which is revoked). . . . But the profound thought is revoked in jest. . . . Just as it comes to the point of giving an explanation, it becomes impatient and revokes it all, saying, 'However, that would be too long drawn out, and too profound.' " [2] English comedy has been characterized by this genial kind of humility. It was in no little part from Cervantes that the eighteenth-century English comic writers learned to write this specifically Christian kind of satire which transforms criticism with charity and which saves the satirist from ever assuming too self-righteous a role. In *Ulysses* Stephen overhears one of his youthful companions repeating laconically a prophecy of Dr. Sigerson, that George Moore is the man to write the national epic, "A knight of the rueful countenance here in Dublin." [3] Joyce, it is clear, had other ideas as to who was best qualified to undertake a work of that sort.

Joyce's two great novels, it seems, could be profitably viewed as masterpieces of this borderline humor, halfway between ethical severity and religious awareness. The dialectic of the profound thought revoked in jest dominates the Protean transformations of the Circe chapter of *Ulysses*. This chapter, which is so vivid and harrowing a vision of hell, is at the same time one of the most comical chapters in Joyce, and in this respect it is in the medieval tradition of hell-representations. Such a decorum can be offensive only to those who flatly deny a hell's existence (or possibility) or who feel sure that if there is a hell they need never go there. The emaciated ghost of Stephen's mother comes back with breath of wetted ashes to plead with Stephen for his soul: "You sang that song to me. *Love's bitter mystery.*" [4] Stephen, to break the spell, crashes his ashplant against the lamp of the brothel. The mother's distraught pleadings are immediately followed by Bloom's shrewd and humorous altercation with the prostitutes about who shall pay, and how

8. Ibid., p. 491.
9. Arthur Koestler, *Insight and Outlook* (New York, Macmillan, 1949), p. 98.
1. "A Defence of Poetry," in Shawcross, ed., *Shelley's Criticism*, p. 131.
2. Kierkegaard, *Postscript*, pp. 491–2.
3. *Ulysses*, p. 190.
4. Ibid., p. 565; cf. p. 11.

much, for the shattered lamp chimney. To conclude from such grotesque juxtapositions, as one sensitive Irish critic, Horace Reynolds, has done, that *Ulysses* is "an original, overpowering, and gigantic structure without a heart" [5] is to perceive the tragic pain of the representation but at the expense of the comic revocation which chooses not to dwell on the pain because it realizes that there is a way out, even though reader and possibly author also may not be inclined to take it.

If Kierkegaard's rationale of the comic is correct, and if Joyce's representation of the comic is satisfactory, then I. A. Richards' assertion that any theological attitude is incompatible with the ironic contemplation of life ("The least touch of . . . theology . . . is fatal") [6] must require serious qualifications. Here if ever Richards can be indicted for oversimplification and for falling himself into a twentieth-century stock response which would render unintelligible a very large area of English literature from Chaucer to Joyce. Jonathan Swift, to judge from his mock-serious "Letter of Advice to a Young Poet," would have had little patience, one imagines, with Richards' dictum. "It has been found, by experience of our professors," Swift writes (prophetically), "that the smallest quantity of religion, like a single drop of malt liquor in claret, will muddy and discompose the brightest poetical genius." [7] Joyce, one imagines, would want to ask Richards: Without at least a "touch of theology" how does one find any deep irony in the human situation? In the Joycean-Viconian *recorso,* the moment of the loss of relevance in theological questions is consistently represented as immediately preceding the thunderclap of wrath.

Joyce's two broadsides, "The Holy Office" and "Gas from a Burner," point early to a comic intention as being the point of control in his literary work:

> Myself unto myself will give
> This name, Katharsis-Purgative. . . .
> Bringing to tavern and to brothel
> The mind of witty Aristotle.[8]

"Steeled in the school of old Aquinas," Joyce constructs in *Ulysses* a modern comedy of ideas, or as he says in the *Wake,* "Acomedy of letters." [9] Aristotle and Aquinas: these two names suggest that Joyce's

---

5. Horace Reynolds, "A Note on *Ulysses,*" *Irish Review* (April 1934), p. 29.

6. I. A. Richards, *Principles of Literary Criticism* (New York, Harcourt, Brace, 1938), p. 246. Explicitly Richards is here speaking of tragedy.

7. Jonathan Swift, "A Letter of Advice to a Young Poet," *Works,* ed. Sir Walter Scott, 2d ed., *11* (Edinburgh, Archibald Constable, 1824), 186. (Letter is dated December 1, 1720.)

8. "The Holy Office," *Portable James Joyce* (New York, Viking, 1949), p. 657.

9. *Finnegans Wake,* p. 425.

conception of comedy is the classical one which regards comedy as a social criticism, an "imitation of nature," but the kind of imitation that perfects, aims to complete nature's intentions which are so often frustrated in the empirical, actual world. Nor was Joyce's interest in the Aristotelian philosophy merely a passing, schoolboy fancy. In a conversation with Georges Borach at Zurich some thirteen or fourteen years after the writing of "The Holy Office," Joyce explained: "In den letzten zweihundert Jahren haben wir keinen grossen Denker gehabt. Mein Ausspruch ist gewagt, denn Kant ist inbegriffen. Alle grossen Denker der letzten Jahrhunderte von Kant bis Benedetto Croce haben nur den Garten umgearbeitet. Der grösste Denker aller Zeiten ist meines Erachtens Aristoteles. Alles ist bei ihm wunderbar klar und einfach definiert. Später hat man Bände geschrieben, um das Gleiche zu definieren." [1]

A defense of *Ulysses* as Aristotelian comedy, which measures the twentieth-century actuality with the Aquinan yardstick of the ideal, is at the greatest possible variance with the views of critics like Richard Aldington and Shane Leslie, for whom *Ulysses* is "an invitation to chaos," "literary bolshevism." [2] Joyce's intention, he told the publisher of *Dubliners,* "was to write a chapter of the moral history of my country and I chose Dublin for the scene because that city seemed to me the centre of paralysis." [3] The eighteen episodes of *Ulysses* would seem to be best situated as so many more chapters in that "moral history." If the comic artist like Joyce cannot change the world for us, he can very much help us to accept the world as it is, to come to terms with it with a certain amount of personal dignity, and to define our own position in it more clearly.

Is it necessary to add that the comic attitude is not the only possible one which a person may take toward life? The point, however, is that it is a possible attitude to take, which may be both profound and sensitive. Shelley's reason in *A Defence of Poetry* for ranking Shakespeare above the great Greek tragedians was precisely this, that Shakespeare combined with his tragic genius a complementary comic sense. [4] May one not go further and add that under certain circumstances the comic attitude is the best possible frame of reference? When things are very badly out of joint with individuals or with society, the comic catharsis may be capable of leading to a serenity of spirit which the catharsis of pity and fear is impotent to effect. Laughter at least will break the tension and clear the air. It is a mistake to look to comedy, as it is to look to any other kind of literature, as the sole interpreter of reality. There are

1. Georges Borach, "Gespräche mit James Joyce," *Omnibus: Almanach auf das Jahr 1932* (Berlin, Verlag der Galerie Flechtheim, 1932), p. 141.
2. Cf. Levin, *James Joyce,* p. 208.
3. Cf. Slocum and Cahoon, *Joyce Bibliography,* p. 13, A, 8.
4. "A Defence of Poetry," in Shawcross, ed., *Shelley's Criticism,* p. 134.

large areas of belief and meaning which comedy does not encompass. But why find fault with comedy because it is not all of life?

In discussing any artist's work as comic it is also well to remember that the comic is almost never found in complete isolation from the tragic. As in life, so in literature, tragedy and comedy are the two great symbolic attitudes which one may take toward reality. Life itself is so manifold and complicated, and reality is so recalcitrant to classification, that rarely will any artistic "imitation" be all-tragic or all-comic. The comic stress of *Ulysses* appears clear once one acknowledges that Joyce's literary control is chiefly social, rationalist, and detached.

From the above point of view, a rapid survey of *Ulysses* in the light of its comic strategy may be useful for narrowing down and testing the more or less general and theoretical remarks so far offered on Joycean comedy. There is no sustained theoretical formulation of the idea of comedy either in Aquinas or in Joyce. The Aquinan texts *de comoedia* or *de risu* would be far too slight a peg on which to hang Joyce's comedy. Joyce's boast in "The Holy Office" that, proud in his Aquinan strength, "I flash my antlers on the air," and his avowal that "not a soul is sober" in his "thomistically drunk" *Wake*-world suggest that the Aquinan basis for Joycean comedy is one of mutual attitudes or common values rather than of textual correspondences. Cecil Maitland, writing in the *New Witness* at a time when this magazine was edited by Chesterton, remarked: "Aquinas would probably be more at home with Freud than, for instance, [with] Mr. G. K. Chesterton. No one who is acquainted with Catholic education in Catholic countries could fail to recognize the source of Mr. Joyce's 'Weltanschauung.' He sees the world as theologians showed it to him. His humour is the cloacal humour of the refectory." [5]

The Aquinan student of Joyce would be rather myopic himself if he did not see that Joyce's vision of the world is in some respects short-sighted and distorted. There is at times an almost cloacal obsession and antisocial stridency in his images which suggest a kind of pathological protest against the human condition itself. Such a posture is not at all Aquinan or even Christian. One could hardly construct a fair picture either of the Thomist synthesis or of the Irish Christian fact if he had nothing else to work with but the Joycean catharsis.

As evidence of an Aquinan *Weltanschauung* and of a social rather than individualist orientation in *Ulysses,* one might begin by pointing out in what way the absorbing preoccupations of the novel are the family, politics, and sex. Unless the comic historian is prepared to disregard all the intangible bonds of society and to accept at face value

5. Cecil Maitland, "Mr. Joyce and the Catholic Tradition," *The New Witness, 20* (Aug. 4, 1922), 71.

Leopold Bloom's definition of a nation ("A nation is the same people living in the same place"),[6] he cannot do better, if he wishes to determine the quality of a nation, than to look at the quality of its family life. Nearly twenty years ago Frank Budgen with critical good sense drew attention to this aspect of *Ulysses:* "Inasmuch as the centre of the stage is held, it is held not by an individual but by a family, a unit of social organization."[7] Admitting with Aristotle and Aquinas that the family is the basic unit of society and that individuals enter society through the family, the novel, without preaching, offers its own plain-spoken commentary on Dublin society as it appeared to the author at the turn of the century, and in doing so obliquely commits itself to a rather thoroughgoing criticism of modern urban society where the family is "lost in the shuffle." Is it not against such a background of the crucial breakdown of the familial society that Joyce arranges for his readers to follow the counterpointed central theme : Stephen's search for a father and Bloom's search for a son? Stephen and Bloom are both cut off from their families : both are outcasts, exiles, outsiders in the land of their birth.

Stephen had left his father's house, as he tells Bloom, in order "to seek misfortune."[8] But the *Liliata rutilantium* of his mother's passing insistently calls him to return home. "I will arise and go to my." Stephen speaks to himself as he runs his fingers over the piano keys in Bella Cohen's brothel, but he cannot bring himself to utter the word "father."[9] The closest perhaps that the novel ever comes to the tragic pathos is Stephen's collision with his sister Dilly at the bookstall: "She is drowning. Agenbite. Save her. Agenbite. All against us. . . . Lank coils of seaweed hair around me, my heart, my soul."[1]

Stephen's absorption in the Hamlet story is like his Sabellianism a manifestation of his spiritual lack of paternity. Sonship like citizenship is a spiritual relationship, "an apostolic succession."[2] Stephen knows this but he is powerless to find it for himself. Like Hamlet he is "the dispossessed son." Stephen tries to find paternity then in himself. So, he reasons, did Hamlet, whose father's voice, Stephen believes, was the "voice heard only in the heart of him who is the substance of his shadow, the son consubstantial with the father."[3] Stephen is self-enclosed. "The note of banishment, banishment from the heart, banishment from home" sounds for him in the tale of the sweet prince of Denmark, as it does for himself in Dublin.[4] His own terrible loneliness ("I spoke to no-one :

6. Ulysses, p. 325.
7. Frank Budgen, *James Joyce and the Making of Ulysses* (New York, Harrison Smith, 1934), p. 131.
8. *Ulysses*, p. 604.
9. Ibid., pp. 12, 24, 188, 506, 688, et passim.
1. Ibid., p. 240.
2. Ibid., p. 204.
3. Ibid., p. 194.
4. Ibid., p. 209.

none to me") [5] drives him to a repudiation of the Catholic Trinitarian theology which he has been taught.

What is the mystery of the Trinitarian life but this: that the Son is completely *ad Patrem,* and the Father completely *ad Filium,* and the Holy Spirit, who proceeds from both, is the consubstantial Love of Son for Father and of Father for Son? Trinitarian theology is a theology of relationships. Aquinas calls the Three Divine Persons three Subsistent Relations. How could Stephen, whose own sense of relationship was so dim, be expected to follow? One works from analogy back to God. Stephen had lost the analogues. He could not see that relationship is an *ens reale.*

Unless you see this you will, in Trinitarian theology, end in Sabellianism.[6] The Father becomes the Son; the Son, the Father. So the relationship perishes, and without these relationships there can be no Holy Spirit, no Subsistent Love. But surely for Stephen there is a comic irony in this: Stephen's search for a father leads him, "battling against hopelessness," to the conclusion that "a father . . . is a necessary evil." [7] Then what happens to society? This much at least may be said for Buck Mulligan, that he is on the side of community: "O, Kinch, thou art in peril." [8] Stephen's own rationalism drives him to admit that so far Buck is right: "He laughed to free his mind from his mind's bondage." [9] Stephen tries too hard "to stress the subjective as mere form." For Kierkegaard, in *Either/Or,* that is comic: "Every isolated individual always becomes comic by stressing his own accidental individuality over against necessary development." [1]

Without ever having once and for always committed Stephen's act of repudiation, Bloom too finds himself without roots and without a home. His has been an aimless drift away from his own tradition. He is an apostate to the Jews, his own people, and at the same time the *Judaeus infidelis* to his Irish countrymen. Bloom, we should remind ourselves, is *the* Ulysses of the novel. The Homeric analogue has its immediate relevance in relation to him. How comically different, though, is the cuckold Bloom's return to adulterous Molly from Odysseus' homecoming to the ingeniously faithful Penelope: Does not the contrast show that Joyce himself appeals to the past as normative? Bloom wants a home but he has rooms in a house of assignation.

Comedy never takes a *parousia* seriously. "A revolution must come on the due instalments plan," [2] Bloom tells Stephen in a sober moment.

5. Ibid., p. 46.
6. Ibid., p. 205.
7. Ibid., p. 204.
8. Ibid., p. 215.
9. Ibid., p. 209.
1. Søren Kierkegaard, *Either/Or,* Vol. I, tr. David F. Swenson and Lillian Marvin Swenson (Princeton, Princeton Univ. Press, 1944), 115–16.
2. *Ulysses,* p. 627.

But what kind of revolution does this modern Ulysses herald? *"Ex quibus . . . Christus* or Bloom his name is, or, after all, any other, *secundum carnem."* [3] It is not toward that kind of indiscriminate sonship, or citizenship, that the cut-off individualist like Stephen gropes. The union of Christians among themselves through Christ their Head is a *Mystical* Body. Generation in this Body is not secundum carnem, but by the Holy Spirit. So much Stephen remembers. Remembering, how can he prize citizenship in a community where, as he sees it, the Reverend Carrion Crow, *"le sacré pigeon,"* has usurped the Holy Spirit's role? [4] "Let my country die for me." [5] Stephen cannot have been unaware of the tautology. What is the quality of citizenship in such a nation: has not the nation already died? "Ireland must be important because it belongs to me." [6] How can you belong to a nation if you cannot get out of yourself?

Sonship and citizenship are mystical states; that is, they exist *secundum spiritum*. Their bonds though intangible are real. Moses led the Israelites, the Chosen People, out of the desert and into the Promised Land. And when the time came for entry, God appointed to Moses that he must remain outside. The Biblical situation is tragic. Bloom's is not, though another writer than Joyce might have so presented it. We leave Bloom, do we not, just as we found him, among the fleshpots of Egypt, in "the house of bondage," [7] before even the trek to the desert begins? We are not meant to take Bloom any more seriously as Moses than we are as Elijah, the prophet who will come back when the world is to end.

The comic artist, who sees the depravity of the present as abnormal, does not look to a distant millennium. Bloomusalem,[8] it sees, is not the goal nor is Stephen's aestheticism the answer. Comedy is too firmly rooted in tradition to do anything but smile when it glimpses the spiritual sterility of the one and the bloodless aridity of the other. A man is not just a body; a man is not just a soul. A man is a soul in a body; a man is a body-soul! For different reasons, neither the Hellenic Stephen nor the Judaic Bloom could accept the Incarnation: "Unto the Jews, indeed, a stumbling-block, and unto the Gentiles, folly!"

Stephen and Bloom have each an odyssey to travel, but *Ulysses* is not the story of either's coming home. Bloom must first go into the desert, and Stephen "must rise and go into his Father's house"—no matter at what cost to his pride. *Ulysses* says that: says it at the same time that its author's eyes are wide open to the desolation of Ithaca. The city is infested with Bloom's and Stephen's enemies; its traditions have been

3. Ibid.
4. Ibid., pp. 580, 509.
5. Ibid., p. 576.
6. Ibid., p. 629.
7. Ibid., p. 121.
8. Ibid., p. 475.

shamelessly violated. Yet the city must prepare for their homecoming. The novel offers no panacea, no blueprints, no parousia, but it is not without hope. LET US HOPE is the headline which helps us see the growth that is going on at least in Stephen: "Dublin. I have much, much to learn." [9]

Like the familial relationships, political and sexual activities are viewed by the comic writer primarily as social, rather than as individual, personalist acts. The situation of *Antigone,* for instance, is quite different from the situation of Stephen Dedalus when he refuses to pray at his dying mother's bedside. Antigone's determination to perform the ceremonial rite of burial for her brother leads her to defy the political order which Creon has imposed on the state. Our sympathies are with Antigone to an extent that they cannot be with Stephen. Each in one sense faces a moral crisis, but only for Antigone does the issue involve tragedy: misfortune and death. Antigone defies a solidly established political order (with legal right at least on its side), and we sympathize with her in her religious act of defiance.

Antigone defies the law, acts in obedience to a higher law. Stephen cannot find any law—without or within—whose dictates he may follow with certitude of doing right. His refusal to pray at his mother's deathbed is not strictly an act of disobedience to the law; it is not by any means an act of obedience to a higher, inward law. For Stephen the law simply is not there. It should be there but it is wanting. We are not inclined to judge (nor are we meant to judge) Stephen for having done right or wrong. His refusal to act is not presented as a positive act. A negation is founded on something positive. Stephen's course of action is not. It is zero: "a micro- and a macrocosm ineluctably constructed upon the incertitude of the void." [1] Renewal, not repudiation, of the tradition is the conclusion toward which the novel works.

With its instinctive allegiance to the family as the unit of society, comedy tends to view as abnormalities all sexual activities or approaches to sex which are not somehow oriented to marriage. Comedy is matter-of-fact about sex, is mostly concerned with sex as a physical act. In this respect *Ulysses* is unqualifiedly comic. The romantic concept of love as a shattering, personal experience of the soul nowhere involves any of its characters. Gerty MacDowell's sentimental eroticism is a kind of Ersatz for romantic idealism, but like all caricatures, Gerty's romanticism is laughable. For all her pitiableness, the new Nausicaa cannot be viewed except as an abnormal, romantic hoax. The extravagant horseplay of the Circe chapter (the funniest chapter on the whole in *Ulysses*) is quite in keeping with the novel's commitment to comedy on the subject of sex.

9. Ibid., p. 142.
1. Ibid., p. 682.

What we may fail to see, however, is that the comic commitment involves us at this point in a fundamentally serious criticism of our contemporary sexual mores. In the *Portrait* Stephen is represented as writing in his diary on the eve of his departure for the Continent: "O life! I go to encounter for the millionth time the reality of experience and to forge in the smithy of my soul the uncreated conscience of my race." [2] Is there not a great comic irony, then, in the fact that the whore who solicits Stephen in Bella Cohen's brothel is called *Zoe* (Life)? But if the dynamism of the novel leads to this negation, that life is not to be found in the brothel—for the bawd Zoe surely cannot stand for the life that Stephen is looking for—is there not by implication an affirmation, namely, that sexual activity which is generative and life-giving is to be found elsewhere? Again we find that the position of *Ulysses* is itself conservative and normative, that it covertly affirms the familial tradition which overtly it seems to attack. In spite of its often unnecessary and sometimes depressing sexual details, the Circe episode is no neutral Kinsey report.

The most convenient rationalist touchstone for *Ulysses* is religion. *Ulysses,* though it is not a religious novel, has much to say about religion. Unlike Dante's *Comedy, Ulysses* is interested in the religious experience from the outside alone. It neither affirms nor denies the validity of the personal religious experience; it neither attacks nor defends the concept of institutionalized religious life in a church. In the comic tradition, its interest in personal or organic religious experience is from the rationalist point of view: How does religious experience affect human behavior? What is its impact on society? What is the effect of institutionalized religion on the community as a whole? As Harry Levin has said very well, Joyce "lost his faith, but he kept his categories." [3]

Between Stephen and Hamlet as characters there is a close affinity even apart from Stephen's absorbing interest in the Hamlet theme. Both young men are haunted with uncertainties: To believe or not to believe in a supernatural order? What is the soul? What is reality? What is seeming? What does it mean to be a son? Hamlet, as a tragic protagonist, comes to grips with the mystery of life in a way in which Stephen cannot. Stephen's questions involve him in a maze of dialectics but do not lead him to the terrible point of deeply felt personal religious experience. Stephen would not be able to see, as Hamlet does so clearly, the ghost on Elsinore's ramparts. Stephen's vision of his mother in the Circe nightmare is something altogether different. She is no more than the projection of Stephen's own troubled spirit and even in his delirium Stephen knows that. Everything was changed for Hamlet after he saw

2. *Portrait,* p. 299.
3. Levin, *James Joyce,* p. 25.

his father's ghost. Stephen's encounter with his mother changes nothing.

Hamlet's flight from reality brings him into collision with nonrationalist forces; Stephen's flight from reality only creates an aesthetic nightmare and a religious void. Stephen is fond of talking about religious experience: "So I carried the boat of incense then at Clongowes. I am another now and yet the same." [4] He often speaks of fatherhood as "a mystical estate," [5] of sonship as an "apostolic succession." [6] He coins (or borrows from Luigi Galvani) a beautiful phrase like "enchantment of the heart" to translate Aquinas' claritas in the exposition of Thomist aesthetics which he attempts in the *Portrait*.[7] His theory of the epiphany both in the *Portrait* and in *Ulysses* makes use of mystical terminology, but Stephen himself is no mystic. His "conversion" in the *Portrait* effects a temporary shift in ideas but does not lead to a surrender of soul to grace. The endeavor of the dialectician to live in the religious climate leads Stephen to scrupulosity, not to a change of heart. His frame of reference at all times is that of the over-rationalist thinker: "But in here it is I must kill the priest and the king." [8]

If we affirm that this rationalist point of view dominates the novel and that the view of life as mystery is seldom developed, we must at the same time acknowledge that *Ulysses* is far from denying the importance of religion in men's lives, both as individuals and as members of society. It is reason itself in the novel which assigns to religion this importance. It is reason too that is most critical of the religious performance, and most ready to laugh at the dismal shortcomings in practice of men committed in principle to high religious ideals. It is of this aspect of *Ulysses* that Edwin Muir has observed: "To see religion with the eyes of comedy is not, of course, to laugh it out of existence, any more than to see sex comically is to destroy it. All that comedy can destroy is strictly the second-rate." [9]

If the Mass is the great central act of Catholic worship, what are we to think, the novel asks, of Catholics "born and bred" who perform the Black Mass with such gusto in Bella Cohen's brothel? Another writer, like Goethe, might concentrate on the blasphemy as diabolical. So, in his

4. *Ulysses*, p. 13.
5. Ibid., p. 204.
6. Ibid.
7. *Portrait*, p. 249.
8. *Ulysses*, p. 574.
9. Edwin Muir, "James Joyce," *Transition: Essays on Contemporary Literature* (London, Hogarth, 1926), p. 31. A. M. Klein has rather ingeniously worked out very close sequential and symbolical correspondences between Joyce's literary technique in *Ulysses* and the Sacrifice of the Mass ("The Black Panther," *Accent, 10,* Spring 1950, 139–55). Whereas Klein maintains that Joyce makes a mockery of the Mass, it seems to me the "mockery," if it exists at all in the parody, is in the Black Mass. Why *must* one "be amused by Thomas Merton's assertion that . . . Joyce's *Ulysses* . . . was one of the influences which brought him into . . . the Church" (p. 151)?

own peculiar religious way, would Baudelaire. The comic perspective of Joyce leads him to a rationalist's critique. Yet from this critique we cannot doubt that reason itself (the "reasoning novel") affirms the liturgical beauty of the true Mass beside the ugliness of the Black Mass to which it is counterpointed.

The same kind of counterpoint is employed in the Nausicaa episode. There is nothing satirical about the opening paragraph of this chapter. Here is the sort of praise of Our Lady that might be found in St. Bernard: "There streamed forth at times upon the stillness the voice of prayer to her who is in her pure radiance a beacon ever to the storm-tossed heart of man, Mary, star of the sea." [1] How cheap and vulgar by contrast seems the actual Catholic woman before us when we have so vivid a portrayal of the ideal of Catholic womanhood. The self-imposed rationalist limits of the comic artist may not allow him to affirm (or deny) the truth of the Catholic's faith in Mary, the Mother of God. His laughter at the behavior of Catholics like Gerty, who do seriously affirm such to be their faith, is, however, an excellent comic purgative. Granting even the religious myopia of the episode, the reasonable Catholic is not so much likely to feel offended as to feel the need to make a serious examination of his own conscience. And the reasonable non-Catholic is asked to consider whether the Marian ideal of purity or Gerty's erotic sentimentality is the better norm by which to evaluate a woman's role in society. The situation is by no means neutral: it calls either for laughter or for tears.

Any portrayal of life in art, be it tragic or comic, exacts some measure of artistic detachment, imposes a need for self-effacement, and presupposes a willingness to be attentive to the intelligible workings of the artwork itself. The control of the artist is "political" rather than "despotic"; he "governs" according to the law intrinsic in the work which he is bringing into being. Roughly that is what Aquinas means by the *integritas* of a work, and roughly that is what we mean when we talk about the "integrity" of an artist. The control of the tragic artist tends, nevertheless, to align him on the side of the protagonist whose downfall or purification through pain he sets out to dramatize or describe. The tragic irony inherent in the classical (Aristotelian) theory of *peripeteia* and *anagnorisis,* where men and women working in ignorance are the architects of their own catastrophe, leads to an engagement of feeling (pity and fear) both in the artist and in the spectator (reader) of the finished work. The comic strategy is different. The role of rationalist critic of human behavior allows the highest possible measure of detachment to the comic artist. He is an idealist at heart, so much so that it is

1. *Ulysses,* p. 340.

ordinarily difficult for us to imagine his ever identifying himself very far in sympathy with any of the imperfect forms of human conduct which he sets out to criticize by the objective yardstick of his ideals. The comic attitude imposes a kind of withdrawal from the maelstrom of life, but its laughter saves it from misanthropy. It may not conduce to pity of weak human nature, but it can and frequently does lead us to love the erring mortal. As William Lynch has pointed out in a perceptive exploration into the problem of comedy, "The one offense . . . which comedy cannot endure is that a man should forget he is man, or should substitute a phony faith for faith in the power of the vulgar and limited finite." [2]

To come back to *Ulysses,* we see that though Joyce succeeds in presenting a searching and exhaustive critique of contemporary society (as reflected in Dublin life on the day of June 16, 1904) the tone of the novel is nowhere that of *saeva indignatio.* Religious mores are satirized and burlesqued, sentimental patriotism is parodied, modern science is mocked, contemporary commercialism and journalism are presented as fraudulent—but at the same time there is an absence of anger. Joyce's own tone is nowhere pleading. He does not set out to deplore the evil; he is content with making us see these deviations from the norm as absurdities. If he throws the light of reason on the dark places in human behavior, he chooses to filter the light through a comic screen so that it does not hurt.[3] For the mature reader, this effort at detachment appears too in the nice neutrality which the novel shows in focus: its light is impartial and evenly dispersed.

It is true that *Ulysses* is a novel without a hero; it is equally true that there is no villain in the piece. Joyce, it may be, refers to Bloom as "our hero," [4] but the characterization is unmistakably comical and ironic. Even the irony is pitched in low key. In his hallucination in the brothel, Bloom seems to perceive the truth which he hides from facing all day: "I stand, so to speak, with an unposted letter bearing the extra regulation fee before the too late box of the general postoffice of human life." [5] Stephen and Bloom and Molly undergo no purification from the encounter with the evil with which they collide as the day wears away. No one is brought to a vision of peace after pain. There is no integration of character. There are moments when resolution of discords seems immi-

2. William F. Lynch, S.J. "Theology and the Imagination, III: The Problem of Comedy," *Thought, 30* (Spring 1955), 24.
3. Oliver St. John Gogarty appears to quarrel with Joyce precisely because he has "filtered" his light through a comic screen: "Joyce has substituted the lampshade for the light" ("James Augustine Joyce," *Dallas Times-Herald Book News,* April 3, 1949, p. 3).
4. *Ulysses,* p. 642.
5. Ibid., p. 516.

nent: when Bloom calls Stephen by his first name,[6] when Stephen and Bloom gaze without speaking into the mirror.[7] But these moments pass. There is no abiding communication. Stephen goes away alone into the darkness; Bloom takes his dumb misery with him into the same old adulterous bed; Molly confusedly remembers the events of the day, which fuse formlessly with similar events of other similar days, but the void is not filled by her memories. The curtain slowly descends, and we see that there has been no growth for any of these Dubliners on this day.

There have been stirrings of change, but the changes, if they come, must come tomorrow—or another day. The book does not record them. Stephen will not go back to the Martello Tower with Haines and Buck Mulligan; Molly will (perhaps) cook breakfast for Bloom tomorrow morning; the furniture in the bedroom at 7 Eccles Street has been shifted about,[8] but the search of the novel has brought no one home. Stephen has not found a father; Bloom has not found a son; Molly has not found happiness. None of these Dubliners has found happiness or wisdom. Stephen and Bloom are not the only "keyless couple" in the book.[9]

If we imagine Joyce smiling in the wings as the curtain falls, it is not to be thought that he is smiling derisively. Neither is it to be thought that Joyce himself is "paring his fingernails." [1] We miss much of the meaning of *Ulysses* when we fail to see through the "comic incognito," when we fail to see that Joyce is himself the severest critic whom Stephen is ever likely to have. *Ulysses* is a story of failure. The most that we can say for all these unhappy men and women in the face of all their frustration and failure is that they have lived the day, have seen it through, that they face the morning of a new day: "Tomorrow is another day." It is in this sense that the artist in Bloom quotes an "adage," as he says, when the day has worn to a close: "Dreaming of fresh fields and pastures new." [2]

Ulysses is not a story of integration. We must also add that it is not a story of disintegration. For all their unhappiness, loneliness, clumsiness, and aimlessness, Stephen and Bloom and Molly (and all these other Dubliners) have held together. They face the morning of June 17 without new understanding, but face it they do. *They go on.*

But, asks Joyce, smiling in the wings, is that enough? Is it enough

6. Ibid., p. 592.
7. Ibid., p. 553.
8. Ibid., p. 690.
9. Ibid., p. 652.
1. *Portrait,* p. 252.
2. *Ulysses,* p. 645. Stephen, walking alone on the Dublin strand, had recalled in the morning another "old adage" from "Lycidas": "Sunk though he be beneath the watery floor" (p. 50). Neither for Bloom nor for Stephen is there a Lycidas rising like the sea-star.

merely "to have sustained no positive loss"? [3] "Where there is a reconciliation, . . . there must have been first a sundering," Stephen remarks at one point in the Library chapter.[4] *Ulysses* is in one sense the story of all men's sundering today. "It is mayhap to relieve the pentup feelings that in common oppress them . . . that birds of a feather laugh together," Joyce remarks in the Sheridan parody in "Oxen of the Sun." [5] To be able to laugh with others at the recognized absurdity of a common tangential position may be a first step in the direction of a reconciliation. So very much more than laughter is necessary, but laughter, it may be, will give us hope.

Joyce does not undertake to point up the serious consequences of any *hamartia*. His are the strokes that lead more easily to laughter than to tears, as when Bloom apologizes for not having a lump of sugar to feed a passing horse: "You could scarcely be prepared for every emergency that might crop up." [6] Molly's soliloquy reveals an utter absence of the sense of sin. Stephen lives committed to his *Non serviam*, but the psychological rather than moral corollaries of his repudiation are the points which the novel on the surface explores. The comic artist, interested though he may be in our moral education, for all of his ethical severity cannot on principle stand before us in the role of professional moralist. His strategy is as objectively as possible to represent the human situation, as it exists, with all its own absurdities, contradictions, abnormalities, and imperfections. The chief "imperfection" of Bloom's "perfect day," as Bloom reviews it, is "a provisional failure to obtain renewal of an advertisement." [7] So it is that Joyce behind the "ironic incognito" brings to tavern and to brothel the mind of witty Aristotle. But unless one sees through the incognito, one can almost totally miss the meaning of the book. The German scholar, E. R. Curtius, though he offers some penetrating insights into *Ulysses,* misses the central clue: "Ein metaphysischer Nihilismus ist die Substanz von Joyces Werk." [8]

Before we characterize Joyce as a metaphysical nihilist, it is for us to ask, and to answer as best we can, of the life symbolized in *Ulysses:* Is this human perfection? Is this rational living? Is this human dignity? Is this the end of the endeavors put forth by the creatures, a little lower than the angels, who are made in the image and the likeness of God?

3. Ibid., p. 660.
4. Ibid., p. 191. Cf. p. 192.
5. Ibid., p. 402.
6. Ibid., p. 646.
7. Ibid., p. 714.
8. E. R. Curtius, *James Joyce und sein* Ulysses (Zurich, Verlag der *Neuen Schweizer Rundschau,* 1929), pp. 60-1. R. P. Blackmur, writing twenty years after Curtius, appears to hold substantially the same view: "Dante tried to put things in order only within reason and tradition, whereas Joyce went ahead anyway, presenting a kind of nihilism of unreasonable order" ("The Jew in Search of a Son," *Virginia Quarterly Review, 24,* Winter 1948, 101).

Molly would never think to ask questions like these; Bloom is incapable of asking them; Stephen is too much confused. But we can ask them. Joyce has been asking them obliquely as the novel went along. Joyce is about as far from nihilism as you can go and still write novels and not "tracts for the times." Nor is he personally committed to the secularist position which claims you can have mores without spiritual roots. *Ulysses* as a symbolic construct of the spirit is at pains to show what happens to mores when these roots in the spirit have withered away.

6

Sabellian Subtleties: The Trinitarian Theme

> *Sabellius, the African, subtlest heresiarch of*
> *all the beasts of the field, held that the Father*
> *was Himself His Own Son. The bulldog of*
> *Aquin, with whom no word shall be impossible,*
> *refutes him. Well: if the father who has not*
> *a son be not a father can the son who has not*
> *a father be a son? When Rutlandbaconsouth-*
> *hamptonshakespeare or another poet of the*
> *same name in the comedy of errors wrote* Hamlet
> *he was not the father of his own son merely*
> *but, being no more a son, he was and felt*
> *himself the father of all his race, the*
> *father of his own grandfather, the father of*
> *his unborn grandson.*
>
> *Ulysses* [1]

THERE are two main themes which Joyce explicitly associates with Aquinas : the aesthetic theme, which is mainly developed in the *Portrait,* and the Trinitarian theme, which keeps recurring insistently in *Ulysses* and in *Finnegans Wake.* Up to the present, critical attention to the "Thomism" of Joyce has concentrated almost exclusively on the aesthetic theme. Perhaps the time has come to ask if Joyce's Thomism, so far as we can isolate it, may not be considered with greater literary relevance in the perspectives of the Trinitarian theme which Joyce in so many words associates with "the bulldog of Aquin."

The most interesting of Aquinas' remarks on beauty which Joyce utilized are found oftener than not in a Trinitarian context and require a rather firm grasp of the Trinitarian import of Aquinas' argument to be at all intelligible. Stephen Dedalus uses one such text as the main springboard for his aesthetic discourse in the *Portrait: "Ad pulchritudinem tria requiruntur integritas, consonantia, claritas."* [2] This is a paraphrase of the *respondeo dicendum quod,* or body (*corpus*), of Aquinas' argument for the suitability of "appropriating," or applying to one Per-

1. P. 205. Unless otherwise indicated, page references to Joyce's works in this chapter are to *Ulysses.*
2. *Portrait,* p. 248.

son in particular in the uncreate Trinity, an attribute or name which is in fact common to all three Divine Persons, since each Person is identical with the divine nature, God. Why, asks Aquinas, does St. Hilary "appropriate" *aeternitas* to the Father? *species,* or image, to the Son? and *usus,* or enjoyment, to the Holy Spirit? [3] Within a single article Aquinas employs as synonyms for *imago* (*imago expressa Patris*) most of the traditional and scriptural names for the eternal Son: *similitudo perfecta, verbum increatum, species* or *splendor intellectus, conceptus sapientiae,* and *sapientia genita.* It is in the light of the suitability (*convenientia*) of these divine names as designations of the Second Person of the Blessed Trinity proceeding by way of intellection from the Father that Aquinas makes his well known remark about the three qualities "required" for beauty. It can hardly have occurred to Aquinas at this point, one imagines, that this incidental statement about the beautiful would subsequently be used as a cornerstone for a Thomist aesthetic.

The point which Aquinas seeks to establish is a theological one: an imago or similitudo is beautiful if it perfectly represents another thing. Inasmuch as the data of revelation present the Son now as the verbum increatum ("In principio erat verbum, et verbum erat apud Deum, et Deus erat verbum," in the opening words of St. John's Gospel), and now as imago (the *imago Dei invisibilis* of St. Paul's Epistle to the Colossians 1 :15), the Son in a very special sense must be conceived of in our minds, says Aquinas, as having a special, if not exclusive, title to the divine name: *beauty.* From our way of looking at things this name in the tradition of Dionysius best describes the fullness of formal, intellectualized representation, and the Son is just such a similitudo, imago expressa, and so forth for the other names.

Aquinas is clearly considering then an uncreated beauty, a beauty purely spiritual (what could be more spiritual than the eternal procession of a Divine Person?), and a beauty which transcends, as God must, sense perception. To apply this text to works of art, like symphonies or poems, which begin in sense perception and are supported by sense faculties—what the eye sees and what the ear hears, and what it enters into the mind of man to imagine—would seem to be reading into the text an aesthetic relevance much beyond what Aquinas could have had in mind. Dorothy Sayers makes a great deal of sense when she points out in her highly instructive and readable book *The Mind of the Maker* that "to complain that man measures God by his own measure is a waste of time; man measures everything by his own experience; he has no other yardstick." [4]

It is important to our understanding of another person's thought to

---

3. *S.T.,* I, q. 39, a. 8, corp.
4. Dorothy Sayers, *The Mind of the Maker* (New York, Harcourt, Brace, 1941), p. 24.

know with what element in our own experience this thinker is trying to take the measurement of God. There is no reason which compels us to exclude at the outset the possibility of God's putting something about Himself into our immediate experience. From the time of St. Augustine, theological tradition, at least, has seen in the human soul the image of the Trinity. It is to an immanent operation of the soul—the procession of the mental word or image—and not to a finished, sensuous work of art, that Aquinas, in line with this age-old Augustinian tradition, primarily appeals when he searches for an analogue that may help us to understand (though, of course, not to establish or to solve) the mystery of the eternal procession of the Son from the Father as a perfect *image* of the Father's perfection, unalloyed and radiant: "Deum de Deo, lumen de lumine, Deum verum de Deo vero," in the words of the Nicene Creed.

It seems logical to suppose that Joyce as he read Aquinas would have perceived the Trinitarian direction in which so very many of Aquinas' remarks on beauty move. In the strangely troubled days of Stephen Dedalus' quasi-conversion to grace in the *Portrait,* Joyce says of him that he found the symbolism and imagery of the divine processions (such as they "were darkly shadowed forth in the books of devotion") "easier of acceptance by his mind by reason of their august incomprehensibility than was the simple fact that God . . . loved his soul. . . ." [5] Whatever may have been the extent or quality of Joyce's own theological enlightenment as a result of his Paris studies, it seems significant that whereas the Stephen Dedalus of the *Portrait* is represented as expanding and refining on Aquinas' texts de pulchro, the sadder and wiser Stephen of *Ulysses* invokes the authority of "the bulldog of Aquin" to support an exegesis of *Hamlet,* and by implication a theory of literature which is based on the Aquinan analysis *fides quaerens intellectum* of what the concepts procession, relation, and person must mean when one applies them to God.

There is no compelling reason why we should accept the Trinitarian theory of literature set forth by Stephen in the Library chapter of *Ulysses* as Joyce's own version of the matter any more than we are compelled to take the aesthetic discourse of the *Portrait* as Joyce's own. So to read the Dedalan theory of *Ulysses* would be especially misleading since Stephen himself is represented as promptly repudiating the theory as soon as John Eglinton inquires about it: "You have brought us all this way to show us a French triangle. Do you believe your own theory?"—"No, Stephen said promptly." [6] Joyce's own title for the Library chapter is "Scylla and Charybdis," which rather pointedly hints at the perils in theological and mystical argument, perils which Joyce represents Bloom as having quite narrowly escaped on his visit to the library while Ste-

5. *Portrait,* p. 172.
6. P. 211.

phen was developing his Shakespeare theory to the astonishment and for the amusement of his young fellow Dubliners. The Stephen of *Ulysses* is not nearly so solemn in his Aquinan exposition as is the Stephen of the *Portrait*. Throughout his long discourse he himself laughs many times, his companions are constantly laughing and interrupting him, and Joyce is at pains to add in parentheses the stage direction: (*Laughter*).[7]

It may serve as a hint of what Joyce intends in these Thomistic discourses of Stephen if one calls to mind that Joyce as an undergraduate had read the metaphysical writings of Giordano Bruno of Nola as well as those of Aquinas.[8] Joyce's first published work, "The Day of the Rabblement," opens with Joyce's taking on the role of Bruno for the twentieth century: "No man, said the Nolan, can be a lover of the true or the good unless he abhors the multitude." [9] This essay was printed privately at Joyce's expense with Joyce as Bruno assuming the name of one of Dublin's leading booksellers, Browne and Nolan (omens of the *Wake*!), when the editor of the University College magazine, *St. Stephen's,* refused to publish it uncensored. Gorman relates that for some time after the publication the students of the College were greatly intrigued and puzzled as to the identity of this supposed ancient Irish chieftain, "The Nolan," whom Joyce quoted so offhandedly as his authority and source.[1] Joyce must have enjoyed their puzzlement and it does not seem altogether farfetched to imagine that at a later date he might have wished to increase it.

Giordano Bruno, as Joyce knew, had spent three years in London as the friend of Sir Philip Sidney, the "defender of poetry," to whom he dedicated two books. Claiming that it was his mission to arouse men out of their "theological stagnation," but wishing at the same time to escape the condemnation of his continental critics, Bruno, a relapsed Dominican, had proceeded to set forth his own personal philosophy under the guise of interpreting and expounding the writings of Thomas Aquinas.[2] Is there not a clue here to the tone to which the wary reader will pay attention in his exegesis of Joyce's Thomism? To say that Joyce here assumes a "comic incognito" is not the same as to agree with Shane Leslie, who says of *Ulysses* as a whole that Joyce has made a gigantic effort "to fool the world of readers and even the Pretorian guard of critics." [3] The fact that Joyce in his last two novels makes a seriocomic use of the metaphysical and historical aspects of the Trinitar-

7. P. 207.

8. Gorman, *James Joyce*, p. 332.

9. *Two Essays:* "A Forgotten Aspect of the University Question," by F. J. C. Skeffington, and "The Day of the Rabblement," by James A. Joyce (Dublin, Gerrard Bros., 1901), p. 7.

1. Gorman, *James Joyce*, p. 71, n. 1.

2. Cf. Charles Dudley Warner, intro. to "The Heroic Enthusiasts" of Giordano Bruno, Library of World's Best Literature (New York, Internat. Society, 1897), *6*, 2613–14.

3. Shane Leslie, *"Ulysses," The Quarterly Review, 238* (Oct. 1922), 220.

ian dogma should not lead us to imagine that Joyce found no serious relevance in the theme, or that the theme cannot be crucial in the text of his works as he patterned them.

Louis Gillet correctly perceives that the essential basis of the Joyce problem is the problem of paternity, "a now ascending, now descending relationship that is entirely extra-sexual, and quite devoid of sensuality." [4] Gillet calls the long meditation of Stephen (in *Ulysses*) on the subject of *Hamlet* "the key to the book." John Courtney Murray in an admirable summary of the complex Trinitarian theology of Aquinas' *Summa Theologiae* calls attention to the fact "that the new 'name' of God as Father, who has an eternal Son, is the very substance of the New Testament—the thing that makes it a *New* Testament." Murray adds that "all Trinitarian heresies have had one thing in common—an attempt to explain away the eternal Father-Son relationship as not of the essence of God." [5] Gillet and Murray are not talking about two different things any more than are Joyce and Aquinas. The mystery of God, as traditional Christianity confronts it, is that God is by intrinsic necessity, *of His own nature*, a Father—and Joyce saw as clearly as Aquinas or Murray does that "this knowledge of what He [God] is in Himself is the ultimate foundation of our hope of what He will be to us." [6] Joyce saw too that the principal Trinitarian heresies may ultimately be reduced to two: Arianism and Sabellianism.

Arius, a fourth-century Alexandrian priest, contended that the Son was not truly a Son of the Father by nature but a kind of intermediary, much more than human but a very great deal less than divine. The Son was not to be regarded as "consubstantial" (*homoousios*); He was "of like substance" (*homoiousios*) with God, but however like, He was not God. But if the Son is not consubstantial (*homoousios*) with God, then God cannot be thought of as by His very nature a Father. If those who opposed Arius made so much of an "iota," it was because that iota made the difference for them between knowing a Son who was an intermediary only and knowing Him as God; between believing in a God who was *like* a true father and believing in a God Who was essentially, irrevocably Father, from Whom all human fatherhood derived its reality and on Whom it founded all its hopes. Arianism was repudiated at Nicea by the first ecumenical council in the year 325, and both the Nicene and Athanasian creeds (or "symbols," as Joyce reminds us they were once called) are explicitly anti-Arian. "Where is poor dear Arius to try conclusions?" Stephen asks himself on the strand. [7]

But Stephen is no Arian. However much he may deplore the sordid

4. Louis Gillet, "Stele for James Joyce," *A James Joyce Yearbook, 1949,* p. 42.
5. John Courtney Murray, S.J., "The Most Blessed Trinity," *Summa Theologiae of St. Thomas Aquinas,* tr. English Dominican Fathers (New York, Benziger, 1948), *3,* 3158, col. 2.
6. Ibid.
7. P. 39.

ending of the "ill-starred heresiarch," as he calls Arius, Stephen has
little sympathy for a theology which would take away the basis of Fatherhood in God. Nor is there any hesitation in Stephen's preference for
the Nicene over the Arian formulation. Stephen lumps Arius with the
enemies of his soul, with Photius (who denied the *Filioque,* or procession of the Holy Spirit from the Son), and with Buck Mulligan: "Photius and the brood of mockers of whom Mulligan was one, and Arius,
warring his life long upon the consubstantiality of the Son with the
Father." [8] Stephen is represented as loving Palestrina's *Mass for Pope
Marcellus,* especially the arrangement of its (Nicene) creed, "symbol
[creed] of the apostles in the mass for pope Marcellus, the voices
blended, singing alone loud in affirmation." [9] Frank Budgen tells us that
Joyce himself loved this Mass, often sang it, and believed that Palestrina
had saved music for the Church by writing it in honor of that Pope,
martyred in the last of the Roman persecutions, who had asserted the
primacy of the Roman See.[1]

Stephen is no Arian, to be sure, but that is mainly because Stephen in
his thinking cannot free himself from the other principal Trinitarian
heresy, Sabellianism, a far subtler, more rationalistic, and quite modern-
istic heresy, the choice (or *hairesis*) of those who wish to hold a trinity
of persons in the Godhead but to do so, at least as Aquinas conceives of
the matter, in purely human terms and entirely on the basis of the content of their human experience of personality rather than on the basis of
God's revelation about Himself. Sabellius, a third-century heresiarch
of Ptolemais in Africa, held that Father, Son, and Holy Spirit were actually no more than "modes," or manifestations, of God in the outer
world. So it is that Stephen refers explicitly to Sabellius as "the subtle
African heresiarch . . . who held that the Father was Himself His own
Son," [2] and characterizes him, when he is not being dialectically pushed
in argument, along with Aquinas' other Trinitarian adversaries as a
"weaver of the wind." For the followers of Sabellius, the Trinity ceases
to be a "mystery," and Aquinas' whole approach to the mystery by way
of "subsistent relationships" appears as illusory. Sabellianism is sometimes called Modalism, since it conceives of the divine Persons as being
no more than *modes* or *modalities* of the Divine Essence. Sometimes too
it is called *Monarchianism,* since it was to save the "divine monarchy,"
as they said, that the Sabellians denied the real distinctions between
the Persons in the Trinity. It is in Sabellianism as Monarchianism that
Stephen finds the link for tying together the story of the murdered king
of Denmark and the dialectical rationalism of a theology that makes the

8. P. 22.
9. Ibid.
1. Budgen, *James Joyce,* pp., 177, 182.
2. P. 22.

Son no more than a specter of the Father. "Is it possible that that player
Shakespeare, a ghost by absence, and in the vesture of buried Denmark,
a ghost by death, speaking his own words to his own son's name (had
Hamnet Shakespeare lived he would have been prince Hamlet's twin)
is it possible, I want to know, or probable that he did not draw or foresee
the logical conclusion of those premises: You are the dispossessed son:
I am the murdered father . . . ?" [3]

It is difficult to see how any reader could follow Stephen as he works
out "the logical conclusion of those premises" unless he possessed some
knowledge of the metaphysics of the Trinitarian theology for which
Aquinas is known as the *princeps theologorum*. A literary study fortu-
nately does not need to adjudicate between theological systems. Suffice
it to say, as John Courtney Murray does, that men of learning have had
no other choice but "to think out their faith in terms of the philosophy
they knew." [4] The attempt of Aquinas to arrive at an understanding of
his faith, *fides quaerens intellectum,* led him to write the most princely
of all his theological expositions, the seventeen questions, *De Personis
Divinis,* in the First Part of the *Summa Theologiae,* Questions 27 to 43.

Aquinas presents his complex Trinitarian exposition with such precision and compression that any attempt more briefly to summarize his
argument must necessarily be unsatisfactory and more or less misleading. Rather than make such an attempt, the literary student will perhaps
be excused if he does no more than call attention by way of outline to the
major steps which Aquinas takes in order to demonstrate that there is no
evident contradiction between the two principles, diversity of Persons
and unity of nature in the Godhead.

In virtue of an analogical rather than a univocal predication, Aquinas
sets out to establish that procession in God implies simply a relationship
of origin between two: for example, the Son is He Who proceeds from
the Father, the Father is He from Whom the Son proceeds. So when
Aquinas says that there are processions in God, he means simply that
there are real relations of origin in God. Moreover since these real relations are *in* God, and there is but one God, Aquinas argues that the
relations must be identified with the one divine substance: in other
words, these relations of origin are subsistent. Since it is the Persons
who proceed, and since processions *in divinis* signify subsistent relations,
Aquinas' argument concludes that the divine Persons are simply the
subsistent relations: for example, the Son consubstantial by proceeding
from the Father, the Holy Spirit consubstantial by proceeding from the
Father and the Son.

Since the second Person is called a Son, His origin must be after the
manner of a "generation," a *begetting;* since He proceeds as the *Ver-*

3. Pp. 186-7.
4. Murray, "The Most Blessed Trinity," *Summa Theologiae, 3,* 3161, col. 2.

bum, He owes His origin to the divine intellect as it is in the Father; and since He proceeds as Image, His eternal origin from the Father is by way of a perfect (consubstantial) likeness to the Father. As for the third Person, since the scriptural data present Him proceeding from the Son and Father as Holy Spirit, Gift, and Love, His names suggest to Aquinas that He owes His origin somehow to the divine will.

A further step leads Aquinas to examine the scriptural data in the light of the traditional Augustinian analogy between the inner life of the human soul and God's own inner life of intelligence and love. In the light of this analogy, the Person who proceeds by way of intellectual operation as the mental word (Verbum) of the Father must be distinct from the Father, just as the mental word "conceived" by the human intellect's understanding of itself must be thought of in human terms as distinct from the intellect itself. (Kant would have conceived of it differently but then Aquinas was not a Kantian.) But, Aquinas resumes, since *in divinis* the Father's infinite understanding of Himself begets a perfect Image, the Person Who thus proceeds by way of intellection (the Son) must be thought of as a perfect Word or Image generated or begotten in the perfect likeness of His progenitor or Conceiver (the Father). Aquinas' presentation at this stage is no more than an orderly exposition in metaphysical terms of the traditional Patristic axiom: "Quo Verbum, eo Imago, et eo ipso Filius."

The fact that Joyce makes literary capital in *Ulysses* of the intricacies of Aquinas' argument is hard to explain unless we suppose that he had studied, with something like the same close attention which he ascribes to Stephen, the Sabellian refutation written by "the bulldog of Aquin." There is not the slightest ambiguity about Stephen's being represented as a close student of the Trinitarian theology directly as it is presented in the text of Aquinas: "Saint Thomas, Stephen, smiling, said, whose gorbellied works I enjoy reading in the original, writing of incest . . . likens it in his wise and curious way to an avarice of the emotions." [5] Throughout his mock-serious lecture on poetics in *Ulysses,* Stephen reveals a knowledge of the subtleties of Trinitarian theology which goes beyond what "the books of devotion which he read" in the *Portrait* could have given him.[6]

Complicating as the admission is, one must yet admit that the Trinitarian current in Joyce's work is constantly being fed by tributary streams of thought and symbolism. For example, to understand the relevance of the Trinitarian theme for the Shakespeare-Hamlet-God-Sun (and Son)-Commercial Traveler theory of literature in *Ulysses,*[7] one must think of this theme as here qualified by at least two other in-

5. P. 203.
6. *Portrait,* p. 172.
7. Cf. p. 494.

tellectual perspectives: George Berkeley's idealism or solipsism, and to some extent by the fin-de-siècle version of German idealistic romanticism (of the Hegelian sort).

The Berkeleyan cast of Stephen's thoughts appears early in the book when Stephen, walking along the strand, watching the tide come in, meditates on the nature of the soul: "Who ever anywhere will read these written words? Signs on a white field. Somewhere to someone in your flutiest voice. The good bishop of Cloyne took the veil of the temple out of his shovel hat." [8] Stephen's allusion to Berkeley, the Irish Protestant bishop of Cloyne, grows out of his own optical experiments as he walks beside the sea, and suggests some familiarity on Joyce's part with Berkeley's "Essay toward a New Theory of Vision," in which Berkeley sets out to establish that the sense-qualities of all things are "inside the head." Whatever may be the merits of Berkeley's radical idealism, *esse est percipi,* he was "on the side of the angels," as Stephen and indeed as Joyce sees it. Berkeley refused at least to settle for the materialism of the "sensationists" (Locke and Hobbes), and combatting what appeared to him as a purely pragmatic, deistic view of reality, sought to bring the mystery of a supernatural, revealed religion back into honor among men.

Joyce's familiarity with his fellow Irishman's writings extended even beyond the "Essay on Vision." The Thomistic version of aesthetics in *Portrait* has not a few verbal echoes of the third of Berkeley's Platonic dialogues in the *Alciphron.*[9] "Everyone knows," says Alciphron, "beauty is that which pleases." [1] "Beauty consists in a certain symmetry or proportion, pleasing to the eye." [2] Euphranon asks, "The parts must be so related and adjusted to one another, as that they may best conspire to the . . . operation of the whole?" And Alciphron leads Euphranon on to acknowledge, "Beauty is an object, not of the eye, but of the mind." [3] The Dedalan aesthetics, sketched in terms of beauty's being perceived in "stages" of the mind's awareness, and "epiphanizing" as "the gropings of a spiritual eye which seeks to adjust its vision to an exact focus" [4] have pronounced Berkeleyan overtones. The druidical brooding of Balkelly at the close of the *Wake* is meant to suggest the idealistic philosophy of George Berkeley, "with a flavoring of Kant," as Campbell and Robinson note in their *Key.*[5]

8. P. 49.
9. Cf. *Works of George Berkeley,* ed. Alexander Campbell Fraser, Vol. *2, Alciphron,* Oxford, Clarendon, 1901.
1. Ibid., p. 132.
2. Ibid., p. 133.
3. Ibid., p. 134.
4. *Stephen Hero, p.* 211.
5. Cf. *Finnegans Wake,* p. 611; and Joseph Campbell and Henry Morton Robinson, *A Skeleton Key to Finnegans Wake* (New York, Harcourt, Brace, 1944), p. 348. The originator in America of the family line of Ralph Waldo Emerson, transcendentalist, was a Peter Bulkeley, who founded Concord in 1636.

"The good bishop of Cloyne" would seem to have influenced Joyce's representation of Stephen as a kind of dialectical, rationalistic Sabellian, whose heart and soul are not in Sabellianism, and whose dialectical maneuver in the "Scylla and Charybdis" episode is executed not so much with the intention of convincing his friends of a "French triangle" theory of Shakespearean authorship as of exorcising the Sabellian triangle, which is not a triangle, from his own soul: "He laughed to free his mind from his mind's bondage." [6] Stephen is represented as a kind of reluctant Sabellian modalist who reinforces and complicates his modalist position by adopting, as if for the sake of argument, the strictly idealistic metaphysics of Berkeley. Sabellius could not see his way to admitting any principle of distinction within the Godhead, but he saw no difficulty in admitting the reality of the extra-mental universe as something quite distinct from a perceiving mind. Berkeley wished to save the tradition of Christian revelation which teaches the existence of a Triune God, but as a theocentric transcendentalist he could not see his way to admitting that the phenomena of this outer world had any reality save insofar as they were perceived by the mind of God. Stephen Dedalus is maneuvered dialectically into the involved situation of trying to hold Berkeley's axiom, esse est percipi, at the same time that he seems forced to hold with Sabellius that in God there is no ground for distinction even between the knowing mind and the object (or Verbum) which the mind begets or knows. Not only is the Son *not* distinct from the Father, but the phenomena of this world are in no way distinct from God. On the basis of such an analogy, the world (or Word) of Shakespeare (or of any other artist's "begetting") cannot be thought of as in any way distinct from the artist's utterly lonely conceiving mind.

As Berkeleyan idealist Stephen must hold on to the only support for reality which has any validity, that is, its existence in the mind; as Sabellian modalist, he cannot admit a real distinction between the Persons in the Uncreate Trinity, nor, by a reverse analogy, between the person of the artist (Shakespeare) and the "words" or "images" which on Sabellian grounds are no more than mere logical distinctions of the mind. The Son is no more than a "mode" or "manifestation" of the Father, but is not really distinct from the Father, and the Holy Ghost, like Hamlet's father's ghost, cannot on any logical grounds (within this system) be conceived of as a distinct person from the Father or the Son, any more than Hamlet's father's ghost can be distinguished as distinct from the father (Hamlet-*père*-Shakespeare) or the son (Hamlet-*fils*-Shakespeare). Stephen, "battling against hopelessness"—his feelings hurt when Buck (Malachi) Mulligan comes into the library and the other lads, hostile to him, make Buck feel welcome—attempts to sum it up:

6. P. 209.

> Brood of mockers: Photius, pseudomalachi. . . . He Who Him-
> self begot, middler the Holy Ghost, and Himself sent Himself,
> Agenbuyer, between Himself and others, Who, put upon by His
> fiends, stripped and whipped, was nailed like bat to barndoor,
> starved on crosstree, Who let Him bury, stood up, harrowed hell,
> fared into heaven and there these nineteen hundred years sitteth on
> the right hand of His Own Self but yet shall come in the latter day
> to doom the quick and dead *when all the quick shall be dead al-
> ready*.[7]

Joyce's main purpose in representing Stephen as a Sabellian idealist,
it need hardly be added, arises less from a desire to establish the theological or philosophical or moral corollaries of such an intellectual position
than from his interest in exploring the consequences for the literary
artist who maintains this position. So it seems necessary at this point to
say a few words about the kind of German romantic and idealistic
aestheticism which was in the air at the turn of the twentieth century
and which no theorist of literature at the time could altogether escape.

The German romantic tradition had reached its high point, it would
seem, in Hegel (d. 1831), and took a new orientation at the end of the
century in the immanent neo-idealism of Croce. This tradition favored a
view of "mystic simultaneity," and tended to break down any principle
of distinction between the artist and his work, between the poet's intuition and his expression of that intuition in poetic utterance. The poet
not only hides himself behind his work, as the Deity hides behind the
universe, but also becomes his work, and his work becomes himself.[8]
(And one suspects that this poet-deity, like Stephen's artist-god of the
creation, is hiding so that he can engage in "paring his fingernails.") [9]
Hegel's theory of symbolic art, "the still unconscious process of the
World-Spirit labored toward artistic utterance," [1] his definition of humor as "romantic irony," [2] and finally his classification of poetry into
the three forms, lyric, epic, and dramatic,[3] are all so clearly echoed at
one point or another in the Dedalan aesthetic that we should find it hard
to believe that if Joyce is not depending directly on the Hegelian texts
he is not at least influenced to the extent of expressing himself, as a child
of his times, in the categories which Hegel's system had made the common stock of writers on art and on poetry.

If it is true that "the reconciliation of opposites" is the essence of
Hegel's doctrine, the Hegelian presumably would find little to quarrel
with in Stephen's conception of Shakespeare: "He is the ghost and the

7. P. 195. (Italics mine.)
8. Cf. Gilbert and Kuhn, *A History of Esthetics,* p. 362.
9. *Portrait,* p. 252.
1. Gilbert and Kuhn, *A History of Esthetics,* p. 444.
2. Cf. ibid., p. 447.
3. Cf. ibid., p. 452.

prince. He is all in all. . . . In *Cymbeline,* in *Othello* he is bawd and
cuckold. He acts and is acted on. . . . His unremitting intellect is the
hornmad Iago ceaselessly willing that the moor in him shall suffer." [4]
Aquinas finds in the Word's procession by intellection as the *Image,* or
flawlessly conceived likeness of the Father, a further intellectual incentive for exploring the datum of revelation so far as it presents the Word
(or Verbum) as the only-begotten Son (*Filius Unigenitus*). An attempted coordination between the two systems, Hegelian and Aquinan,
is part of Stephen's own dialectical maneuver, and there is no reason to
believe that Joyce (or even Stephen) commits himself to it as proved—
or provable. (In the interior monologue which he carries on with himself at the same time that he is developing his theory aloud, Stephen
comments shortly before he invokes the authority of Saint Thomas : "I
think you're getting on very nicely. Just mix up a mixture of theolologic-
icophilolological. *Mingo, minxi, mictum, mingere.*" [5] A modern theorist
of the arts summarizes the aesthetic position of the Hegelians (among
whom he includes Benedetto Croce) : "They conceive of art, and of all
life and civilization, as a process of 'self-expression' by the Cosmic Mind.
The thoughts in an individual artist's mind . . . are all parts of this
process of divine expression. Croce affirms that 'art is vision or intuition,' and not a physical fact of any kind, since 'physical facts do not
possess reality.' " [6]

In the light of the above summary of the Hegelian position, as well as
in the light of Berkeley's principle, "esse est percipi," it should not be too
difficult to see what Joyce intends in representing Stephen as Sabellian
exegete of Shakespeare : "He goes back, weary of the creation he has
piled up to hide him from himself, an old dog licking an old sore. But,
because loss is his gain, he passes on towards eternity in undiminished
personality, untaught by the wisdom he has written or by the laws he
has revealed. His beaver is up. He is a ghost, a shadow now, the wind
by Elsinore's rocks or what you will, the sea's voice, a voice heard only
in the heart of him who is the substance of his shadow, the son consubstantial with the father." [7]

"Or what you will—." Quite logically, Stephen perceives that if
Sabellius and Berkeley and the Hegelians are all three right, then
Aquinas must be wrong. For Aquinas' Triune God, in that case, has
been vanquished and "rests, disarmed of fatherhood," [8] a *"dio boia,*

4. P. 210. Compare Keats' words (in a letter to Woodhouse, Oct. 27, 1818) : "As
to the poetical character itself . . . it is not itself—it has no self—it is everything and
nothing—it has no character . . . it has as much delight in conceiving an Iago as an
Imogen" (quoted by Mario Praz, *The Romantic Agony,* tr. Angus Davidson, 2d ed.
London, Oxford Univ. Press, 1951, foreword, p. xii).

5. P. 202.
6. Munro, *The Arts and Their Interrelations,* p. 79.
7. P. 194.
8. P. 204.

hangman god" in a new sense which the Italians, "most Roman of catholics," never intended, "in all of us ostler and butcher . . . an androgynous angel, being a wife unto himself." [9] And if the Father-hood of God has been vanquished, if "a father . . . is a necessary evil," [1] what grounds are there for holding a human father in reverence, or for setting one's heart on the cruel and impossible bourne of an "at-one-ment" with God? If, as Stephen says, all fatherhood is necessarily evil, is not Stephen's hopeless characterization of this age quite valid: "It is an age of exhausted whoredom groping for its god"? [2] "Paternity may be a legal fiction. Who is the father of any son that any son should love him or he any son?" [3] That is Stephen's question, and by implica-tion it is the artist's question at the point where it occurs in the Shake-speare argument. Joyce represents Stephen as stating his conclusion provisionally. "Paternity may be a legal fiction." Even in the heat of argument Stephen feels the need to qualify.

Having turned on its head the Aquinan Trinitarian analogy from creature to creator, Stephen as Sabellian idealist faces the dialectical situation where he must hold that all the artist's images are the pure and simple self-idealizations of a lonely Deity, no longer inclined to communicate selfhood or life to another, self-enclosed, and indeed "in-cestuous," whose love "is covetously withheld from some stranger who, it may be, hungers for it." [4] It is well enough to speak of the artist's world as a self-projection, to conceive of all the varied verbal images and character symbols of literature as one might of a Son (the Verbum) begotten of the Father, but what happens in such a theory when the ultimate theological and metaphysical grounds for fatherhood have given way and vanished? Speaking of Shakespeare, Stephen states the answer logically enough: "He found in the world without as actual what was in his world within as possible. Maeterlinck says: *If Socrates leave his house today he will find the sage seated on his doorsteps. If Judas go forth tonight it is to Judas his steps will tend.* Every life is many days, day after day. We walk through ourselves, meeting robbers, ghosts, giants, old men, young men, wives, widows, brothers-in-love. But al-ways meeting ourselves." [5]

But Stephen's answer does not explain Shakespeare's world, and Stephen is well aware that it does not do so. "O Lord, help my unbelief," he adds to himself when the dull-witted Eglinton shows signs of taking his theory seriously. "That is, help me to believe or help me to un-believe." [6] What is belief? That is the crux of Stephen's sufferings.

9. P. 210.
1. P. 204.
2. Ibid.
3. P. 205.
4. P. 203.
5. P. 210.
6. P. 211.

"What useful discovery did Socrates learn from Xanthippe?" Eglinton had asked Stephen earlier. And Stephen had not needed to search long for an answer: "Dialectic, Stephen answered: and from his mother how to bring thoughts into the world." But of what Socrates had learned from Myrto, the death-goddess, Stephen had added, "No man . . . will ever know." [7] If we find Stephen's theory confusing, it is not likely that we find it half as confusing as Stephen found it himself. "What the hell are you driving at?" he exclaims to himself at another point when he is under full sail, shortly before he invokes the winds of rhetoric to carry him further along: *"Amplius. Adhuc. Iterum. Postea."* [8]

The world of art need not be so lonely a world as the world of our humdrum lives. Shakespeare does not actually leave us, even in the world of *Hamlet,* at the brink of the grave, as one side of Stephen's mind asserts: "The motion is ended. Grave-diggers bury Hamlet *père* and Hamlet *fils.* A king and a prince at last in death, with incidental music." [9] Shakespeare's *Hamlet* ends with the arrival of Fortinbras, the exorcism of Denmark, and with "soldiers' music" for the funeral of the king's son who had proved himself a soldier by accepting the war within. Stephen has yet to learn soldiering. The plight of Stephen is not so much that he cannot find in Bloom a father as that he cannot find in his art a son, or image. It took Joyce, the mature artist, to conceive the image of Stephen Dedalus, the artist as a young man, which Stephen as a young man suffering from dialectical paralysis was impotent to beget.

Allen Tate in a suggestive study, "Poe and the Power of Words," calls attention to the fact that Poe "represents that part of our experience which we are least able to face up to: the Dark Night of Sense." [1] Later, speaking of Poe's conception in *The Colloquy of Monos and Una* of the poet's ability to participate through language in "the creative power of God," Tate makes a point which needs badly to be made: to speak of man's *spoken* or *written* word as a participation in the absolute creative power of the Word Eternal is "an extravagant and slippery pun on the Logos." [2] The Shakespearean theory of poetry sketched in *Ulysses* would make more sense to us if we were to realize that Stephen, as Joyce represents him, is carrying to their furthest limits the dialectical and rhetorical possibilities inherent in this "extravagant and slippery pun." There is Patristic precedent for distinguishing between the Word *conceived,* and the Word *uttered* at the Creation and at the Incarnation, the *logos endiathetos* and the *logos prophorikos.* But the theological argument for the procession of the second Person of the Trinity as the

7. P. 188.
8. P. 205.
9. P. 210.
1. Allen Tate, "The Angelic Imagination," *Kenyon Review, 14* (Summer 1952), 455. (This essay was first delivered as an address at Boston College, Feb. 11, 1951.)
2. Ibid., p. 468.

Son (since He proceeds as the Logos) is invariably founded on the Augustinian analogy of the conception of the *inner word,* the soul's knowledge of itself, and not upon the outward utterance of a word spoken or written.

To perceive the "extravagance" and "slipperiness" of Stephen's punning is not the same as totally to disqualify Stephen's literary theory, as a literary (not theological) theory, nor is it the same as to assert that Joyce had no precedent at all for his representation. German aesthetic metaphysicians of the romantic tradition speak of God as "the immediate cause of all art" and describe "poetic genius" as the "presence of the divinity in man, the gift that enables the individual to translate the ideal world into objectivity." [3] The procession of the inner word or image from the poet's mind is, to be sure, a kind of self-communication which may serve as a human analogue or exemplar to illustrate the divine processions since it suggests at least at another level the possibility of distinctness of persons within a perfectly unique consubstantiality of nature. Yet the Divine Word does not proceed as created, but as eternally uncreate.

No poet may dare hope to give himself so perfectly to his poems as the divine Father gives Himself to His consubstantial Son. The agony of poets "in creation" and their many sad avowals of failure confirm this inherent limitation on human operation which is imitative of but by no means identical with the divine. Joyce would be the last poet to deny this limitation. But that does not prevent Joyce from representing Stephen Dedalus as prepared to suffer as poet in the face of this very human limitation on his art. A poet may project or beget an image of his interior life, now as an Iago, now as an Othello, but these images which arise from the conscious and unconscious depths of his personality cannot each be full self-communication. It is in the nature of man-the-artist to beget still other images—for example, a Desdemona or a Cassio. Besides, for poetry, the mediation of art is always required. Artistic self-portrayal is not inevitable or unthwartable. The Trinitarian analogy is not the unique theological analogy which may be invoked to shed light on the reality of the experience embodied in a literary work of art. This literary experience, it may be, could be more easily explored on the analogy of a "Creation" or an "Incarnation." Stephen Dedalus prefers in his theory of Shakespeare to keep the Trinitarian analogy central. In doing so he chooses the harder part: for he possesses enough theological acumen to recognize that the eternal Son's procession as the Word or Image of the Father is quite independent of there being a Creation or an Incarnation at all: *"In the beginning* was the Word." The Stephen of *Ulysses,* having so miserably failed to create any art at all "in the smithy of his soul," finds little comfort in the thought of Creation—even on the

3. Cf. Gilbert and Kuhn, *A History of Esthetics,* p. 432.

Flaubertian principle of the *Portrait* that the artist like God is every-where present but nowhere visible in his works.

"Fabulous artificer, the hawklike man" [4] comes into the Library chapter of *Ulysses* as a forlorn, ironic echo of the disillusioned hopes that were so triumphantly, indeed arrogantly, represented in Stephen's diary at the end of the *Portrait:* "I go to encounter for the millionth time the reality of experience and to forge in the smithy of my soul the uncreated conscience of my race." [5] Surely it is no accident at this point that Joyce should have represented Stephen as a Father and a Son fused, as it were, into one: the Daedalus of the labyrinth perfectly (indeed numerically) one with the Icarus of the waxen wings. With no little sorrow, Stephen recalls the inevitable human awakening to reality: "Icarus. *Pater, ait.* Seabedabbled, fallen, weltering. Lapwing you are. Lapwing he." [6] The lapwing, it may be worth noting, is a faker, a bird which bluffs you and leads you away from its nest by falsely luring you on. The Shakespearean theory of poetry outlined in the library affords Stephen an opportunity to diagnose the nature of his own artistic malady, and to put his finger on what it was in his hopes to be an artist that somehow went wrong.

A brief diagrammatic representation may help at this point to recapitulate, or retrace, the principal elements that enter into the intellectual labyrinth which the Sabellian-decoyed Dedalus of *Ulysses* has constructed to explain Shakespeare, and, through Shakespeare, to explain art or poetry in general. Since Joyce was so precise in his use of symbols, it may not be irrelevant to recall here that the Cretan Daedalus, after whom Stephen is named, was confined for a long time in his own tortuous labyrinth and, no god he, only escaped when a natural-born son from outside the labyrinth came to take him away. The following schematization, though it labors under the defect of oversimplification common to all schemata, may clarify what Stephen has in mind when he brings the three themes, Father, *Hamlet,* and Shakespeare, into a single focus:

I. Stephen is *not* interested in "natural" sonship, which he equates with bodily generation, and which he depressingly characterizes as "a bodily shame," "an instant of blind rut." [7]

So the following Father-Son relationships are dismissed as unreal, devoid of honor or sense (though, in the third, Stephen "hedges") :

    1. Simon Dedalus   Stephen Dedalus
       (father)   (son)

4. P. 208.
5. *Portrait*, p. 299.
6. P. 208.
7. P. 205.

2. John Shakespeare   William Shakespeare
  (father)   (son)

3. William Shakespeare   Hamnet Shakespeare
  (father)   (son)

Whatever may ultimately have been Stephen's grounds (Berkeleyan? Hegelian?) for repudiating "natural sonship," the repudiation is his own and certainly not that of Aquinas.

II. Stephen *is* interested in sonship as "a mystical estate, an apostolic succession," as he says,[8] by which he means that he is interested in sonship so far as "the son [is] consubstantial with the father," [9] in the spirit, but not in the flesh.

So the following Father-Son relationship is examined under two aspects as meaningful and real:

1. God (the divine   God (the Divine, Consub-
  Father)   stantial Son)

2. God (the Father) as   God (the Son) as the
  begetting the Word   Word or begotten Image
  or Image   of the Father

The Aquinan Triune analogues at this point are evidently crucial to Stephen's argument. The Son's conception as the Word (Logos), or consubstantial image, is according to some intellectual operation of the Father. The Father knows Himself perfectly in His Son.

On the periphery here is the mental "sonship" ("kinship" would be a more accurate word) which Stephen half senses with Bloom, or even with his sister Dilly: "Shadow of my mind." [1] Some existence they certainly do have for him, so far at least as he identifies them with the self-existence of his own mind: esse est percipi.

III. Stephen, conceiving of the artistic process as self-expression by the cosmic mind, and not as a physical fact of any kind, explores the following Father-Son (that is, Father-Word) relationships as typical of the "ideal" relationships which alone make sense to the artistic mind:

1. Shakespeare (or   *Hamlet* (that is, Hamlet
  image-begetting   père as well as Hamlet
  artist-father)   fils) so far as both are
                     Shakespeare's image of
                     himself. Here one might

8. P. 204.
9. P. 194.
1. P. 239.

	add Iago, Othello, Prospero, and others—even Gertrude and Imogene—for all are "begotten" images of Shakespeare's self.
2. Stephen Dedalus (the artist-father confined in his own too artfully constructed maze)	*Stephen Hero* as projected (the Icarus, or Son-as-Image—the book which might enable Stephen Dedalus to escape from his maze)
3. Bous Stephanoumenos—"Lord and giver of their life" [2]— Stephen Dedalus' projection of himself into the future	All the phantom-sons, the ghost-characters (men and women) in the books which Stephen will *never* write [3]

The Trinitarian doctrine of the procession of the Second Person is still operative at this point in Stephen's theory, "Quo Verbum, eo Imago, et eo ipso, Filius," but the doctrine is now radically distorted by "interference" coming in from the fin-de-siècle version of German romantic idealism, the *Philosophie der Kunst.*" (The doctrine is modified by Berkeleyanism too.)

IV. Through the excessive assimilation of human artistic experience to the divine Trinitarian processions, the Aquinan (Hebraic-Christian) doctrine of God as Father breaks down completely. Stephen, no longer agonizingly polarized between the Aquinan and Sabellian concepts of the Trinity, now adheres fully to a Sabellian rationalism which he had earlier described to the free-thinking Englishman Haines with disgust, the rationalism of "the subtle African heresiarch Sabellius who held that the Father was Himself His own Son," [4] the collapse and identity of the human and the divine. The Sabellian, purely metaphorical, or modal, Father-Son relationship (for how can you have a real relationship without two really distinct terms?) is the only possible relationship in which Stephen can now find any relevance as an artist. Art, as he now conceives of it and phrases it, is the impossible "conscious . . . begetting" or intuitive self-expression of the conscious mind which, known to God

2. P. 408.
3. Ibid.
4. P. 22.

(the artist), is "unknown to man." [5] The following collapse of art into the artist, of the Son (or Image) into the Father, is complete:

The "divinely" conscious artist-father, eternally in possession of himself in mystic simultaneity: the "All in all" ("bawd and cuckold" in all of us). "He acts and is acted on." [6] *A hangman God:* His name may be Shakespeare, but it might just as well be Bizet, or Oscar Wilde, or Dumas (père or fils), or either of the brothers Grimm. This lonely deity might even be called Stephen Dedalus.

The "folio of this world" which is written badly—[7] Hamlet (père and fils, ghost and son), José and Carmen, all the men and women who have ever lived: Ann Hathaway, Hamnet Shakespeare, and the Shakespeare brothers: Gilbert, Edmund, Richard: [8] all the characters who have ever been conceived (that is, "begotten") in the likeness (*qua imagines*) of the father-artist. All the "possible" (that is, ghost) men and women, and all their phantom "images." [9]

All principle of distinction between a son and a father has broken down. The son is the father; the father is the son. Stephen is Bloom; Bloom is Stephen: *"Christus* or Bloom his name is, or, after all, any other, *secundum carnem."* [1] Shakespeare is the ghost. Shakespeare is Hamlet's unborn grandson. Paternity in God has been vanquished. Man's "at-onement" with the Father annihilates man's personality and eliminates art. The "images" of God in this world, "a badly written folio," like the molecules in men's bodies, are no more substantial than the constantly "woven and unwoven" formless self-portrayals of the lonely deity whom Stephen represents as spinning purposelessly from all eternity at his shuttle: "Through the ghost of the unquiet father the image of the unliving son looks forth." [2] Art has become impossible. As the Arian Buck Mulligan (the pseudo-Malachi) predicted to Haines in the first episode of the novel, Stephen "proves by algebra that Ham-

5. P. 204.
6. P. 210.
7. Ibid.
8. P. 206.
9. P. 408.
1. P. 627.
2. P. 192.

let's grandson is Shakespeare's grandfather and that he himself is the
ghost of his own father." [3] In doing so, Stephen uses, as Buck, shouting
in pain, predicted that he would, "the fifty-five reasons" of Thomas
Aquinas to prop up his argument.

Paul Tillich, speaking of "the courage to be," makes an observation
which seems applicable to Joyce's portrayal of "the Dedalus": "Courage
always includes a risk, it is always threatened by nonbeing, whether the
risk of losing oneself and becoming a thing within the whole of things or
of losing one's world in an empty self-relatedness." [4] In this sense of the
word, Stephen is not courageous; he will not take the risk; he is a good
example of the man who loses his life because he holds on to it too
avariciously. Unlike Hamlet, he has no title to a soldier's funeral.[5] He
ends up without God, and he ends up without the world. He ends up
without actualizing the potentialities of being in himself. Esthete that
he is, he ends up, to be sure, without art.

Shakespeare at one point in *The Winter's Tale* represents a father,
Leontes, reflecting that in his son, Mamillius, he has begotten a perfect
image of himself.[6] But Leontes does not think of Mamillius as a dialectic
projection of his intellect, positing as it were its own antithesis, but
rather as the substantial gift of love itself. In spite of the pastoral peace
which pervades the scene of reconciliation at the end of the play, Shakespeare, in no mood of mystic simultaneity, does not quite let us forget
that "in this wide gap of time" the sundering of love between Leontes
and Hermione had cost them both a son: for Mamillius at the end of
the play is dead.

In the Aquinan perspectives, echoed from afar in Shakespeare, it is
the child proceeding from the parents' love for one another which more
closely than any other subsistent human analogue reflects the eternal
procession of the Holy Spirit—as the gift of the Father to the Son and
of the Son to the Father. The world of *Ulysses,* as Joyce surveys it, is a
world where the Holy Spirit no longer breathes upon the waters. This is
perhaps only another way of saying the same thing Jung says of *Ulysses*
in the course of his penetrating Joycean study: "It is the picture of a
world that could give one a bad dream and plunge one into a mood
befitting a cosmic Ash Wednesday." [7]

3. P. 19.

4. Paul Tillich, *The Courage to Be* (New Haven, Yale Univ. Press, 1952), p. 155.

5. Cf. Maynard Mack, "The World of Hamlet," *Yale Review, 41* (Summer 1952),
523: "I think we understand by the close of Shakespeare's *Hamlet* why it is that unlike
the other tragic heroes he is given a soldier's rites upon the stage. For as William Butler
Yeats once said, 'Why should we honor those who die on the field of battle? A man
may show as reckless a courage in entering into the abyss of himself.'"

6. *The Winter's Tale,* Act I, sc. ii, ll. 129–35, 153–8.

7. Jung, *"Ulysses:* A Monologue," tr. W. Stanley Dell, Reprint of the Analytical
Psychology Club of New York (Spring 1949), p. 16.

Stephen on the strand recalls reading "the fading prophecies of Joachim Abbas," [8] who thought that all men, through the power of divine love, would shortly be gods. The prophecies of Joachim, before Buck Mulligan's mockery, are fading for Stephen in more ways than one. So it is that Stephen transfers the title *Abbas* (Father) to Swift, the "furious dean," [9] who taught that all men already are dogs. Stephen can no longer think of his own conception as the gift of love which has the procession of the Holy Spirit as its prime analogate, or exemplar: "Wombed in sin darkness I was too, made not begotten. . . . They clasped and sundered, did the coupler's will. . . . Is that then the divine substance wherein Father and Son are consubstantial?" [1] For Bloom and for Molly, the story of their lost son Rudy's conception is depressingly the same: "We came together when I was watching the two dogs . . . in the middle of the naked street that disheartened me altogether." [2] Denis de Rougement in the course of his discussion of "Religion and the Mission of the Artist" asks a very intelligent question which it never occurs to Stephen to ask himself: "Do I project into the cosmos the forms of my spirit, or is it rather that I espouse by the spirit some of the objective forms of the real?" [3] Stephen walking on the strand recalls a remark of Dryden's to Swift, "Cousin Swift, you will never be a poet," and he applies this remark with a difference to himself: "Cousin Stephen, you will never be a saint." [4] But Stephen need not have made the difference. Cousin Stephen, so long as he conceives of poetry after the exemplar of Sabellius' modal Trinity, will never be a poet either nor escape out of the labyrinth where a lifeless image and an unquiet imager are one. [5]

8. P. 40.
9. Ibid.
1. P. 39.
2. P. 763.
3. Denis de Rougement, "Religion and the Mission of the Artist," *Spiritual Problems in Contemporary Literature,* ed. S. R. Hopper (New York, Harper, 1952), p. 185.
4. P. 41.
5. P. 192.

7

The Wrunes of the World: The Theme of Creation

> *But the world, mind, is, was and will be*
> *writing its own wrunes for ever, man, on all*
> *matters that fall under the ban of our infra-*
> *rational senses.*
>
> *Finnegans Wake* [1]

STEPHEN DEDALUS accepts the characterization of his aesthetic theory in the *Portrait* as "applied Aquinas." But he goes on to say that so far as the phenomena of artistic conception and reproduction are concerned, he requires "a new terminology and a new personal experience." [2] The newness of the terminology and of the personal experience seeks at the same time to operate so far as it can upon a traditionally Aquinan axis: the concept that the artist (or maker) is to his work as God is to His creation. The aesthetic discourse of the *Portrait* concludes by Stephen's invoking this analogy of the artist as creator to sanction the "impersonal" theory of poetry which he has taken such pains to develop: "The esthetic image in the dramatic form is life purified in and reprojected from the human imagination. The mystery of esthetic like that of material creation is accomplished. The artist, like the God of the creation, remains within or behind or beyond or above his handiwork, invisible, refined out of existence, indifferent, paring his fingernails." [3]

No Thomist, much less St. Thomas himself, would accept Stephen's final metaphor of the Creator "paring his nails" as a just vehicle to signify either the creative activity of the poet or the Fatherly activity of the transcendent God of the creation. When the issue is drawn and Stephen recurs to this analogy in the privacy of his diary (at the end of the *Portrait*), he no longer feels the need to pose as he has done before Lynch as a "fingernail paring" artist but speaks quite earnestly of forging *in the smithy of his soul* the uncreated conscience of his race. [4]

The comparison between the poet and the God of the creation is by

1. Pp. 19–20. Unless otherwise indicated, page references to Joyce's works in this chapter refer to *Finnegans Wake*.
2. *Portrait*, pp. 245–6.
3. Ibid., p. 252.
4. Ibid., p. 299.

no means original either with Aquinas or with those who hold the Christian dogma of creation. The view that the poet somehow participates in the divine prerogative of creation is a commonplace of poetic theory from Plato's day to our own. Yet as soon as one begins to reflect modestly on what creation implies in theological perspectives, one begins to wonder how any exact or realistic theorist of literature could make use of this analogy to throw light on the essentially finite and necessarily imitative act of so-called "creative" poetic expression.

The poet certainly does not produce something out of nothing. The world as most of us experience it must be given, must be there, long before the poet can set out to interpret it, discover it, or represent it symbolically. To a greater or a lesser extent, and usually to a greater, the poet is dependent on centuries-old traditions, conventions of genres and of metaphor, ready-made exigencies of diction and style. Language is something which the poet can hope to modify or purify at a certain high level of literacy—"Donner un sens plus pur aux mots de la tribu" —but not even a Mallarmé or an Eliot has been able to construct a language ex nihilo. Oftener than not the pressures of "the tribe" determine the shape of things to come, in language as in everything else, more effectively than the self-conscious productions of the poetry makers. Not a little important poetry is apt to strike us as an achievement in coping with a world, inside poetry as well as outside it, rather than as an achievement in creating one. Shaun the Postman's indictment of Shem the Penman in the *Wake* contains such a large measure of truth applicable to all poets that it need not surprise us that Shem makes no effort to evade it. Shaun (*Justius*) says to Shem (*Mercius*) : "O, you were excruciated, in honour bound to the cross of your own cruelfiction!" [5]

The fact remains that, for Aquinas on theological grounds and for Joyce on poetic grounds, it seemed meaningful and indispensable to liken the work of the poet to the work of the God of the creation. Joyce's use of the creation theme or analogy, unlike other elements in his Thomism, becomes more rather than less prominent and operative as he advances from the *Portrait* to the *Wake*. Between the Thomist perspectives of the early work and the Viconian perspectives of the later work, there is on this point of the creation analogy not nearly so radical a difference as one might at first suppose. As Joyce from his own experience was in a position to see, Vico's reaction against Scholasticism was in no sense a repudiation of Thomism (hardly known in Vico's day) but rather a dissent from the nominalistic, excessively rationalistic tradition of thought which developed at a time when the open structure of Aquinas' own system was in the shadow and in decline. Few if any Scholastics today would care to take up the cudgels in defense of the eighteenth-century *Aufklärung* version of Scholastic thought. If Joyce

5. P. 192.

found in Giambattista Vico ("Mr. John Baptister Vickar," as he calls him in the *Wake*) [6] a philosophic spirit congenial to the poetic aims which he set for himself in regard to the treatment of history and the symbol, language and the myth, there is no necessary reason to suppose that his poetic susceptibilities were therefore being "reconstructed," or that he looked upon the new orientation as a process of breaking with the categories of Thomist thought.

Nothing is more evident in regard to Joyce's indebtedness to Vico than that he found in Vico's theme of the *corso-ricorso* movement of history, as developed in the *Scienza Nuova,* a very spacious symbol which could be conveniently taken over for the rehabilitation of history, the soul-and-body history of Everyman which is at the center of the *Wake*. There are fundamental differences of perspective, it is obvious, between Aquinas' work and Vico's. Nothing. but an acute astigmatism could produce a vision of the *Summa Theologiae* and the *Scienza Nuova* on the same plane. It would be misleading and farfetched to suggest that Joyce adopted Vico's corso-ricorso movement for the *Wake* precisely because he saw in it an analogy to the exitus and reditus rhythm of Aquinas' *Summa Theologiae*.[7] There is no way of telling now if on a theoretical level Joyce ever consciously adverted to the correspondence at all—though he of all men was most likely to be sensitive to correspondences of this sort. Certainly at the practical level of poetic structure he explored the analogy fully, and it is in terms of this double law of creation, exitus et reditus, the coming forth and the turning back, that Vico's corso-ricorso rhythm unifies the complex thematic pattern of the *Wake*. Vico's system had a symbolic value for Joyce mostly because it was a system open, like the *Summa,* to history, sacred as well as profane, and in his manipulation of the symbol, Joyce is inclined to accentuate not so much the immanent, natural movement of a four-part cycle as the transcendent rhythm of the ever-recurring thunderclap which comes from outside the cycle to awaken men to the claims of the supernatural and the need of grace.[8]

6. P. 255.
7. Cf. M. D. Chenu, O.P., "The Plan of St. Thomas' *Summa Theologiae*," tr. Ellen Bremner, *Cross Currents, 2* (Winter 1952), 72.
8. Cf. Thomas J. Fitzmorris, "Vico Adamant and Some Pillars of Salt," *Catholic World, 156* (Feb. 1943), 568–77. Fitzmorris points out, "It is ironical that controversy should have raged over Vico's orthodoxy. Personally, he was a devout, almost a scrupulous Catholic" (569). And Fitzmorris goes on to show that Vico's warfare was not against the Scholastics but against "Hobbes, Locke, Spinoza and all those who find the origin of society in a social contract" (570). Though Fitzmorris asserts that "between the Neapolitan and Joyce there is a gap not of years but of eternity" (577), he maintains that "Joyce has distorted Vico's nobly conceived theory with less surface violence and bitterness than Spengler" (577). Cf. A. Robert Caponigri's magisterial study, *Time and Idea: The Theory of History in Giambattista Vico* (Chicago, Henry Regnery, 1953), especially the discussion (ch. 5) of Vico's doctrine of Providence, his "unequivocal theism" (p. 100) : "There is an unbridgeable gulf between the Crocean and the Vichian aesthetic, the Crocean and the Vichian ethics" (p. 106).

If the poet, unlike the God of creation, cannot hope to produce ex nihilo a new being where there was no being before, he can very well imitate the fatherly act of God in bringing order and light out of chaos and darkness, and in giving things their proper names.[9] Within the cosmic unity, as Aquinas thought of it, a transcendent God is the principle of origin and the point of ultimate return. "In our end is our beginning" is only another way of saying "in our beginning is our end." God's ultimate reason for creating, as Aquinas argues, cannot have been other than the divine goodness itself: "God Who is the first cause of all things does not so act in creating as to *acquire* something by His action that He did not possess before: He acts rather so as *to make a gift*, as it were, to another, in virtue solely of His own creative action." [1] The highest communication of His intrinsic goodness which such a transcendent God could give to His creatures would be, as Aquinas sees it, a title to share in some way according to their respective natures in the divine life and happiness, a participation quite gratuitous and the effect solely of His love forever free.

The poet's ability to imitate in parable this aspect of God's fatherly act of creation cannot be more than symbolic, for like all analogies with the infinite, finite human making is always enigmatic and at best but a shadow of the divine analogate. Yet every poem enables us to share in some way in the personal subjectivity of its maker and to enter into communion with the poet's interior life. "Immi ammi Semmi," Joyce remarks shyly at one point in the *Wake*.[2] This quite natural identification of himself with Shem the Penman, Shem the poet, further accentuated by his punning on his own name, Jim or *Jacobus* ("Shem is as short for Shemus as Jem is joky for Jacob"),[3] does not cancel out the fact that all the other characters (including Shaun the Postman, Shem's twin brother, the other half of his soul) are created similitudes of the Joycean personality, each one quite distinct objectively from its maker's personality but each one participating to some degree in that personality which underlies and fashions all the characters, brings them into being.

When the corso-ricorso movement of the *Wake* has come full circle, Joyce describes the return of the flowing river Liffey back to the sea in such a way as unmistakably to symbolize at another level the return, or reditus, of Anna Livia Plurabelle, the psyche or soul of (Everyman) Earwicker, to the Father of origins, the Father of the Creation: "Carry me along, taddy, like you done through the toy fair! If I seen him bearing down on me now under whitespread wings like he'd come from

9. Cf. Albert Béguin, *L'âme romantique et le rêve. Essai sur le romantisme allemand et la poésie française* (nouv. éd. Paris, Librairie Jose Corti, 1946), p. 380.

1. *Contra Gentes,* Lib. III, c. 18 (italics mine) : "Deus autem, qui est primum agens omnium rerum, non sic agit quasi sua actione aliquid acquirat, sed quasi sua actione aliquid largiatur."

2. P. 258.

3. P. 169.

Arkangels, I sink I'd die down over his feet, humbly dumbly, only to washup. Yes, tid. There's where. First. We pass through grass behush the bush to. Whish! A gull. Gulls. Far calls. Coming, far! End here. Us then. Finn, again!" [4]

This final page of the *Wake* succeeds first in suggesting an important theological or Aquinan point about the soul's return to the Father in an economy where sin has come in to distort the soul's Father-likeness, where man's union with God in worship begins as a rule with an act of "washing-up." It also illustrates Joyce's acceptance of the Augustinian-Aquinan outlook on history in which the future, not the past, is conceived of as coming first, a teleological picture of time which represents the past and the present as of importance (for tears or for laughter) only insofar as they are a fulfillment of the circle of the future which God at the center has already circumscribed. Finally the page suggests that at this final moment Joyce, the poet of the finished work, is content that the world of this poem has within human limits made perfectly manifest the worth (value or goodness) of his own creative, poetic resourcefulness—for with Joyce the gull over the waters is a symbol of poetry.

The Jewish critic Jean de Menasce, speaking in *La revue juive* of the world of *Ulysses,* makes an interesting assertion which is even better applicable to the *Wake,* an assertion which goes a long way toward explaining how it is that with Joyce in "the mystery of esthetic" the God of the creation remains at the same time both "within" and "beyond" his handiwork: "Et comme de la divinité, dont on se demande pourquoi elle a créé, on se doit convaincre que Joyce n'a pu créer les personnages d'*Ulysses* que, par un étrange amour unilateral. . . . Dans cette oeuvre décentrée, ou, plus exactement, acentrique, le créateur n'a pas eu à laisser sa marque, puisqu'il lui est immanent." [5]

Recourse on the level of poetics to a theological concept of creation for the purposes of illustrating what happens in art will sooner or later enter that area of "explosive union" (in the words of Erich Przywara) where the concepts of transcendence and immanence seem to collide.[6] If God is at the center of the circle (of the creation, of history), how may one speak as if He were outside the circle, as if His work (or a work made with His as exemplar) were "décentrée, ou plus exactement, acentrique"? In theological terms the polarity, as Przywara puts it, is that between a "God in me" (immanence) and a "God over me" (transcendence), the known unknown. Hence arises the continuous movement between the two given poles of "love in union" and "reverence from

4. P. 628.
5. Jean de Menasce, *"Ulysses," La revue juive, 1* (Nov. 1925), 761.
6. Erich Przywara, S.J., *Polarity. A German Catholic's Interpretation of Religion,* tr. A. C. Bouquet (London, Oxford Univ. Press, 1935), p. 37.

afar." In Joycean aesthetic terms, the polarity, by analogy, may be illustrated by pointing to that polarity which exists in his work between the autobiographical and the impersonal strands. On the one hand, we have all the autobiographical allusions (sometimes lyrical, sometimes ironic) present on almost every page of his work from *Stephen Hero* through the *Wake,* and represented in his ceaseless preoccupation with but one subject, "dear, dirty Dublin." "Every journey from Ireland is a flight into Egypt," states a late comment of Joyce on the *Portrait* in one of the large Paris Library notebooks. Counterpointing all this, especially in the *Wake,* there is the complete neutrality of *persona,* an impersonality of poetic utterance which all but succeeds in the end through comic detachment in refining the author altogether out of any existence in the poem. What more can we say about Joyce, the author of the *Wake,* creator of its world, than that he is a "known unknown"? Tindall notes this latter aspect of impersonality, or "transcendence," in Joyce's work, and uses it as the key to Joyce's meaning much as Jean de Menasce uses the aspect of "immanence." Tindall writes of Joyce's achievement in the *Wake:* "Joyce found the absolute in time and thereby reconciled it with eternity. He found eternity in the historical pattern, the family, and man. Above all things, he found eternity in art. The work of art, in which all things are reconciled, is an image of the absolute. . . . Formal, complete, at once in time and out of it, *Finnegans Wake* is a symbol of eternity." [7]

"Immanence" or "transcendence"? Once the poet (or critic) approaches poetry with the theological analogy of creation more or less consciously in mind, both concepts are involved. Within the analogy, it is not possible to illustrate the one without at least by implication invoking the other. It is no wonder that Joyce's conception of the artist-creator, derived as it is from the Thomist conception of Deity, should oscillate between the maximum form of personality and that of impersonality in relation to the "created" work.[8] Tindall's description of the *Wake* as a "symbol of eternity" is apt in view of the simultaneity of occurrence which Joyce manages between all the recorded events of human history and all the events of prehistorical antiquity, the forgotten past.

The thundering voice of Deity which breaks into the *Wake* above the din of the tavern [9] and over the uproar of Phoenix Park (Eden) [1] cannot belong to the sublimely indifferent "fingernail paring" Lord of Creation Who is described in the *Portrait.* The doctrine of metempsy-

7. Tindall, *James Joyce,* p. 93.

8. Cf. Przywara, *Polarity,* p. 70, and Paul Henry, S.J., "The Christian Philosophy of History," translated from the French text of the Philip Maurice Deneke Lecture at Lady Margaret Hall, Oxford, Feb. 23, 1950, *Theological Studies, 13* (Sept. 1952), 425.

9. P. 314.

1. P. 90.

chosis, of the soul's perpetual return and perpetual rebeginning, is one of the dominant themes of *Ulysses*. Inherent in this doctrine are a determinism and pessimism which might well turn history into a nightmare, as Stephen perceives: "What if that nightmare gave you a back kick?" [2] Although the *Wake* takes over Vico's cyclic view of history, there is in the *Wake* (as in Vico) an optimistic effort to penetrate the meaning of history, which postulates beyond the time-bound the presence of the timeless transcendent One, Who cares for man, for his laughter and tears.[3]

If the work of art "above all things" is an "image of the absolute," it must be because a work of art more successfully than other images contrived by man reflects the immanence of personality at the same time that it symbolizes an impersonality of transcendent timelessness. The metaphorical creations of the poets give an insight into the human situation, an insight which will remain valid so long as the human situation lasts. Is it not in this way that eternity in art is beyond the fashions and the categories of time?

The dreamer of the *Wake* would have had no dream at all unless Joyce had dreamed it first, or should we say, unless Joyce were "dreaming" simultaneously? But if we say that, we must distinguish between the artlessness of the unconscious *Wake*-dreamer's dream and the artfulness of Joyce's symbolic dream. It is in the dream as symbol that the transcendence of eternity is found. It was in order to construct the symbol that Joyce ransacked the resources of the forgotten and recorded past and of the posthistorical eschatological future, sacred and mythological: the events of the imagination, what goes on in a dream, what comes to pass in a song. It would be difficult to think of a better analogy than the *Wake* to illustrate at a poetic level what Aquinas means when at the beginning of the tenth quaestio of the *Summa Theologiae,* he defines the eternity of the transcendent God in the words of Boethius, as "a perfection of life, without beginning or end, possessed simultaneously and without any flaw" ("Interminabilis vitae tota simul et perfecta possessio").[4] From an analogously atemporal vantage point, the "transcendent" poet-maker of the *Wake* takes in with one steady, sweeping glance the temporal events real and imaginary of past, present, and future, and expresses himself most fully by a work in which all these

2. *Ulysses*, p. 35.

3. Cf. *The New Science of Giambattista Vico,* tr. from 3d. ed. (1744) by Thomas Goddard Bergin and Max Harold Fisch (Ithaca, Cornell Univ. Press, 1948), p. 99 (Bk. II, ch. 1, Nicolini para. 366): "Divine providence has so conducted human affairs that, starting from the poetic theology which regulated them by certain sensible signs, . . . and by means of the natural theology which demonstrates providence by eternal reasons which do not fall under the senses, the nations were disposed to receive [revealed] theology in virtue of a supernatural faith, superior not only to the senses but to human reason itself."

4. Cf. *S.T.*, I, q. 10, a. 1, obj. 1.

events have their own quite special existence as interrelated parts of his poem: for example, Adam's fall from grace in the Garden of Eden; the fall of the hod carrier Tim Finnegan from his ladder; Earwicker's fall from respectability in Phoenix Park, Dublin; Humpty Dumpty's fall from his perch on the wall; Everyman's daily fall from grace. Within this single, atemporal dimension all the temporal consequences of the fall, in guilt and in sorrow, are comprehensively included: the frustrated love of Tristram and Iseult, of Swift and Vanessa, Earwicker's nameless, unconfessed love for his own adolescent daughter. Confronted with the vision of the core of pain at the heart of things human, at the center of the created being of his poetry, the poet-maker of the *Wake* is not troubled: "O foenix culprit," he says, for having seen the end he sees the contradiction canceled. "Remember, maid [thou who art *made*], thou dust art powder but Cinderella thou must return." [5] Like Aquinas' "exitus et reditus," Joyce's "Vico road goes round and round to meet where terms begin." [6]

At the poetic level, it is precisely where terms or words begin that the creative polarity between transcendence and immanence begins to operate. God's world ceaselessly writes its own runes, it may be without any assistance from the poets; if we pay attention to its writings, the world may tell us many things not only about itself but also about its maker. God is revealing Himself in the world; the poet or mythmaker has to interpret that revelation; the poet in the process reveals himself. If the poet wishes to reveal himself as a poet, he must know how to hide himself in the "wrunes" of language. These wrunes may afford no more than a partial revelation, but without them there would be no poetic revelation or image at all. The poet writes his image in language much as God writes his image in man.

When Aquinas has finished his discourse on God as He is in Himself (in the First Part of the *Summa Theologiae*), he turns to a consideration of man (in the Second Part) with the following comment by way of transition: "Now that there has been a treatment of the Exemplar, that is God, it remains for us to consider His image, man." [7] It is through the creative word of God that this image, man, comes into being. It is through the creative word of the poet that the image of the poet comes alive in the poem. The more the poet's creative resourcefulness resembles at its level of language the creative resourcefulness of God, the more coherently complex and diversified will his language images be.

An interesting point about all Joyce's artist-portraits is the signif-

5. P. 440.
6. P. 452.
7. *S.T.*, I–II, Prolog.: "Postquam praedictum est de exemplari, scilicet de Deo . . . restat ut consideremus de eius imagine, idest, de homine."

icant fact that save for poor Shem the Penman's writing with "gallic acid" on the "only foolscap available, his own body," [8] and save for a few of Stephen's languid fin-de-siècle verses (to Emma Clery—E.C.) at the end of the *Portrait*,[9] these hero-artists (including the Stephen of *Ulysses*) are almost never portrayed as writing any poetry, as creating any art. These images (or portraits) of the poet do not themselves write poems. It would not, of course, be necessary to conceive of the God of the creation as immanent in His universe if the universe had never come into being. The question of the poet's immanence in his poetry can become relevant only when his poems have been written, when they have reached a status where they have an existence of their own. Having become thus totally immanent, he is in a position where we can speak of his having "refined himself out of existence" to such an extent as not to *seem* present at all.

The comparison between God's act of creation and the act of the poet involves a very special analogy between the divine act and the unconscious part of the poet's activity. "God is an artist first and an engineer afterwards," says Gilby.[1] And Aquinas at one point calls attention to the role of poetic analogies in "seducing the reason" (*similitudinibus ratio seducatur*),[2] in leading the reason to a grasp of reality which is below the threshold of conscious, conceptual thought. At another point Aquinas asserts that human knowledge, in comparison with the divine knowledge of the eternal *Word,* is always a case of light with a more or less generous admixture of shadows ("Ipsa cognitio creaturae, tenebris est admixta").[3]

From beginning to end the *Wake* is concerned with the *poesis* of this shadow-side of life. At its simplest level the whole book tells the story of the tavern keeper Earwicker's dream in which he faces for the first time the humiliation of acknowledging that in the depths of his unconscious he is in love with his own daughter Isobel, that his love for his wife Maggie is no longer more than a mask of consciousness which he wears to hide from his daytime self the guilt of his love "without a name." "Tisn't only tonight you're anacheronistic!" [4] he tells himself with sorrow at one moment in the shifting dream sequence as he thinks of his wife, no longer as she is now beside him in bed but as she was

8. P. 185.
9. *Portrait,* pp. 260–3. Cf. R. P. Blackmur, "The Artist as a Hero: A Disconsolate Chimera," *Art News, 50* (Sept. 1951), 19, col. 1.
1. Thomas Gilby, O.P., *Phoenix and Turtle. The Unity of Knowing and Being* (New York, Longmans, Green, 1950), p. 149.
2. *I Sent.*, Prolog., q. 1, a. 5, ad 3ᵐ.
3. *De Pot.*, q. 4, a. 2, ad 14ᵐ.
4. P. 202.

when she too was young like Isobel, the Iseult of his dreams: "Just a young thin pale soft shy slim slip of a thing then, sauntering, by silva-moonlake." [5] But having faced his guilt and taken on its sorrow in the burden of his dream, Earwicker wakes up to face the new day with equanimity, for in the poesis of dreaming his soul had found a way of accepting by artistic projection that side of his life on which the shadows lay. With the sun rising on a new morning, his dream comes to a close with the victory of St. Patrick over the druids: "Lo, the laud of laurens now orielising benedictively when saint and sage have said their say." [6]

In the perspectives of the *Wake,* the poet ("Shem Macadamson," as Joyce calls him) [7] participates like other men, like Earwicker for example, in the consequences of a long-ago fall from grace. In the light and shadow of his guilt-consciousness, his poesis, imitative at best of God's creative act from afar, will inevitably lead him at times to actualize by symbol making the *tenebrae possibilitatis* (in Aquinas' words) [8] which make up the dream stuff of his own not always reasoning soul. Unless the analogy between poetry making and world making can account for the activity of the unconscious in Shem Macadamson's poetry making, that analogy must somehow seem inadequate as an approach to the symbols which Shem creates. Is there any sense in which the unconscious can be likened to God?

The English Dominican Victor White in his study *God and the Unconscious* has noted how many of the nineteenth-century pre-Jungian psychologists ascribed to the unconscious almost all of the attributes which most religious traditions have ascribed to the deity: They speak of it as ceaselessly operative, untiring, and sleepless, unfettered by the categories of time or space.[9] Gustav Carus in his *Psyche* (1848) described the unconscious as the source of all consciousness itself, and speaks of it as "the source of all *können*," of all possibility and power, infinite, unfathomable, and never directly to be known as it is in itself. In discussing Eduard von Hartmann's *Philosophy of the Unconscious,* White remarks that von Hartmann's unconscious "is hardly distinguishable from the 'God' of the traditional natural theology of, for example, St. Thomas Aquinas." [1]

The religious and prophetic poets have not failed to look within their own souls in order to find a witness to deity. To the "dark, deep thoroughfare" within, which modern psychiatrists call "the unconscious," they often enough gave the name of God. "Stand forth, O soul, stand

5. Ibid.
6. P. 613.
7. P. 187.
8. *De Pot.,* q. 4, a. 2, ad 14[m].
9. Victor White, O.P., *God and the Unconscious* (London, Haverhill, 1952), p. 30.
1. Ibid., p. 31.

forth and give thy witness," Tertullian enjoined the early Christians: "Look into thy soul and you will find that God is everywhere." [2]

The poet who chooses to accept the postulate of an unconscious and to exploit it as a conscious part of his art puts himself in a very special way in need of a coherent formulation of psychic experience already available on the language level. One way to express that need in the modern idiom is to say that the poet of the unconscious (as all imaginative poets are to some extent) is in need of a myth. In the privately printed edition of *A Vision,* which appeared in 1925, Yeats explains, "I wished for a system of thought that would leave my imagination free to create as it chose and yet make all it created, or could create, part of the one history, and that the soul's." [3]

Unlike Yeats, Joyce never took time out from poetry to construct his own private, independent myth. But in the poetry of the *Wake* itself (a work which is at the same time monomyth and vision) one finds Joyce's final version of his own poetic effort to create out of the stuff of language an adequate history of the soul's unconscious life: "For that (the rapt one warns) is what papyr is meed of, made of, hides and hints and misses in prints." [4] Rather than attempt to construct outside of poetry an imaginative pattern or symbolic organization of unconscious psychic life, Joyce preferred to tap the vast resources of myth and psychic symbolism which already existed in all the world's literatures which he knew. By cutting in a main here and leading out a conduit there, he sought to make each reservoir feed into his own vast dam of metaphor and myth. "It is not a miseffectual whyacinthinous riot of blots and blurs . . . it only looks as like it as damn it." [5] This dam of allegory and metaphor, of myth and symbolism, is brimful, as Joyce is at pains to tell us, of plunderings "even to the hidmost coignings of the earth." [6] Joyce represents the poet of the *Wake* as a qualified "spickspookspokesman of our spectresque silentiousness" [7] who has authority to speak for us in the present because he "has acquired accretions of terricious matter whilst loitering in the past." [8]

Joyce takes his myths seriously but not solemnly. He expects his readers to take them in the same way: "I would rather spinooze you

2. Cf. Tertullian's *Apologia* for Christianity in "De Testimonio Animae," *The Writings of Tertullian,* Ante-Nicene Library, *1,* 37 ff. (Translation adopted in this essay is from White's *God and the Unconscious,* p. 39.) Cf. Frederick A. Pottle, "Wordsworth and Freud, or the Theology of the Unconscious," Commencement Address, May 26, 1948, at General Theological Seminary, reprinted in *Bulletin of the General Theological Seminary* (June 1948), p. 6.

3. Cf. Cleanth Brooks, "Yeats: The Poet as Myth-Maker," *Modern Poetry and the Tradition* (Chapel Hill, Univ. of North Carolina Press, 1939), pp. 175–6.

4. P. 20.

5. P. 118.

6. Pp. 118–9.

7. P. 427.

8. P. 114

one from the grimm gests of Jacko and Esaup, fable one, feeble too." [9]
At the same time one could not make "a more freudful mistake," to use
Joyce's expression,[1] than to imagine that one might penetrate to the
significance of the *Wake's* "idioglossary" [2] by a kind of unconscious
intuition. However much these myths in their dream-logic and dream-
grammar may seem to resemble the fantasy of sleep, the alert reader
soon perceives that the illusion which Joyce is striving to create is not
the product of incoherent dreaming but of most consciously controlled
and patterned comic art. The illusion comes as much from the comedy
as the comedy from the illusion: out of the stasis of arrested contemplation (not loitering, but reconnoitering) the illusion and the comedy
both arise.

It might appear at first sight as if Joyce's interest in the language of
the unconscious and of the myth was a relatively late development, a
sign that the influences of his Zurich residence had been in this respect
decisive in the development of his later style. It is not at first sight
obvious how the complex linguistic experiments of his maturity are, at
a theoretical level, in line with the early Thomist formulation of his
aesthetics and with his early conception of the poet as somehow participating in and imitating the creative action (the causing a passage
from nonbeing to being, which is *poièsis*) of the God of the creation.
There is a passage in the *Portrait,* however, which is strongly prophetic
of the development Joyce's own style was later to take and of the particular sense in which Joyce would later utilize the analogy of creation
to justify that development. Stephen is represented in the *Portrait,* on
the eve of his departure from Ireland, as gazing upward at the sight of
the wild geese in flight (a symbol of his own projected exile) : "A sense
of fear of the unknown moved in the heart of his weariness, a fear of
symbols and portents, of the hawklike man whose name he bore soaring
out of his captivity on osier woven wings, of Thoth, the god of writers,
writing with a reed upon a tablet and bearing on his narrow ibis head
the cusped moon." [3]

Joyce is not the Stephen Dedalus of the *Portrait* passage, but the pas-

9. P. 414.
1. P. 411.
2. P. 423.
3. *Portrait,* p. 264. Cf. Plato's *Phaedrus,* toward the end, where Socrates recounts the
myth of Theuth (or Thoth), "the father of written letters," in his effort to convince
Phaedrus of the superiority of the spoken to the written word. Socrates argues that
"the man who fancies . . . that something clear and certain will issue from his writing"
must "be a very simple person," and that whereas the written word lacks the necessary
assistance of its *father* (the author) to defend itself, the spoken word may call upon
its father (the speaker) to defend it, help it, and tell it to whom to address itself, and
to whom not to do so. Thamus tells Theuth: "O most ingenious Theuth, one man can
bring an art to birth, but it takes another to judge what share of harm or benefit the
art may have for those who are going to use it." (I have used Lane Cooper's translation of the *Phaedrus,* Ithaca, Cornell Univ. Press, 1948, pp. 65–6, *Steph.* 275.)

sage is at least illuminating since it presents an early portrait of a word-
artist called after Daedalus, the contriver of the labyrinth, who sees no
necessary incompatibility at the practical level of poesis between "the
symbols and portents" of the mythological unknown and the aesthetic
principles of poetry as "making," which in the *Portrait* are derivative
in no small part from Aquinas' metaphysics of creation. Aquinas in his
commentary on Aristotle's *Metaphysics* speaks with praise of the *poetae
theologizantes* of antiquity, and points out that even the philosopher,
like the poet, must be to some extent (*aliqualiter*) a friend or lover of
the fable ("Philomythes, idest amator fabulae, quod proprium est poetarum").[4] Aquinas assumes, without seeing any need to prove it, that
the poets are necessarily myth lovers and mythmakers. The reason which
Aquinas gives to support his belief that the philosopher must be "to
some extent" interested in mythology is that philosophy like poetry
begins in wonder, in the unknown wonderful causes of things (*principia
mirabila rerum*).[5] The most interesting point about these texts for the
student of poetics is that Aquinas takes it so much for granted that
poetry when it assumes for its theme the wonderful (*circa miranda
versatur*) will sooner or later come to an invocation of the myth. Modern theories of poetic idiom would seem to have arisen out of the need
which modern criticism felt for a new literary tool to control the discussions of a poetry which, more overtly than before, had cut its moor-
ings with the conscious (the rationalistic, the scientific, that part of
the mind which is disconcerted by mystery and incongruity) and was
sailing the uncharted seas of mythic symbolism, the "enchafèd flood" of
wonder and of the unconscious.

In *Criterion* in 1927 John Middleton Murry asserted that the time
had come for setting over against the scientific philosophism of the post-
Renaissance, "not indeed the conscious philosophy, but the unconscious,
or semi-conscious, assumptions of art." [6] Writing some twenty years
earlier, the French Jesuit Rousselot in *L'intellectualisme de saint
Thomas* had concluded that in the perspectives of Aquinas' intellectual-
ism these unconscious assumptions above all others were the proper

4. "Cum enim aliquos manifestos effectus videamus, quorum causa nos latet, eorum
tunc causam admiramur. Et ex quo admiratio fuit causa inducens ad philosophiam, patet
quod philosophus est aliqualiter philomythes, idest amator fabulae, quod proprium. est
poetarum. Unde primi, qui per modum quemdam fabularem de principiis rerum tracta-
verunt, dicti sunt poetae theologizantes. . . . Causa autem, quare philosophus compara-
tur poetae, est ista, quia uterque circa miranda versatur. Nam fabulae, circa quas
versantur poetae, ex quibusdam mirabilibus constituuntur." *I Lib. Metaphys.*, lect.
3.

5. Cf. *II Lib. Sent.*, dist. 18, q. 1, a. 3, solutio: "Admiratio ex duobus causatur; scilicet
ex hoc quod alicujus effectus causa occulta est, et ex eo quod aliquid in re videtur per
quod aliter esse deberet."

6. John Middleton Murry, "Towards a Synthesis," *Criterion*, 5 (June 1927), 302.

province of poetry: "La poésie ne persuade pas l'intelligence, mais incline la cogitative." [7]

Literary critics and theorists have not been alone in giving attention
to the vast areas of the unconscious which make up in large part the life
of most men and peoples, areas which modern literature (the poetry, let
us say, of the *Wake,* or the prose of Kafka's novels) sets out quite consciously to exploit and to explore. Theologians no less than others have
been sensitive to the import and importance of this shadow-side of life.
The German Protestant theologian Hans Schaer says of the "collective
unconscious": "It *re-presents* the memories not only of the individual
man but of all mankind. In it are contained the instincts and their psychic analogues—the archetypes." [8] Having accepted such a postulate,
adds Schaer, theology cannot afford not to take cognizance of the myth
since for those to whom myth is a living thing, it functions primarily as
"the experience and expression of what happens in the soul." [9] The
German Catholic theologian Romano Guardini declares: "C'est l'homme
déchu qui s'exprime par le mythe." [1] Guardini distinguishes, as does
Aquinas, between the concepts mythology and revelation; like Aquinas,
Guardini absolves literature (the literature of the myth) from the responsibility of performing the function of Scripture. Neither Aquinas
nor Guardini looks to the symbols and metaphors of mythology to give
us a scriptural revelation.

As Aquinas conceived of the matter, the "literal," that is, the natural,
truth of poetry *was* its "poetic" truth, the best that it could aspire to,
and he was content if a poem said poetically what it had to say, since he
did not look to poetry to supply moral, allegorical, or anagogic meanings
in the religious sense.[2] Supernatural faith is not required to read literature, not even to read the Scriptures as literature. It *is required,* at least
so far as Aquinas (or Guardini) conceives of the matter, to assent to any
part of Scripture, however literal *or* metaphorical the expression, as part
of the deposit of a supernatural revelation, especially when this part is
not self-evidently true. The relevance of the myth to poetry might be
clearer if we paid less attention to our modern distinction between truth
that is "literal" (by which we usually mean "factual") and truth that is
"poetic" (by which we seem to mean something like "imaginative").

7. Pierre Rousselot, S.J., *L'intellectualisme de saint Thomas* (Paris, Librairies Félix
Alcan et Guillaumin Réunies, 1908), p. 174.

8. Hans Schaer, *Religion and the Cure of Souls in Jung's Psychology,* tr. R. F. C.
Hull (London, Routledge and Kegan Paul, 1951), p. 69.

9. Ibid., p. 70

1. Romano Guardini, "Le mythe et la vérité de la révélation," tr. Jeanne Ancelet-
Houstache, *Recherches de science religieuse, 37* (1950), 174. Cf. trans. in Eng. by Marie-
Christine Hellin and Sally S. Cunneen, *Cross Currents, 1* (Winter 1951), 3–12.

2. *Quodl.,* VII, q. 16, a. 15.

Instead we might talk, with poetry in mind, of the distinction between "dogmatic" and "imaginative" truths. The myth in that case is an important "imaginative" or "poetic" truth which theology itself would not care to ignore.

By keeping the myth on the side of the imagination, one keeps it on the side of poetry: at the same time one preserves a domain of "dogmatic" or "revealed" truths which the poet, if he chooses to, can journey into with little loss as a rule to his poetry. Whether one accepts these "dogmas" or "revelations" as one's own or not is another question—a question which concerns theology very much but which poetics does not need to be able to answer. At least it never has answered, and it has had a long career.

Poetry has never been the gainer by a collapse of theology into myth. English poets who have made the most meaningful use of theological perspectives (poets like Spenser, Milton, Vaughan, or Hopkins) have invariably accorded theology a privileged position, which is qualitatively different from the status of myth. When men did "put their faith in myth," they were under the impression that they were putting their faith in something more than a poetic fiction. It does not aid progress in poetics to talk about the need of a "new myth" when what one means is the need of a new or revived faith in dogma, a more alert awareness of the importance or value of theological points of view, even when these points of view, it may be, are not one's own.

When Aquinas speaks of the fictiones poeticae,[3] he is not being derogatory to "fiction," or myth, or poetry. Nor is he setting up a wall of exclusion between poetry and revelation, myth and theology. In one of the hymns on the Blessed Sacrament commonly attributed to Aquinas, the poet makes use of the pelican "fiction" to symbolize an aspect of the Eucharistic Christ. The presence of Christ in the Eucharist was for Aquinas no fictio poetica (like the pelican) but a revealed truth (veritas) which led him to accord it an intellectual assent rather than merely an imaginative sympathy:

> Credo quidquid dixit Dei Filius,
> Nil hoc verbo Veritatis verius.

Whatever the reader of his poem may think about the Eucharist (and many modern readers presumably think differently), an understanding of the poem will be distorted unless one sees that within the poem the

---

3. *Quodl.*, VII, q. 6, a. 16, ad 2^m. With Aquinas' characterization of the poets' work as fictiones poeticae, compare Vico's remark in *The New Science*, p. 292 (Bk. III, Sec. II, ch. 16; Nicolini para. 891) : ". . . Horace avows himself to be no poet because he lacks the knack or the wit to maintain what he calls the colors of words, *colores operum*, which means the same thing as the poetic untruths of Aristotle's phrase, for in Plautus we find *obtinere colorem* in the sense of telling a lie that under every aspect has the appearance of truth, which is what a good fable must be."

Eucharist is taken not at the level of myth (as Yeats, for example, takes the "phases of the moon" in his poetry) but at the level of the supernatural *revelabile,* a revealed reality inviting intellectual assent and exploration first, and imaginative representation after that.

The literary critic will hardly wish to insist that the reader must hold the same theological beliefs which Aquinas held concerning the Eucharist in order to read the *Adoro Te Devote* and to judge that it is a good poem. Nor is the reader who holds the same theological beliefs as Aquinas thereby prevented from appreciating the poetry of the *Wake,* at those points ("Tavernry in Feast," for example) where the theme of the eating of the god is developed in mythical symbols and terms: "All we wants is to get peace for possession. We dinned unnerstunned why you sassad about thirteen to aloafen, sor, kindly repeat! . . . And smotther-mock Gramm's laws! . . . In the buginning is the woid, in the muddle is the sound-dance and thereinofter you're in the unbewised again." [4] Nevertheless the achievement of Joyce's poetry, even at such comic points, has a gravity that seems to transcend the purely mythic dimension, a gravity that comes from theological perspectives which are to be read not purely as fictions. We look not to the Grimms' fairy tales ("smotther-mock Gramm's laws!") but to the story of the Last Supper, which the story of the eating of Earwicker, the victimized tavern keeper, can possibly parallel in allegory or parody but never itself call to life.

There appears to be this double equivocation about most of Joyce's myths: (1) the profound equivocation inherent in myth itself and (2) the added equivocation in Joyce's handling or tone: Is not the myth constantly being taken, or at least treated as if taken, at a level of significance where it is a shadow or symbol of a reality (maybe a lost reality) which has "substance" outside of mythology, outside of the poem? The theologically minded poet, like the theologically minded reader, operates on the assumption that between myth and revelation ("the truths of theology") there are frontiers, if not exactly a wall of exclusion. It is not poetry's business to define these frontiers, but poetry has never lost anything by recognizing their existence. The passing back and forth between the frontiers creates, it may be, an equivocation, but if the equivocation makes possible a new theological dimension to poetry, poetry need not fear losing anything by the transaction. If I am correct in my surmise that there exists a double equivocation in most of

When Aquinas says (*I Post. Analyt.,* lect. 1) that a certain (good) food can *seem* loathsome if it is represented in a loathsome manner, and adds, "Ad hoc ordinatur Poetica," his context makes it clear that he means to insist that a lofty (or religious) subject must be well represented verbally or it will seem "flat." Religious subjects more than others exact skilful poetic representation. "Religious" poetry often fails quite dismally—at least as poetry—from a lack of "imaginative color" in the language.

4. P. 378. Cf. Michel Butor, "Petite croisière préliminaire à une reconnaissance de l'archipel Joyce," *La vie intellectuelle, 16* (Mai, 1948), 104–35. Butor calls *Finnegans Wake* "ce burlesque mystère de mort et de résurrection" (128).

Joyce's myths, and that this equivocation involves a theological dimension in Joyce's mythopoesis, it would seem natural to attribute this added dimension to Joyce's theological categories, which for the most part, in substance, if not always in derivation, are those of Aquinan thought.

Theological discussion of the myth, as of the symbol, not seldom circles back much in the same way as does poetics to the question of the polarity between transcendence and immanence in the act of creation. Guardini says that the primitive myth (if we accept his hypothesis that such a thing can be identified) has two sources, both immanent: "l'une dans la réalité de la nature, l'autre dans la profondeur inconsciente de l'âme." [5] Primitive myth, taking the world and man's own soul as the sources for its account of actuality, can have had but a dim understanding of the concept of a transcendent God, outside the world, not part of it, not the effect of the soul's self-expression but the ultimate cause and ground of the soul's being able to operate at all. Few poets, if any, are able to take myth today in the same primitively immanent terms. In practice, if not always in theory, most poets make use of the symbols of myth much as Joyce does the "wrunes of the world" to suggest quite consciously a suprasensible reality, to introduce perspectives of transcendence and by so doing to awaken resonances as much theological as poetic. As Owen Barfield has pointed out in *Poetic Diction,* we are no longer "primitive men," and "our poets can no longer write poetry of the *instinctive* kind." The kind of poetry for which the individual poet becomes increasingly responsible implies the operation of the reason rather than of unconscious principle. As Barfield notes, the bare fact of verbal expression always implies, and always has implied, that the poet is at work making meaning in some *conscious* sense.[6] The more sophisticated and cultivated and critical our culture becomes, the less and less satisfactory becomes primitive myth as the natural expression of man's being and consciousness, and the more conscious must the poet become of his responsibility to "create meaning" out of language itself.

The poet today, as Barfield says, "has in certain respects to fight *against* language, making up the poetic deficit [in words as we now use them] out of his private balance." [7] If Barfield is right, it would seem to follow that a poet like Joyce would be in an initially favorable position since so many of the words and symbols which made up his experience of reality and language had a privileged theological resonance; they

5. Guardini, "Le mythe et la vérité de la révélation," *Recherches de science religieuse,* 37 (1950), 168.

6. Owen Barfield, *Poetic Diction* (London, Faber and Gwyer, 1928), pp. 103, 110, 174.

7. Ibid., p. 110.

were "in possession" of the tradition. The "private balance" of Joyce's verbal resources was not meager. The "ancestral words" which he inherited possessed not only the ordinary metaphorical virtualities but also latent theological values, a "richness of usage" that had been given to them by the speech and poetry of many theologically minded men who had gone before. Here were resources which he could tap in externalizing through language his own experience, and in making conscious meaning out of the unconscious maelstrom of shadowy thought and shifting dream imagery.

There is certainly nothing "primitive" or "unconscious" about Joyce's employment of myth. In the mythopoesis of *Finnegans Wake,* he is the most sophisticated, self-conscious, and deliberate of artists. Myth may be initially an unconscious projection of the mind's psychic contents, but Joyce, not "patient" to myth but most active in its creation, controls at every moment the movement of his mythical, symbolic projections. The point of control is largely theological. The avowal of personal faith is not explicit in the book and seems in the main to be absent, but the whole mythic material in the poetry revolves around a core of theological acceptance.

8

The Root Language of Shem

As often as I think of that unbloody
housewarmer, Shem Skrivenitch, always cutting
my prhose to please his phrase, bogorror, I
declare I get the jawache! . . . He's weird,
I tell you, and middayevil down to his
vegetable soul. . . . He used to be avowdeed as
he ought to be vitandist. . . .
   —But for what, thrice truthful teller,
Shaun of grace? . . .
   —For his root language, if you ask me
whys, Shaun replied . . .
                Finnegans Wake [1]

"I SHOULD imagine that the name Hermes has to do with speech, and signifies that he is the interpreter, or messenger, or thief, or liar, or bargainer; all that sort of thing has a great deal to do with language." [2] So Plato represents Socrates discoursing half jocularly with Hermogenes at one point in the *Cratylus*. Hermogenes like Shaun is not amused by farfetched etymologies.

Socrates can hardly be said at any point in the dialogue to treat etymology as a serious category of thought, but throughout he shows a qualified poetic admiration for this species of linguistic fact: "Yes, my dear friend; but then you know that the original names have been long ago buried and disguised by people sticking on and stripping off letters for the sake of euphony, and bedizening them in all sorts of ways." [3]

No serious student of phonology or morphology in Plato's day or in our own has had much to learn, it may be, from Socrates' etymologies in the *Cratylus*. As a study in poetic diction they are not without their relevance. Nature, art, and chance all come into play in the poet's formation of his language. Poets like Shem do not use different words from the rest of us but they tend to take our common words at the "root"

1. Pp. 423–4 (emphasis mine). Unless otherwise indicated, page references to Joyce's works in this chapter refer to *Finnegans Wake*.
2. *Dialogues of Plato*, tr. B. Jowett, *1* (New York, Macmillan, 1892), 351 (*Steph.* 408).
3. Ibid., p. 358 (*Steph.* 414).

level, and consequently at a level deeper down than most of us ordinarily have the patience or the art ourselves to go. Down at this root level the lines of analogy everywhere intersect more closely and the metaphysical, moral, mythological, and historical interpenetrations of meaning are more easily uncovered for the seeing eye to notice.

As recent linguistic studies show more and more clearly, the root meanings of words tend deviously to proliferate in usage. Dwight L. Bolinger has pointed out, for example, that the whims of linguistic reality cannot be realistically described without taking into account what he describes as "root-forming morphemes" and "root-forming phones-themes," that is, basic units of variable meaning within any given word which are capable (because of some sight or sound resemblance to other units) of entering into new combinations and making new sense: "Most speakers of English, when they hear ambush, are likely to think of some-one hiding in the *bushes*. Likewise with *hierarchy,* one tends to hear the element *higher*." [4]

How much nonsense is constitutive of the fictio poetica (as Aquinas describes metaphor), of the "fibfib fabrications" [5] which Shem is out to set down in the ". . . soundscript" language [6] of the *Wake?* Shaun's characterization of Shem as "middayevil" is not without its point. E. R. Curtius has called the *Etymologiarum libri* "the basic book of the entire Middle Ages." [7] The "Etymologies" of Isidore of Seville, like the ety-mologies of the *Cratylus,* are certainly farfetched "fables" if one is look-ing for the matter-of-fact (or "matter of fict," as Shem puts it) [8] philo-logical history of a word. As essays in the poetic perception of analogies, these etymologies are almost always interesting. Rousselot maintains that it was at the "fable" or "poetic" level rather than at the level of metaphysics that these etymologies were honored by the serious thinkers of the high Middle Ages.[9] Be that as it may, there are few questions which Aquinas ever turns to where he does not sooner or later invoke the authority of *Isidorus*. Frequently enough Aquinas invokes Isidore's authority only to dispute it, as when somebody argues from the *Etymol-ogies* that superstition (*superstitio*) is not a vice contrary to religion since Cicero speaks of parents who prayed to God that their children might be *superstites,* or survivors.[1] In general one might say that Aqui-

---

4. Dwight L. Bolinger, "Rime, Assonance, and Morpheme Analysis," *Word* (Journal of the Linguistic Circle of New York), 6 (Aug. 1950), 128. Cf. Bolinger, "On Defin-ing the Morpheme," *Word, 4* (April 1948), 18–23.

5. P. 36.

6. P. 219.

7. Curtius, *European Literature,* p. 496.

8. P. 532.

9. Rousselot, *L'intellectualisme de saint Thomas,* p. 172.

1. *S.T.,* II–II, q. 92, a. 1, ad 2ᵐ. In his commentary on Aristotle's *De Anima,* Bk. III, ch. iii (428ᵇ 10–429ᵃ 9), Aquinas observes (lectio 6) that the name for the imagination (*phantasia*) is from the Greek *phos* for light, "whence comes *phanos,* i.e. 'appearance'

nas appeals to the etymological argument whenever it favors his own, and that he disputes it whenever his own argument has anything to lose thereby.[2]

In either case it is clear that Aquinas considered these "etymological" arguments to be indubitably in possession in the contemporary tradition and that he himself was deeply appreciative, at least qua artist, of Isidore's poetic resourcefulness. Gilson maintains against Rousselot that the great medieval thinkers took these "etymologies" as seriously as everybody else. At one point in Les idées et les lettres, Gilson describes the etymological methods of the medieval exegetes of Scripture in such a way as to furnish Shaun with good justification for labeling his brother Shem the Punman as "middayevil down to his vegetable soul." In his essay, "De quelques raisonnements scriptuaires usités au moyen âge," Gilson remarks: "En fait, les étymologistes du moyen âge ont été victimes des analogies morphologiques les plus accidentelles et les plus extérieures, et le passage des mots aux idées s'effectue constamment chez eux sur la foi de ces ressemblances superficielles. . . . La règle, pour tout penseur médiéval, est que lorsque deux mots se ressemblent, les choses qu'ils désignent se ressemblent, de sorte que l'on peut toujours passer de l'un de ces mots à la signification de l'autre." [3]

To pass from sound to sense may not be good logic but it is to some degree characteristic of the language of all poetry and indeed of any kind of vital speech. Accidental and superficial resemblances in the spoken or written forms of words may not be a good basis on which to argue philosophically to analogies in being or essence, but the poet has ever found such resemblances a blessing: "Every letter is a godsend," [4] as Shem the Penman, Shem the Punman, knows. The "argument" of poetry need not be nearly so rigorous as the arguments of philosophy. The nonsequiturs of metaphysics often open up interesting sequences of poetic rationality. The logic of poetic phrasing can be very thin. Behind

---

or 'enlightening,' and phantasia." Cf. Aristotle's De Anima (with the Commentary of St. Thomas Aquinas), tr. Kenelm Foster, O.P., and Silvester Humphries, O.P. (New Haven, Yale Univ. Press, 1951), pp. 398–9, No. 668.

2. Modern arguments from etymology tend to move with the same partiality. Cf. "Letters" in Time, Vol. 62 (Nov. 30, 1953): A. Haas amusingly argues: "Take the word Presbyterian itself (from Greek presbyteros, comparative of presbys, old). It would seem to mean 'of or pertaining to the elders.' Thus any old people's home, of whatever religion, becomes by definition a presbyterian . . . establishment; and the Elders of Zion have, by the same token, as good a right to the adjective as the Kirk of Scotland."

3. Étienne Gilson, Les idées et les lettres (Paris, Librairie Philosophique J. Vrin, 1932), p. 166.

4. P. 269. Is not this "godsend" of sound leading into sense one of the most happy "accidents" of rime? The examples are legion, but see how Chaucer capitalizes on the aural and ocular resemblances of "cloystre" and "oystre" in his description of the Monk in the General Prologue to the Canterbury Tales. Cf. Lucky Strike "Sticklers" for week of Nov. 25, 1956: "What is a hide-away for shellfish?" "Oyster Cloister."

the happy accident of the linguistic resemblance, it may be, there is some affinity of metaphor which it is the poet's right to explore. In an essay which goes a long way in exploring Joyce's indebtedness to a trivium-quadrivium program of studies ("We've had our day at triv and quad and writ our bit as intermidgets"),[5] Marshall McLuhan begins by calling attention to Joyce's puns: "He means literally that his puns are crossroads of meaning in his communication network, and that his techniques for managing the flow of messages in his network were taken from the traditional disciplines of grammar, logic, rhetoric, on one hand, and of arithmetic, geometry, music, and astronomy, on the other." [6] Poetry itself in the medieval tradition was not regarded as one of the beaux-arts but was connected by long usage with the practical Scholastic disciplines (*artes*) of grammar (which Dante calls *la prima arte*), rhetoric, and logic.[7]

When is a pun a good pun? When does a pun become "poetic" and cease to be a mere linguistic homophone, a kind of irrelevant phonetic accident which is beneath the notice of poetry altogether? Both these questions would have sounded like begging questions to the "reasonable" Augustan, Joseph Addison, who defined *"true* wit," the poetic principle of his day, as the resemblance (or opposition) of *ideas* (not of words), and who insisted that the basis of all (true) wit in poetry is truth, not "bargaining or lying," and that "no thought can be valuable, of which good sense is not the ground-work." [8] The Addisons of the twentieth century, like those of the eighteenth, can have little patience with anything like "this allnights newseryreel" [9] which Shem the Punman likes to keep projecting on every page of *Finnegans Wake*.

Shem was not out for "truth" in the same limited sense of reason and good sense as Addison. Being himself a poet, Shem was quite content to exploit the resources of his language as he could unearth them, and was quite willing to capitalize on the extravagant witty riches of spoken or written words, with their ubiquitous aural or ocular intimations or suggestions of related meanings (which almost always precede the full statement of the literal sense). "To concentrate solely on the literal sense . . . to the sore neglect of the enveloping facts" of language is, as he says in his poetics, "just as hurtful to sound sense (and let it be added to the truest taste)" as visualizing a lady (to whom one has just

5. P. 306.
6. Marshall McLuhan, "James Joyce: Trivial and Quadrivial," *Thought, 28* (Spring 1953), 75. Cf. two excellent studies on this subject of medieval poetics by Walter J. Ong, S.J., "The Province of Rhetoric and Poetic,"*Modern Schoolman, 19* (Jan. 1942), 24–7, and "Wit and Mystery," *Speculum, 22* (July, 1947), 310–41.
7. Cf. Curtius, *European Literature*, pp. 42, 480.
8. "Spectator," No. 62 (Friday, May 11, 1711), *The Spectator, 1* (London, Thos. Bosworth, 1853), 198, 200.
9. P. 489.

been introduced) in her "natural altogether." [1] Shem definitely puts the pun on the side of literary decorum.

It is not likely that Shem would have had any more patience with outright "false wit" than Addison had, though he certainly would not have made this domain so inclusive, and he would by no means have included the literary, or poetic, pun within its boundaries. The pun, as Shem employs it, is never merely a linguistic homophone or a sheer phonetic accident. However extravagant or obscure the sense or "idea" correspondence may be, the patient reader invariably discovers ("with surprise and delight," as Addison would say) several intimations or suggestions of related properties in the beings upon which the pun is founded. The pun, as Shem conceives of it, is not entirely a means of fabricating the resemblance but of starkly pointing to the resemblance already obscurely manifest on the language level, which the reader, it is assumed, had never stopped to notice or think of before. "You may be as practical as is predicable," Shem says in summary of his puns, "but you must have *the proper sort of accident* to meet that kind of a *being* with a difference." [2]

Joyce's manner of speaking for Shem at this point is so very much akin to Scholastic discussions of analogies (or *aequivocationes a consilio,* as they are sometimes called) that it is difficult to imagine that he has not chosen here to speak of Shem's punning, his "doublecrossing twofold thruths," [3] with something of the "middayevil" Schoolmen's accent and lore. It may be worth noting that Aquinas, who did not have much esteem for puns as mere phonetic accidents, the *aequivoca a casu,* as he sometimes called them (for example, in his Commentary on Aristotle's *Ethics*),[4] was nevertheless not prepared even at this merely "accidental" level to hold that the pun had no significance at all. The trouble with the pun which is not founded on "the proper sort of accident" is not, as Aquinas expresses it in his Commentary on the *Perihermenias,* that it signifies nothing but that it signifies too much: "Dictio aequivoca non nihil significat; sed multa significat: et quandoque hoc, quandoque illud per ipsam accipitur." [5] In a successful pun there should always be something held back, some latent potential of meaning left for the mind itself to explore (or "explode out of darkness") and bring to light.

It would be much too complicated and on the whole illusory to search for any strict illustrations of Aquinas' threefold types of analogy in the "Shamwork" punning of the *Wake.*[6] The most perhaps that one might

1. P. 109.
2. P. 269. (Italics mine.)
3. P. 288.
4. *I Ethic.,* lect. 7, finis.
5. *I Perih.,* lect. 5, finis.
6. P. 613. Cf. Francis Fergusson, *The Idea of a Theater* (Garden City, Doubleday, 1953), "The Notion of Analogy" (pp. 248–50), an excellent appendix in partial sum-

look for in Joyce's mingle-mangle of language is the awareness that just
as analogy is a mode of discovering on the level of metaphysical abstraction a likeness in the very differences of beings and of discovering simultaneously a difference in the very likeness, so the "witty" pun reveals
and reflects on the verbal level some significant likeness-difference proportion. Penido in his study of the role of analogy in dogmatic theology
has a sentence which might well have cheered up Shem in the midst of
Shaun's polemic: "Si les métaphores peuvent être simples jeux de plume,
elles peuvent aussi atteindre vraiment quelque chose en Dieu, participer
aux gloires de la règne des analogies." [7]

Simple jeu de plume is not a bad definition of the kind of pun which
Shem tries to rehabilitate for poetry: "chanching letters for them vice
o'verse." [8] A pun as such is not a metaphor and not an analogy; the
"formalities," as the Schoolmen say, are not the same. But a good pun,
a literary or poetic pun, is apparently never unrelated to analogy. The
distinction between a mere phonetic or orthographic accident and "the
proper sort of accident" in terms of which one meets "being with a
difference" [9] can invariably be made, it would seem, on the basis of the
absence or the presence of an implied analogy in the situation which the
phonetic or orthographic accident fortuitously, as it were, highlights or
"sparks" with energy. Actually, as W. H. Auden has noted, the "witty"
pun is never fortuitous, nor must it appear to be such. Always it must
appear to be (and be) a quite deliberate exploitation of a providential
similarity in the sound or in the appearance of words, which reflects or
captures an unexpected similarity in the manner in which two or more
beings indicated by the words exist. The resourceful poet manages by a
kind of verbal legerdemain to make two counterpointing meanings each
simultaneously present in one word formation.[1] All puns exploit the
linguistic affinities given by the conventions and traditions of words as
language-facts; a successful pun unexpectedly calls attention to some
affinity, however remote and unconventional, in the facts of being. Bad
puns are tiresome even in Shakespeare, and a bad pun can be detected
by the lack of any significant analogy in being or reality sufficient to
justify the verbal jeu de plume. "Laughter arises from the diction (or
expression) as well as from the content," as the peripatetic author of the
Tractatus Coislinianus long ago observed.[2] Shaun's prejudice against

mary of Aquinas' three main types of analogy (*attribution, inequality,* and *proportion-
ality*) as explained by M. T. L. Penido in his magisterial study, *Le rôle de l'analogie en
théologie dogmatique,* Paris, Librairie Philosophique J. Vrin, 1931.

7. Penido, p. 101.

8. P. 288.

9. P. 269.

1. W. H. Auden, "Notes on the Comic," *Thought, 27* (Spring 1952), 66.

2. Cf. Lane Cooper's translation, pp. 224–6, of the *Tractatus Coislinianus, An Aristotelian Theory of Comedy* (New York, Harcourt, Brace, 1922), p. 225.

Shem's poetry is partly motivated by Shem's knowing that his brother is, as Shem himself puts it, a "conformed aceticist and aristotaller." [3]

So far in this chapter the punning of the *Wake* has been ascribed not to Joyce but to Shem, "the shamshemshowman." [4] Such an ascription may seem to be very largely fictitious, but the fiction at least is Joyce's own, and there may be advantages in preserving it not unlike the advantages of preserving a distinction between Joyce and Stephen Dedalus. Joyce saw as clearly as anyone that the concentration required to meet a climax or crisis of meaning in almost every single unit of expression is likely to be more than the ordinary reader can endure. In the process of breaking down so many complex chords of language for analysis and comprehension, the ordinary reader cannot or will not go beyond a certain point. The *Wake* itself abounds with ironic criticism at the expense of its own mode of self-expression; it may be this reflex irony partly justifies the experiment and cheers the reader on: "Where in the waste is the wisdom?" [5]

Vico's *Scienza Nuova* suggests a reason why Joyce should have made so much literary capital of the intersecting analogies in Shem's "root language." This Viconian reason is felt not so much in such stylistic strategies as the pun as in the organization of the work as a whole on the theme of thunder, often expressed in variations of the hundred-letter word: "Ullhodturdenweirmudgaardgringnirurdrmolnirfenrirlukkilokki-baugimandodrrerinsurtkrinmgernrackinarockar!" Vico makes much of the notion that the earliest language arose out of man's efforts to formulate the meaning of the primeval thunderclap of God's wrath. Shaun's reason for hating Shem's "root language" is developed in these terms. Shaun hears the thunder and realizes at once in fear and trembling that the divine power inherent in language is not his birthright but that of his brother, the poet Shem: "Thor's for yo!" [6]

It has been argued that Joyce's situation of the pun at the center of his communications network is a particular stylistic version of Vico's argument in the *Scienza Nuova* that language is the best of all practical tools to use in a reconstruction of the vanished past.[7] Almost every critic of Joyce's language sooner or later comes around to mentioning the theory of Giambattista Vico, who held that language in its origin is to be regarded as an expression of poetic wisdom: "The philosophers and philologians should all have begun to treat of the origins of languages and letters from the following principles. (1) That the first men

3. P. 417.
4. P. 530.
5. P. 114.
6. P. 424.
7. McLuhan, "James Joyce: Trivial and Quadrivial," *Thought*, *28* (Spring 1953), 76.

of the Gentile world conceived ideas of things by imaginative characters of animate and mute substances. (2) That they expressed themselves by means of gesture or physical objects which had natural relations with the ideas; for example, three ears of grain, or acting as if swinging a scythe three times to signify three years. (3) That they thus expressed themselves by a language with natural significations." [8]

In evaluating the influence of Vico's theory of the origin of language on Joyce's polyphonic interweaving of themes in the *Wake* some qualifications need to be made. Joyce certainly was not writing a primitive language. Nor did he have any illusions about inventing a new synthetic language of his own (a kind of poetic Esperanto) as so many of the contributors to the *Exagmination* symposium assert.[9] As Marxist critic Margaret Schlauch goes so far as to say that it is actually "better to forget all about Vico in approaching the linguistic problem" in Joyce.[1] Walter Taplin, the English critic, in his essay "James Joyce Wrote English," asks very pertinently: "If James Joyce did not write English, what did he write? . . . The overwhelming majority of the words in *Finnegans Wake* are English words. The grammar and syntax are English—and, what is more, for the greater part of the book they are regular and orthodox." [2] Joyce himself asserts in the *Wake* that his "lingo" is "basically English." [3] Still we have to ask what peculiar thing he does with this "basic English."

Early in the *Wake* Joyce advises his readers to stop ("stoop"), "if

8. Vico, *The New Science*, p. 125–6 (Nicolini para. 431).

9. *Our Exagmination Round His Factification for Incamination of Work in Progress*, London, Faber and Faber, 1929. Cf. Eugène Jolas, "The Revolution of Language and James Joyce": "Language is being *born anew* before our eyes" (p. 89); John Rodker, "Joyce and His Dynamic": "To show still more obviously that he is *creating* a language" (p. 114); Thomas McGreevy, "The Catholic Element in *Work in Progress*": "In spite of the difficulty of having to *invent* a new language as he writes" (p. 120); Robert McAlmon, "Mr. Joyce Directs an Irish Word Ballet": "To him language does not mean the English language" (p. 106). (Italics mine throughout.)

1. Margaret Schlauch, "The Language of James Joyce," *Science and Society, 3* (Fall 1939), 496.

2. Walter Taplin, "James Joyce Wrote English," *The Critic* (Spring 1947), p. 12. Donald Davie in a recent valuable inquiry into the function of syntax in English poetry, *Articulate Energy* (London, Routledge and Kegan Paul, 1955), argues convincingly that "the abandonment of syntax" in much modern poetry "testifies to a failure of the poet's nerve, a loss of confidence in the intelligible structure of the conscious mind, and the validity of its activity" (p. 129). Davie makes use (*passim*) of *Finnegans Wake* as a prime example of the sort of breakdown in the articulating power of language which occurs when "the syntactical weave" (p. 110) of words is no longer regarded as an essential factor in poetic discourse. Although Davie's inquiry is a much needed and salutary antidote to the virus of much recent symbolistic and imagistic criticism which tends to disregard the "silent eloquence" (pp. 25, 34) of syntax, one may wonder if there is not a greater pattern of complexity than Davie seems to discern in the comic syntax of the *Wake*: "Have your little sintalks in the dunk of subjunctions, dual in duel and prude with pruriel. . . . It's a wild's kitten, my dear, who can tell a wilkling from a warthog" (p. 269).

3. P. 116.

you are *abcd*minded." [4] He then goes on to describe his own poetic process as a search for the "nameform that whets the wits that convey contacts that sweeten sensation . . . that entails the ensuance of existentiality." [5] There is a sense in which you must know and love your instrument, words, for their own sake, if you ever hope to use them for the construction of poetry, or for entry into an already constructed poem.

This notion of the instrumental causality of language is much more operative in the *Wake* than is any concept of words as mere speculative signs. Not unrelated to it is Joyce's tendency to regard words as gestures or epiphanies of being, gestures whose meaningfulness consists in the disclosure of the secret, wordless essence itself. For though the essence lies beyond the gesture, there is between the two the closest possible rapport; without the gesture, the essence would not be manifest at all. The words of "a true friend" will tell us much more about himself, says Joyce, than we will ever learn, for instance, by studying his footwear.[6] The *Wake* is full of many good-natured counsels to the reader to cut short his reading if he cannot accept Joyce's attitude that words must be taken as intrinsically interesting "gestures of being" rather than as mere signals of concepts to inform us by a kind of shorthand of what is going on: "Please stop if you're a B.C. minding missy, please do." [7] Or again, "Begin to forget it. It will remember itself from every sides, with all gestures, in each our word. Today's truth, tomorrow's trend." [8]

The Thomist-minded critic may well be inclined to wonder if Joyce's ready willingness to capitalize on the contemporary Viconian emphasis given to words as tools and gestures really marks a new departure either in Joyce's theory of style or in his stylistic practice. Enough has been said earlier in this chapter about the medieval delight in etymologies to suggest that Joyce might have derived his respect for words as instrumental gestures as easily from the "middayevil" Schoolmen as from the eighteenth-century Vico, or from the nineteenth-century *Gestalt* students of primitive language cultures. Rousselot's appraisal of Aquinas' debt to Isidore of Seville, "le précepteur du moyen âge," suggests that Aquinas found the *Etymologies* interesting and important not because he imagined that they were scientifically proved or provable but because each word performed the important role of gesturing to the essence, as the essence came to be analogously manifested in the emblematic word. "Les Scholastiques donc, et s. Thomas comme les autres, vont de l'étymologie à la nature. Un certain rapport intime est supposé entre le nom et l'être; le mot sert comme de clé pour ouvrir cette boîte mystérieuse qui est l'essence de l'objet." [9]

4. P. 18. (Italics mine.)
5. Ibid.
6. P. 115.
7. P. 272.
8. P. 614.
9. Rousselot, *L'intellectualisme de saint Thomas*, p. 176.

When Joyce speaks of finding "in the ignorance that implies impression . . . the nameform that whets the wits," [1] he appears to be using the "nameform" as a key to unlock the essence much as Aquinas does when he stops so often to explore (or refute) the implications of Isidore's etymological "gestures," founded though they were so often on the sheerest of morphological accidents. The gesture meant a great deal as gesture, personal and dramatic, even when its meaning was a fiction or fictitiously derived. Strange as Joyce's language on the page looks to the eye, there may be on the score of gesture good Thomistic reason to justify the strangeness. But then one must be willing to look at the words as gestures of the spirit, and not be in a hurry just to "get on" with the story. Joyce says apropos of the *Wake* that "each word that would not pass away" has its "squidself." "This exists that isits after having been said we know." [2]

As for a word's being a tool or instrument, it scarcely seems credible that Joyce needed to wait until he had read the *Scienza Nuova* before he could appropriate this notion as his own. There is undeniably a Viconian accentuation in the outright manner in which Joyce pursues this notion of verbal instrumentality in the *Wake*. But a similar notion is prominent in the religious tradition in which Joyce was reared from childhood. Crucial to the whole Catholic concept of strict sacramentality is the notion that the Sacraments are not merely signs but practical and efficacious *instruments* which effect what they signify, the conferring of grace. The theological formula insists upon the causality as *ex opere operato* rather than as *ex opere operantis,* two phrases in medieval Latin which are hard to render in English. They are a kind of ecclesiastical shorthand which represents the sacramental rites as working effectively from their own intrinsic causality (as energized, of course, by God) rather than as signs manifest only of God's action or of man's reaction to the conferring of grace.

As Aquinas conceives of the sacramental rite, the word (*verbum vitae*) is the formal cause, the determining and perfecting principle, which gives meaning and instrumental efficacy to the sacramental actions. These actions (for example, the pouring of the water in Baptism, the anointings with oil in Extreme Unction) are regarded by Aquinas as the (proximate) matter, or the material cause, which come to have significance and efficacy by their conjunction with the word: "per verba perficitur significatio rerum." [3]

All of this, of course, is not equivalent to claiming some supernatural efficacy at the instrumental level for the words of the poets, nor is there any indication that Joyce so conceived (or misconceived) the notion of Aquinas. Obviously the instrumentality of the *poetic* word is not that

1. P. 18.
2. P. 186.
3. *S.T.,* III, q. 60, a. 6, ad 2^m; Cf. *IV Sent.,* dist. 3, q. 1, a. 1, q. 4, ad 2^m, ad 3^m

it confers supernatural grace but rather that it effects within a structure of analogies some more or less natural modification of being-as-realized, some change in the situation or object which the language *re-presents*. When Aquinas refers to a word as a *similitudo varia, repraesentatio,* or image of an object,[4] there is no reason to believe that he conceives of the object as something which *must* exist ontologically separate from the word and outside the mind. The object, of which the spoken or written word is the image may, as very often happens in poetry, have no other existence than as a creative construction of the mind itself.

Since Aquinas is willing to allow that in some respects a sculptured statue or a stained-glass window has no other meaningful existence save that which the mind itself imparts,[5] is there any reason to believe that he would always exact more of the verbal images which go into the making of a poem? For the resourceful poet one of the greatest of values inherent in words is that their very denseness and their often shifting planes of imagery enable him to effect a meaningful expression of the complex reality which he is constructing through their instrumentality in his own mind. To no little extent he can make words mean what he wants them to mean. The construction and the expression go hand in hand. Shaun says (though Shem is the brother who has the right to say it, as false Shaun knows), "Every dimmed letter in it is a copy and not a few of the 'silbils and wholly words I can show you in my Kingdom of Heaven." [6]

Unlike Croce, the expressionistic monist, Aquinas distinguishes between intuition and expression though he does not, as some discussions of Thomist realism might lead us to believe, push the two notions so far apart as to make the word merely a kind of surrogate for some reality (for example, a tree or a stone) which the user of the word must always be able to discover in the "outside" world. For poetics it may be important sometimes to insist upon the elementary and the obvious: every tree and every stone which gets into poetry by verbal representation (whether we use the words *tree, arbre, Baum; stone, pierre, Stein,* or any one of a thousand possible metaphorical indications: "Telmetale of *stem* [tree] or *stone*") [7] is a very particular tree or stone which has

4. *S.T.,* I, q. 1, a. 9.

5. Cf. *S.T.,* III, q. 25, a. 3, corp.: "Duplex est motus animae in imaginem: unus quidem in ipsam imaginem, secundum quod res quaedam est; alio modo in imaginem, inquantum est imago alterius; et inter hos duos motus est haec differentia, quia primus motus quo quis movetur in imaginem, ut est res quaedam, est alius a motu qui est in rem; secundus autem motus, qui est in imaginem, inquantum est imago, est unus et idem cum illo qui est in rem."

Cf. *De Ver.,* q. 12, a. 7, ad 5[m]: "Sicut in eo qui ex signis scientiam accipit, signorum cognitio est via ducens ad res ipsas; ita e converso in eo qui significat aliquid, cognitio rei significandae praesupponitur ad formationem signorum, non enim potest aliquis rei quam ignorat, congrua signa adhibere."

6. P. 424.

7. P. 216. (Italics mine.)

somehow gotten first into the poet's imaginative mind and has subsequently entered into some context with other words. As Aquinas perceives the matter at one point in the *De Veritate,* the mind must fashion some sensible expression of its interior concepts (which Aquinas here significantly calls not bare "concepts" but "the thoughts of the heart") in order that the reality behind these concepts may become manifest even to the mind itself: "Oportet quod ad interiores conceptus exprimendos quaedam sensibilia signa aptentur, quibus cognitiones cordium nobis manifestentur." [8]

There is enough drama, it would seem, in every good poem to justify the conclusion on Aquinan grounds that by calling attention to themselves words call attention to the psychic situation (the cognitiones cordium) which the poet has chosen to act out in language and which the reader is invited to the limit of his own verbal resources to re-enact. One of the favorite modern ways of expressing this reciprocal interaction between word and situation is to speak metaphorically of the poet's struggle or fight against words. Much of poetry is said to consist in this "war with words." "The war is in words and the wood is the world," Joyce remarks of the psychic drama which the *Wake* re-enacts.[9] On still other pages he describes more fully this wood into which he has led us as the wood of "sphoenix spark" where "the sombrer opacities of the gloom are sphanished." [1] It is the wood of the *word* made flesh ("wold made fresh").[2] Or to return, within a domestic context, to the metaphor of warfare with which we started out: "The word is my Wife, to expone and expound, to vend and to velnerate. . . . Till Breath us depart!" [3]

To read the *Wake* sympathetically requires great mental strength in order to keep up the struggle with language. A kind of ritualistic or ceremonial attitude toward language is also a prime requisite (even when the word is thought of as one's wife). This "war in words" is conducted at all times with an elaborate decorum: "The ring man in the rong shop but the *rite* words by the *rote* order!" [4] Unless the reader delights in the very ceremonial of the "rite" language warfare, he will soon tire. Joyce, one imagines, would be very much disappointed if the "rite" words were any less resistant than they are. Unless the reader on his part shares to a considerable extent Joyce's own delight in the "rote" order of *how* a thing is being said, in spite of the difficulties, as well as in *what* is being said, there would be little point in undertaking "to war" against the language of *Finnegans Wake.*

8. *De Ver.,* q. 9, a. 4, corp.
9. P. 98.
1. P. 473.
2. P. 336.
3. P. 167.
4. Ibid. (Italics mine.)

In his ceaseless striving to manipulate words much as if they were iconic or hieroglyphic counters, Joyce attempts throughout the *Wake* a quasi-infinite (or *n*-dimensional) symbolic resonance in notation. Still, the inherent symbolizing function of a word is neither satisfactorily nor wholly accounted for at the hieroglyphic level alone. Even if one agrees with Aquinas that words are the "most expressive" of signs,[5] one has to keep always in mind that there are countless other kinds of things, "natural" and "conventional," which have symbol-making power too. "Signa autem exteriora non solum sunt verba, sed etiam facta." [6] In respect to words, there is a very special reason for keeping the symbolic power of these other facta in mind because the word is constantly joining forces with one or the other nonverbal symbol. Much of the strength which we attribute to words as symbols might prove upon analysis to be a power *in things,* a power which the word has appropriated for itself.

Shadow of a shadow, does the word itself step aside when the non-verbal symbol has been called into being and set to work within the psychic situation which the poem re-enacts? Sometimes, it seems, yes! But not always: for the word never really withdraws from a poem's situation, and sometimes by the slightest of *verbal* movements the nonverbal symbol will undergo the most substantial of changes and start functioning in a diametrically opposite sense.

For this reason it may not be very helpful to poetics to insist that the sense of symbols is ever very firmly or specifically set. Daniélou maintains that the range of meanings for a given symbol is not indeterminate, that "symbols have a natural, objective power [presumably unchanging] of reference in themselves." [7] Outside of poetry such symbols possibly may be found. In poetic contexts it is difficult to discover them. For poetry it is obvious that the same reality can be refracted through quite different words. As attempts to translate poetry from one language to another show, the refraction of words does something to the reality. A gull over the waters is a symbol (a word-symbol) in Joyce for poetry itself.[8] (The gull over the waters is also a symbol of exile, in the *Portrait.*) [9] But the dominant symbol for poetry in *Finnegans Wake* is not the gull upon the waters (though it occurs as such at the end) but the hen, Belinda of the Dorans (Biddy Doran), digging up the letter from the dump-heap of the world: "Lead, kindly fowl! They always did: ask

5. *S.T.,* II–II, q. 174, a. 3, corp.
6. *S.T.,* II–II, q. 111, a. 1, corp.
7. Jean Daniélou, S.J., "The Problem of Symbolism," *Thought 25* (Sept. 1950), 426.
8. Sometimes this symbol is given an ironic twist in *Finnegans Wake,* as at the beginning of Bk. II, ch. 4: "Bride-Ship and Gulls," p. 383, where the sea gulls over the water are used to parody the romantic poetry of Tristram and Isolde, "Three quarks for Muster Mark! Sure he hasn't got much of a bark. . . . Fowls, up! Tristy's the spry young spark . . ." (Campbell and Robinson's *A Skeleton Key to Finnegan's Wake* is the authority here for the chapter title.)
9. *Portrait,* pp. 263–5: "Symbol of departure or of loneliness?" (p. 265.)

the ages." [1] If anyone is inclined to think that the hen has an inevitable or limited symbolic reference to the wisdom of poetry, it may not be irrelevant here to recall that Christ chose the barnyard hen, "the kindly fowl," as the symbol of God's ever anxious, ever tender love and care for His people: "How often have I been ready to gather thy children together, as a hen gathers her chickens under her wings: and thou didst refuse it" (Matt. 23:37). Recourse to the speaker's or writer's intentions to explain the analogical appropriateness of any natural object (a gull or a hen) to symbolize something else still leaves open the question how this symbolism is to be effected through the more or less established semantic connections already present in words.

The example of the hen as a symbol now of poetry, now of the divine compassion, may be instructive so far as it illustrates the extent to which the situating of a natural object within a verbal structure may actuate, or even at times seemingly create, a symbolic potentiality in the natural object which it would otherwise lack. It is not, at any rate, very obvious how "that original hen" [2] in the barnyard is a "natural" symbol either of poetry or of God's ever solicitous care. The barnyard hen is, to be sure, no "arbitrary" symbol of anything: she is just herself, a hen. But let the poet see her through the refracting lenses of words, and although she can never become a symbol of "fearful symmetry" like Blake's tiger, she can become a number of interesting things which, without the words, we might never think were possible. In *A Tale of a Tub* Swift sees her (ironically, to be sure) as a symbol of wisdom: "Wisdom is a hen, whose cackling we must value and consider, because it is attended with an egg." [3] Through the words of the *Wake,* the hen becomes, as we have said, the symbol of the *Wake*-poetry itself: "But how many of her readers," asks Joyce, "realise that she is not out to dizzledazzle"? [4]

No poet, no matter how resourceful or sensitive, can hope to actuate symbolically all the "infinite variety" in words. In *The Tempest,* when the *Shamwork* of Prospero's revels is over, Prospero speaks of breaking his staff and drowning his book. On the last page but four of *Finnegans Wake* Joyce has Anna Livia say: "Sometime then, somewhere there, I wrote me hopes and buried the page." [5] It is the gulls crying over the water as the poem comes to its unfinished ending which call our attention to the page buried somewhere in sea or in "copsjute (dump for

1. P. 112.
2. P. 110.
3. Jonathan Swift, *A Tale of a Tub,* Sec. I, Intro., in *Works* ed. Sir Walter Scott, 2d ed., *10* (Boston, Houghton, Mifflin, 1833), 71. Virginia Woolf in *To the Lighthouse* (New York, Harcourt, Brace, 1927) introduces the hen and her chicks to symbolize "an odd illumination" of the heart at the end of a friendship (pp. 34-5).
4. Pp. 112-3.
5. P. 624.

short)" [6] on which Shem in "root language" has given, as he says, "the keys of dreamland," "the keys of me heart." [7]

A rapid glance back over the poetry making of Joyce would show that a "middayevil" fascination with words, their history and their symbolism, was a dominant characteristic of his poetics from the start. Certain words intrigued him apparently just for their sounds. J. F. Byrne, who as we know was the Cranly of the *Portrait,* writes in his memoirs, "He liked the name, the word, the sound of it. He liked the word 'Cranly' as much as, if not more than, any other word spoken or written. As for anything else about it, or connected with it, he didn't really care." [8] The Stephen Dedalus of the *Portrait* is almost as much enchanted by the strange power of language as the Shem Skrivenitch of the *Wake*. "My soul frets in the shadow of his language," Stephen thinks to himself in the presence of the English dean with whom he converses. "The language in which we are speaking is his before it is mine. How different are the words *home, Christ, ale, master,* on his lips and on mine! . . . His language, so familiar and so foreign, will always be for me an acquired speech. I have not made or accepted its words." [9] From beginning to end of the *Portrait* there is no question more frequently raised than that of the "associations of legend and colour" which are present in words.[1] Stephen speaks of words as refractors, of seeing "the glowing sensible world through the prism of a language manycoloured and richly storied." [2] The little boy at Clongowes Wood is represented as weeping over the sadness and beauty in language: "He wanted to cry quietly but not for himself: for the words, so beautiful and sad, like music." [3] Later, the restless university student, "his mind, in the vesture of a doubting monk," continues his search for the essence of things "amid the spectral words of Aristotle or Aquinas," [4] and he comes close again to weeping, so much is "his soul shrivelled up sighing with age as he walked on in a lane among heaps of dead language." [5]

The metaphorical, metaphysical experimentation with language at the root level in the *Wake* is perhaps best understood as an effort to bring life back into these heaps of dead language, to show that a man could ratify by personal insight and vital metaphorical usage his own acceptance at the root level of the words which his language already possessed.

6. P. 110.
7. Pp. 615, 626.
8. Byrne, *The Silent Years,* p. 44.
9. *Portrait,* p. 221.
1. Ibid., p. 193.
2. Ibid., p. 194.
3. Ibid., p. 22.
4. Ibid., p. 205.
5. Ibid., pp. 207–8.

The principal Aquinan themes which make their presence felt in the writings of Joyce come to a focus sooner or later, unless this study is mistaken, in the question of the meaning of language and the mystery of words. In the understanding and illustration of epiphanies there is a great advance from the almost wordless gestures of the early schoolboy notebooks (entitled "Epiphanies") to the verbally resourceful "culious epiphanies" of *Finnegans Wake*. In the development and transformation of the "epiphanic" notion, many other influences besides that of Aquinas were patently at work: French Symbolist literature, Freudian and Jungian theories of unconscious verbal associations, Vico's postulate that language manifests the total human drama of history, present and past. The principal shift in meaning of epiphany occurs at a time when, as the Paris notebooks testify, Joyce was reading Aquinas and was noting the poetic implications of Aquinas' remarks on symbolism, tied in as these remarks so often are with remarks on metaphor and myth. It is at this time that the *Stephen Hero* theory of epiphany ("a sudden spiritual manifestation" focused by "the gropings of a spiritual eye") [6] becomes substantially modified by a theory of epiphany as a verbal strategy or symbolic technique of verbal art, to capture the "inside true inwardness of reality" through the "sextuple gloria of light actually retained" *in words!* [7] To put these "signatures of existence" in order, as McLuhan observes, the artist must discover "the orchestral analogies in things themselves." [8]

The problem of paternity, so crucial to *Ulysses* (and scarcely less crucial to the *Wake*—"Who were Shem and Shaun the living sons or daughters of?") [9]—comes to a focus for Stephen in terms of the Augustinian-Aquinan Trinitarian axiom, "Quo Verbum, eo Imago, et eo ipso Filius." In spite of the theological extravagances of Stephen's rhetorical distortion of the axiom, Joyce himself seems seriously concerned to understand, and to turn to poetic account, the relevance for poetics which lies in this analogy between sonship and the utterance of a word. The other Aquinan analogy between poesis and the act of *creation* is explored in Joyce with less explicit invocation of the authority of the "bulldog of Aquin," possibly because it is less polemical and more generally

6. *Stephen Hero*, p. 211.

7. P. 611.

8. Marshall McLuhan, "Joyce, Mallarmé, and the Press," *Sewanee Review, 62* (Winter 1954), 49. Cf. Ellsworth Mason, "Joyce's Categories," ibid., *61* (Summer 1953), 427–32. Mason concludes that the road from the early *Portrait* categories (dramatic, lyric, epic, comedy, tragedy) to *Ulysses* and *Finnegans Wake* is a straight line: "His definitions of the categories set up five requirements for the perfect work of art. It should be comedy; it should be concerned with character, rather than narrative; it should work with material drawn from the artist's experience with life around him; it should contain the author's emotions depersonalized; it should be written with conscious artistry" (p. 432).

9. P. 216.

conceded. But for Joyce the analogy reveals itself, as in Aquinas, in terms of actuation of new being through the utterance of a creative word. The "middayevil" poesis of Shem the Penman, Shem the Punman, carries on the same enterprise through the instrumentality of the analogies which are grounded in "root language," a process of tapping the vitality buried in the original and metaphorical root meanings of words.

Joyce never committed himself as a poet to the "Thomistic system," any more than he did to any other philosophical system—Berkeleyan, Freudian, Viconian, or what you will. He took from each system he encountered what proved most helpful to him as a writer, as a poet, either by way of organizing insight or by way of theme or image which he could incorporate into the structure of his own work. Sometimes he qualified what he found; often he dramatized it, earnestly or ironically; almost always he combined it with something else. The fact that Joyce found Aquinas as helpful as he did is at one and the same time a sign, it would seem, of the vitality of the *philosophia perennis* and of Joyce's own vast resourcefulness.

Index

(Parentheses indicate titles mentioned but not discussed)

THE YALE PAPERBOUNDS